KB169891

나의 토익 Listening 목표 달성기

나의 목표 점수	나의 학습 플랜
	☐ [400점 이상] 2주 완성 학습 플랜
	☐ [300~395점] 3주 완성 학습 플랜
_____ 점	☐ [295점 이하] 4주 완성 학습 플랜

* 일 단위의 상세 학습 플랜은 p.20에 있습니다.

각 Test를 마친 후, 해당 Test의 점수를 ● 으로 표시하여 자신의 점수 변화를 확인하세요.

토익의 고수!

고득점은 이제 시간 문제!

토익 감 잡았어!

토익 초보예요!

	TEST 01	TEST 02	TEST 03	TEST 04	TEST 05	TEST 06	TEST 07	TEST 08	TEST 09	TEST 10
학습일	/	/	/	/	/	/	/	/	/	/
맞은 개수	개	개	개	개	개	개	개	개	개	개
환산점수	점	점	점	점	점	점	점	점	점	점

* 리스닝 점수 환산표는 p.167에 있습니다.

해커스 토익 LC

실전 1000제 1
LISTENING

문제집

해커스 어학연구소

최신 토익 경향을 완벽하게 반영한
해커스 토익 실전 1000제 1 LISTENING 문제집을 내면서

해커스 토익이 항상 독보적인 베스트셀러의 자리를 지킬 수 있는 것은 늘 **처음과 같은 마음으로** 더 좋은 책을 만들기 위해 고민하고, **최신 경향을 반영하기 위해 끊임없이 노력**하기 때문입니다.

그리고 이러한 노력 끝에 **최신 토익 경향을 반영한 《해커스 토익 실전 1000제 1 Listening 문제집》(최신 개정 판)**을 출간하게 되었습니다.

최신 출제 경향 완벽 반영!

최신 출제 경향을 철저히 분석하여 실전과 가장 유사한 지문과 문제 10회분을 수록하였습니다. 수록한 모든 문제는 실전과 동일한 환경에서 풀 수 있도록 실제 토익 문제지와 동일하게 구성하였으며, Answer Sheet를 수록하여 시간 관리 연습과 더불어 실전 감각을 보다 높일 수 있도록 하였습니다.

점수를 올려주는 학습 구성과 학습 자료로 토익 고득점 달성!

모든 문제의 정답과 함께 스크립트를 수록하였으며, 해커스토익(Hackers.co.kr)에서 '문제 해석'을 무료로 제공합니다. 문제의 정확한 이해를 통해 토익 리스닝 점수를 향상할 수 있으며, 토익 고득점 달성이 가능합니다.

《해커스 토익 실전 1000제 1 Listening 문제집》은 별매되는 해설집과 함께 학습할 때 보다 효과적으로 학습할 수 있습니다. 또한, 해커스인강(HackersIngang.com)에서 '온라인 실전모의고사 1회분'과 '단어암기 PDF&MP3'를 무료로 제공하며, 토익 스타 강사의 파트별 해설강의를 수강할 수 있습니다.

《**해커스 토익 실전 1000제 1 Listening** 문제집》이 여러분의 토익 목표 점수 달성에 확실한 해결책이 되고 영어 실력 향상, 나아가 여러분의 꿈을 향한 길에 믿음직한 동반자가 되기를 소망합니다.

해커스 어학연구소

CONTENTS

무료 해석 바로 보기

토익, 이렇게 공부하면
확실하게 고득점 잡는다!

01
토익에 완벽하게 대비한다!

최신 토익 출제 경향을 반영한 실전 10회분 수록

시험 경향에 맞지 않는 문제들만 풀면, 실전에서는 연습했던 문제와 달라 당황할 수 있습니다. ≪해커스 토익 실전 1000제 1 Listening 문제집≫에 수록된 모든 문제는 **최신 출제 경향과 난이도를 반영하여** 실전에 철저하게 대비할 수 있도록 하였습니다.

실전과 동일한 구성!

≪해커스 토익 실전 1000제 1 Listening 문제집≫에 수록된 모든 문제는 **실전 문제지와 동일하게 구성**되었으며, **미국·캐나다·영국·호주식의 국가별 발음** 또한 실전과 동일한 비율로 구성되었습니다. 또한 영국·호주식 실전 버전 MP3로 까다로운 영국·호주식 발음에 확실히 대비할 수 있으며, 고사장/매미 버전 MP3로 실전 감각을 극대화할 수 있습니다. 이와 더불어 **교재 뒤에 수록된 Answer Sheet**으로 실제 시험처럼 답안 마킹을 연습하면서 시간 관리 방법을 익힐 수 있습니다.

02

한 문제를 풀어도, 정확하게 이해하고 푼다!

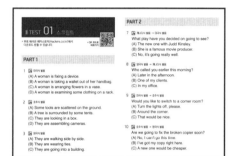

스크립트

수록된 모든 문제에 대한 스크립트를 교재 뒤에 수록하였습니다. 테스트를 마친 후 문제를 풀 때 음성을 정확히 이해하면서 풀었는지, 틀린 문제의 경우 어떤 부분을 놓쳤는지 등을 **스크립트를 통해 꼼꼼히 확인하고 다시 듣는 연습**을 통해 리스닝 실력을 향상할 수 있도록 하였습니다.

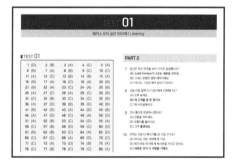

무료 해석 PDF

수록된 모든 지문 및 모든 문제에 대한 정확한 해석을 **해커스토익 (Hackers.co.kr) 사이트에서 무료로 제공**합니다. 이를 통해 테스트를 마친 후, 스크립트를 봐도 잘 이해가 되지 않거나 해석이 어려운 문제를 확인하여 **지문과 문제를 보다 정확하게 이해**할 수 있도록 하였습니다.

Self 체크 리스트

각 테스트 마지막 페이지에는 Self 체크 리스트를 수록하여 **테스트를 마친 후 자신의 문제 풀이 방식과 태도를 스스로 점검**할 수 있도록 하였습니다. 이를 통해 효과적인 복습과 더불어 목표 점수를 달성하기 위해 개선해야 할 습관 및 부족한 점을 찾아 보완해나갈 수 있습니다.

03

내 실력을 확실하게 파악한다!

점수 환산표

교재 부록으로 점수 환산표를 수록하여, 학습자들이 테스트를 마치고 채점을 한 후 바로 점수를 확인하여 자신의 **실력을 정확하게 파악**할 수 있도록 하였습니다. 환산 점수를 교재 첫 장의 목표 달성 그래프에 표시하여 실력의 변화를 확인하고, 학습 계획을 세울 수 있습니다.

무료 온라인 실전모의고사

교재에 수록된 테스트 외에 해커스인강(HackersIngang.com) 사이트에서 온라인 실전모의고사 1회분을 추가로 무료 제공합니다. 이를 통해 토익 시험 전, 학습자들이 자신의 실력을 마지막으로 점검해볼 수 있도록 하였습니다.

인공지능 1:1 토익어플 '빅플'

교재의 문제를 풀고 답안을 입력하기만 하면, 인공지능 어플 '해커스토익 빅플'이 **자동 채점은 물론 성적분석표와 취약 유형 심층 분석까지 제공**합니다. 이를 통해, 자신이 가장 많이 틀리는 취약 유형이 무엇인지 확인하고, 관련 문제들을 추가로 학습하며 취약 유형을 집중 공략하여 약점을 보완할 수 있습니다.

04 다양한 학습 자료를 활용한다!

단어암기 PDF&MP3 / 정답녹음 MP3

해커스인강(HackersIngang.com) 사이트에서 단어암기 PDF와 MP3를 무료로 제공하여, 교재에 수록된 테스트의 중요 단어를 복습하고 암기할 수 있도록 하였습니다. 또한 정답녹음 MP3 파일을 제공하여 학습자들이 보다 편리하게 채점할 수 있도록 하였습니다.

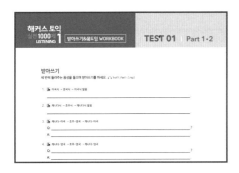

받아쓰기&쉐도잉 워크북 / 받아쓰기&쉐도잉 프로그램

해커스인강(HackersIngang.com) 사이트에서 무료로 제공되는 받아쓰기&쉐도잉 워크북과 MP3를 통해 ≪해커스 토익 실전 1000제 1 Listening 문제집≫ 교재의 파트별 핵심 문장을 반복 학습할 수 있습니다. 동일한 기능의 받아쓰기&쉐도잉 프로그램 또한 무료로 이용 가능하며, 받아쓰기와 쉐도잉을 통해 영어 듣기를 마스터할 수 있게 하였습니다.

방대한 무료 학습 자료(Hackers.co.kr) / 동영상강의(HackersIngang.com)

해커스토익(Hackers.co.kr) 사이트에서는 토익 적중 예상특강을 비롯한 방대하고 유용한 토익 학습 자료를 무료로 이용할 수 있습니다. 또한 온라인 교육 포털 사이트인 해커스인강(HackersIngang.com) 사이트에서 교재 동영상강의를 수강하면, 보다 깊이 있는 학습이 가능합니다.

해설집 미리보기

<해설집 별매>

01 정답과 오답의 이유를 확인하여 Part 1&2 문제 완벽 정복!

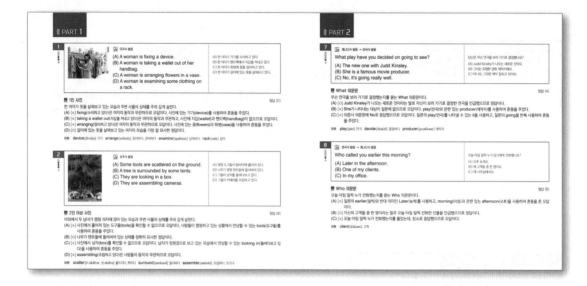

1 문제 및 문제 해석

최신 토익 출제 경향이 반영된 문제를 해설집에도 그대로 수록해, 해설을 보기 전 문제를 다시 한번 풀어보며 자신이 어떤 과정으로 정답을 선택했는지 되짚어 볼 수 있습니다. 함께 수록된 정확한 해석을 보며 문장 구조를 꼼꼼하게 파악하여 문제를 완벽하게 이해할 수 있습니다.

2 문제 유형 및 난이도

모든 문제마다 문제 유형을 제시하여 자주 틀리는 문제 유형을 쉽게 파악할 수 있고, 사전 테스트를 거쳐 검증된 문제별 난이도를 확인하여 자신의 실력과 학습 목표에 따라 학습할 수 있습니다. 문제 유형은 모두 《해커스 토익 Listening》의 목차 목록과 동일하여, 보완 학습이 필요할 경우 쉽게 참고할 수 있습니다.

3 상세한 해설 및 어휘

문제 유형별로 가장 효과적인 해결 방법을 제시하며, 오답 보기가 오답이 되는 이유까지 상세하게 설명하여 틀린 문제의 원인을 파악하고 보완할 수 있습니다. 또한, 영국·호주식 발음으로 들려준 지문문제에서 어휘의 국가별 발음이 다를 경우, 미국·영국식 발음 기호를 모두 수록하여 국가별 발음 차이까지 익힐 수 있도록 하였습니다.

02 효율적인 Part 3&4 문제풀이 전략으로 고득점 달성!

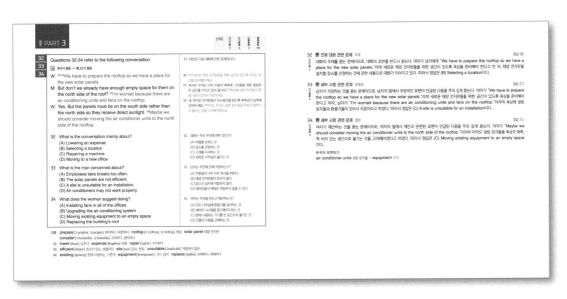

1 지문, 문제, 해석, 정답의 단서

최신 토익 출제 경향이 반영된 지문 및 문제와 함께 수록된 정확한 해석을 보며 지문 및 문제의 내용을 완벽하게 이해할 수 있습니다. 또한, 각 문제별로 표시된 정답의 단서를 확인하여, 모든 문제에 대한 정답의 근거를 정확하게 파악하는 연습을 할 수 있습니다.

2 문제 유형별 상세한 해설 및 문제 풀이 방법

질문 유형별로 가장 효율적인 해결 방법이 적용된 문제 풀이 방법을 제시하였습니다. 대화/지문에서 주의 깊게 들어야 할 부분이나 파악해야 할 사항을 확인하는 단계부터 대화/지문을 들으며 정답을 선택하는 문제 풀이 과정을 읽는 것만으로도 자연스럽게 Part 3 · 4의 문제 풀이 전략을 익힐 수 있습니다.

3 바꾸어 표현하기

대화/지문의 내용이 질문이나 정답 보기에서 바꾸어 표현된 경우, [대화/지문의 표현 → 정답 보기의 표현] 혹은 [질문의 표현 → 대화/지문의 표현]으로 정리하여 한눈에 확인할 수 있도록 하였습니다. 이를 통해 Part 3 · 4 풀이 전략을 익히고 나아가 고득점 달성이 가능하도록 하였습니다.

토익 소개 및 시험장 Tips

토익이란 무엇인가?

TOEIC은 **Test Of English for International Communication**의 약자로 영어가 모국어가 아닌 사람들을 대상으로 언어 본래의 기능인 '커뮤니케이션' 능력에 중점을 두고 일상생활 또는 국제 업무 등에 필요한 실용영어 능력을 평가하는 시험입니다. 토익은 일상생활 및 비즈니스 현장에서 필요로 하는 내용을 평가하기 위해 개발되었고 다음과 같은 실용적인 주제들을 주로 다룹니다.

- 협력 개발: 연구, 제품 개발
- 재무 회계: 대출, 투자, 세금, 회계, 은행 업무
- 일반 업무: 계약, 협상, 마케팅, 판매
- 기술 영역: 전기, 공업 기술, 컴퓨터, 실험실
- 사무 영역: 회의, 서류 업무
- 물품 구입: 쇼핑, 물건 주문, 대금 지불

- 식사: 레스토랑, 회식, 만찬
- 문화: 극장, 스포츠, 피크닉
- 건강: 의료 보험, 병원 진료, 치과
- 제조: 생산 조립 라인, 공장 경영
- 직원: 채용, 은퇴, 급여, 진급, 고용 기회
- 주택: 부동산, 이사, 기업 부지

토익의 파트별 구성

구성		내용	문항 수	시간	배점
Listening Test	Part 1	사진 묘사	6문항 (1번~6번)	45분	495점
	Part 2	질의 응답	25문항 (7번~31번)		
	Part 3	짧은 대화	39문항, 13지문 (32번~70번)		
	Part 4	짧은 담화	30문항, 10지문 (71번~100번)		
Reading Test	Part 5	단문 빈칸 채우기 (문법/어휘)	30문항 (101번~130번)	75분	495점
	Part 6	장문 빈칸 채우기 (문법/어휘/문장 고르기)	16문항, 4지문 (131번~146번)		
	Part 7	지문 읽고 문제 풀기(독해) - 단일 지문 (Single Passage) - 이중 지문 (Double Passages) - 삼중 지문 (Triple Passages)	54문항, 15지문 (147번~200번) - 29문항, 10지문 (147번~175번) - 10문항, 2지문 (176번~185번) - 15문항, 3지문 (186번~200번)		
Total		7 Parts	200문항	120분	990점

토익 접수 방법 및 성적 확인

1. 접수 방법
- 접수 기간을 TOEIC위원회 인터넷 사이트(www.toeic.co.kr) 혹은 공식 애플리케이션에서 확인하고 접수합니다.
- 접수 시 jpg형식의 사진 파일이 필요하므로 미리 준비합니다.

2. 성적 확인
- 시험일로부터 약 10일 이후 TOEIC위원회 인터넷 사이트(www.toeic.co.kr) 혹은 공식 애플리케이션에서 확인합니다. (성적 발표 기간은 회차마다 상이함)
- 시험 접수 시, 우편 수령과 온라인 출력 중 성적 수령 방법을 선택할 수 있습니다.
  *온라인 출력은 성적 발표 즉시 발급 가능하나, 우편 수령은 약 7일가량의 발송 기간이 소요될 수 있습니다.

시험 당일 준비물

신분증	연필&지우개	시계	수험번호를 적어둔 메모	오답노트&단어암기장

* 시험 당일 신분증이 없으면 시험에 응시할 수 없으므로, 반드시 ETS에서 요구하는 신분증(주민등록증, 운전면허증, 공무원증 등)을 지참해야 합니다.
  ETS에서 인정하는 신분증 종류는 TOEIC위원회 인터넷 사이트(www.toeic.co.kr)에서 확인 가능합니다.

시험 진행 순서

정기시험/추가시험(오전)	추가시험(오후)	진행내용	유의사항
AM 9:30 - 9:45	PM 2:30 - 2:45	답안지 작성 오리엔테이션	10분 전에 고사장에 도착하여, 이름과 수험번호로 고사실을 확인합니다.
AM 9:45 - 9:50	PM 2:45 - 2:50	쉬는 시간	준비해간 오답노트나 단어암기장으로 최종 정리를 합니다. 시험 중간에는 쉬는 시간이 없으므로 화장실에 꼭 다녀오도록 합니다.
AM 9:50 - 10:10	PM 2:50 - 3:10	신분 확인 및 문제지 배부	
AM 10:10 - 10:55	PM 3:10 - 3:55	Listening Test	Part 1과 Part 2는 문제를 풀면서 정답을 바로 답안지에 마킹합니다. Part 3와 Part 4는 문제의 정답 보기 옆에 살짝 표시해두고, Listening Test가 끝난 후 한꺼번에 마킹합니다.
AM 10:55 - 12:10	PM 3:55 - 5:10	Reading Test	각 문제를 풀 때 바로 정답을 마킹합니다.

* 추가시험은 토요일 오전 또는 오후에 시행되므로 이 사항도 꼼꼼히 확인합니다.
* 당일 진행 순서에 대한 더 자세한 내용은 해커스토익(Hackers.co.kr) 사이트에서 확인할 수 있습니다.

▌Part 1 사진 묘사 (6문제)

사진을 가장 잘 묘사한 문장을 4개의 보기 중에서 고르는 유형

문제 형태

문제지	음성
1. 	Number 1. Look at the picture marked number 1 in your test book. (A) He is writing on a sheet of paper. (B) He is reaching for a glass. (C) He is seated near a window. (D) He is opening up a laptop computer.

해설 남자가 창문 근처에 앉아 있는 모습을 seated near a window(창문 근처에 앉아 있다)로 묘사한 (C)가 정답이다.

문제 풀이 전략

1. 보기를 듣기 전에 사진을 묘사할 수 있는 표현을 미리 연상합니다.

보기를 듣기 전에 사진을 보면서 사용 가능한 주어와 등장 인물의 동작이나 사물을 나타내는 동사 및 명사를 미리 연상합니다. 표현을 미리 연상하는 과정에서 사진의 내용을 정확하게 확인하게 되며, 연상했던 표현이 보기에서 사용될 경우 훨씬 명확하게 들을 수 있어 정답 선택이 수월해집니다.

2. 사진을 완벽하게 묘사한 것이 아니라 가장 적절하게 묘사한 보기를 선택합니다.

Part 1은 사진을 완벽하게 묘사한 보기가 아니라 가장 적절하게 묘사한 보기를 선택해야 합니다. 이를 위해 Part 1의 문제를 풀 때 ○, ×를 표시하면서 보기를 들으면 오답 보기를 확실히 제거할 수 있어 정확히 정답을 선택할 수 있습니다. 특별히 Part 1에서 자주 출제되는 오답 유형을 알아두면 ×를 표시하면서 훨씬 수월하게 정답을 선택할 수 있습니다.

Part 1 빈출 오답 유형

· 사진 속 사람의 동작을 잘못 묘사한 오답
· 사진에 없는 사람이나 사물을 언급한 오답
· 사진 속 사물의 상태나 위치를 잘못 묘사한 오답
· 사물의 상태를 사람의 동작으로 잘못 묘사한 오답
· 사진에서는 알 수 없는 사실을 진술한 오답
· 혼동하기 쉬운 어휘를 이용한 오답

* 실제 시험을 볼 때, Part 1 디렉션이 나오는 동안 Part 5 문제를 최대한 많이 풀면 전체 시험 시간 조절에 도움이 됩니다. 하지만 "Now, Part 1 will begin"이라는 음성이 들리면 바로 Part 1으로 돌아가서 문제를 풀도록 합니다.

Part 2 질의 응답 (25문제)

영어로 된 질문을 듣고 가장 적절한 응답을 3개의 보기 중에서 고르는 유형

문제 형태

문제지	음성
7. Mark your answer on your answer sheet.	Number 7. When is the presentation going to be held? (A) I'm going to discuss sales levels. (B) Sometime on Tuesday. (C) He handled the preparations.

해설 의문사 When을 이용하여 발표가 진행될 시기를 묻고 있는 문제이므로 Sometime on Tuesday라는 시점을 언급한 (B)가 정답이다.

문제 풀이 전략

1. 질문의 첫 단어는 절대 놓치지 않도록 합니다.

Part 2의 문제 유형은 질문의 첫 단어로 결정되므로 절대 첫 단어를 놓치지 않아야 합니다. Part 2에서 평균 11문제 정도 출제되는 의문사 의문문은 첫 단어인 의문사만 들으면 대부분 정답을 선택할 수 있습니다. 그리고 다른 유형의 문제도 첫 단어를 통하여 유형, 시제, 주어 등 문제 풀이와 관련된 기본적인 정보를 파악할 수 있습니다.

2. 오답 유형을 숙지하여 오답 제거 방법을 100% 활용하도록 합니다.

Part 2에서는 오답의 유형이 어느 정도 일정한 패턴으로 사용되고 있습니다. 따라서 오답 유형을 숙지해두어 문제를 풀 때마다 오답 제거 방법을 최대한 활용하도록 합니다. 이를 위해 Part 2의 문제를 풀 때 O, ×를 표시하면서 보기를 들으면 오답 보기를 확실히 제거할 수 있어 정확히 정답을 선택할 수 있습니다.

Part 2 빈출 오답 유형

· 질문에 등장한 단어를 반복하거나, 발음이 유사한 어휘를 사용한 오답
· 동의어, 관련 어휘, 다의어를 사용한 오답
· 주체나 시제를 혼동한 오답
· 정보를 묻는 의문사 의문문에 Yes/No로 응답한 오답

* 실제 시험을 볼 때, Part 2 디렉션이 나오는 동안 Part 5 문제를 최대한 많이 풀면 전체 시험 시간 조절에 도움이 됩니다. 하지만 "Now, let us begin with question number 7"이라는 음성이 들리면 바로 Part 2로 돌아가서 문제를 풀도록 합니다.

Part 3 짧은 대화 (39문제)

· 2~3명이 주고받는 짧은 대화를 듣고 관련 질문에 대한 정답을 고르는 유형
· 구성: 총 13개의 대화에 39문제 출제 (한 대화 당 3문제, 일부 대화는 3문제와 함께 시각 자료가 출제)

문제 형태

문제지	음성
32. What are the speakers mainly discussing? (A) Finding a venue (B) Scheduling a renovation (C) Choosing a menu (D) Organizing a conference 33. What does the woman offer to do? (A) Visit a nearby event hall (B) Revise a travel itinerary (C) Proceed with a booking (D) Contact a facility manager 34. What does the woman mean when she says, "we're all set"? (A) Some furniture will be arranged. (B) Some memos will be circulated. (C) An update will be installed. (D) An area will be large enough.	Questions 32 through 34 refer to the following conversation. W: Joseph, I'm worried it'll be too chilly for the outdoor luncheon we've planned for Wednesday. M: I agree. We'd better book an event hall instead. W: How about Wolford Hall? I'm looking at its Web site now, and it appears to be available. M: Oh, that'd be ideal. That place is near our office, so staff won't have to travel far. W: I can book the hall now, if you want. We need it from 11 A.M. to 2 P.M., right? M: Yeah. Just make sure it can accommodate 50 people. W: It says it'll hold up to 70, so we're all set. M: Perfect. I'll send staff an e-mail with the updated details. Number 32. What are the speakers mainly discussing? Number 33. What does the woman offer to do? Number 34. What does the woman mean when she says, "we're all set"?

해설 32. 대화의 주제를 묻는 문제이다. 여자가 it'll be too chilly for the outdoor luncheon이라며 야외 오찬을 하기에는 날씨가 너무 쌀쌀할 것 같다고 하자, 남자가 We'd better book an event hall instead라며 대신 행사장을 예약하는 것이 낫겠다고 한 뒤, 행사를 위한 장소를 찾는 것에 관한 내용으로 대화가 이어지고 있다. 따라서 정답은 (A)이다.

33. 여자가 해주겠다고 제안하는 것을 묻는 문제이다. 여자가 I can book the hall now라며 지금 자신이 그 행사장을 예약할 수 있다고 하였다. 따라서 정답은 (C)이다.

34. 여자가 하는 말의 의도를 묻는 문제이다. 남자가 Just make sure it[hall] can accommodate 50 people이라며 행사장이 50명의 사람들을 수용할 수 있는지만 확인하라고 하자, 여자가 it'll hold up to 70, so we're all set이라며 그것은 70명까지 수용할 것이니 우리는 준비가 다 되었다고 한 말을 통해 행사장의 공간이 충분히 클 것임을 알 수 있다. 따라서 정답은 (D)이다.

문제 풀이 전략

1. 대화를 듣기 전에 반드시 질문과 보기를 먼저 읽어야 합니다.

① Part 3의 디렉션을 들려줄 때 32번부터 34번까지의 질문과 보기를 읽으면, 이후 계속해서 대화를 듣기 전에 질문과 보기를 미리 읽을 수 있습니다.

② 질문을 읽을 때에는 질문 유형을 파악한 후, 해당 유형에 따라 어느 부분을 들을지와 어떤 내용을 들을지 듣기 전략을 세웁니다. 시각 자료가 출제된 대화의 경우, 시각 자료를 함께 확인하면서 시각 자료의 종류와 그 내용을 파악합니다.

③ 보기를 읽을 때에는 각 보기를 다르게 구별해주는 어휘를 선택적으로 읽어야 합니다. 특별히 보기가 문장일 경우, 주어가 모두 다르면 주어를, 주어가 모두 같으면 동사 또는 목적어 등의 중요 어휘를 키워드로 결정합니다.

2. 대화를 들으면서 동시에 정답을 선택합니다.

① 질문과 보기를 읽으며 세운 듣기 전략을 토대로, 대화를 들으면서 동시에 각 문제의 정답을 선택합니다.

② 3인 대화의 경우, 대화가 시작하기 전에 "Questions ~ refer to the following conversation with three speakers."라는 음성이 재생되므로 각 대화별 디렉션에도 집중해야 합니다.

③ 대화가 끝난 후 관련된 3개의 질문을 읽어줄 때 다음 대화와 관련된 3개의 질문과 보기를 재빨리 읽으면서 듣기 전략을 다시 세워야 합니다.

④ 만약 대화가 다 끝났는데도 정답을 선택하지 못했다면 가장 정답인 것 같은 보기를 선택하고, 곧바로 다음 대화에 해당하는 질문과 보기를 읽기 시작하는 것이 오답률을 줄이는 현명한 방법입니다.

3. 대화의 초반은 반드시 들어야 합니다.

① 대화에서 초반에 언급된 내용 중 80% 이상이 문제로 출제되므로 대화의 초반은 반드시 들어야 합니다.

② 특별히 대화의 주제를 묻는 문제, 대화자의 직업, 대화의 장소를 묻는 문제에 대한 정답의 단서는 대부분 대화의 초반에 언급됩니다.

③ 초반을 듣지 못하고 놓칠 경우 대화 후반에서 언급된 특정 표현을 사용한 보기를 정답으로 선택하는 오류를 범할 수 있으므로 각별히 주의해야 합니다.

Part 4 짧은 담화 (30문제)

· 짧은 담화를 듣고 관련 질문에 대한 정답을 고르는 유형
· 구성: 총 10개의 지문에 30문제 출제 (한 지문 당 3문제, 일부 지문은 3문제와 함께 시각 자료가 출제)

문제 형태

문제지	음성

문제지

Department	Manager
Accounting	Janet Lee
Sales	Sarah Bedford
Human Resources	David Weber
Marketing	Michael Brenner

95. What is the purpose of the announcement?

(A) To explain a new project
(B) To describe a job opening
(C) To discuss a recent hire
(D) To verify a policy change

96. Look at the graphic. Which department will Shannon Clark manage?

(A) Accounting
(B) Sales
(C) Human Resources
(D) Marketing

97. What will probably happen on September 1?

(A) A job interview
(B) A product launch
(C) A staff gathering
(D) An employee evaluation

음성

Questions 95 through 97 refer to the following announcement and list.

May I have your attention, please? I just received an e-mail from David Weber in human resources regarding a new manager. Shannon Clark will begin working here next month. Ms. Clark has over a decade of experience working for multinational corporations, so she brings a wealth of knowledge to our company. She will be replacing Michael Brenner, who is retiring this month. One of the other department managers . . . um, Janet Lee . . . has arranged a get-together on September 1 to introduce Ms. Clark. Food and beverages will be provided. Please give her a warm welcome.

Number 95.
What is the purpose of the announcement?

Number 96.
Look at the graphic. Which department will Shannon Clark manage?

Number 97.
What will probably happen on September 1?

해설 95. 공지의 목적을 묻는 문제이다. I just received an e-mail ~ regarding a new manager. Shannon Clark will begin working here next month이라며 새로운 관리자에 관련된 이메일을 방금 받았으며, Shannon Clark가 다음 달에 이곳에서 근무를 시작할 것이라고 하였다. 따라서 정답은 (C)이다.

96. Shannon Clark가 관리할 부서를 묻는 문제이다. She[Shannon Clark] will be replacing Michael Brenner, who is retiring this month이라며 Shannon Clark은 이달에 은퇴하는 Michael Brenner를 대신할 것이라고 하였으므로, Michael Brenner가 관리자로 일하던 마케팅 부서를 관리하게 될 것임을 표에서 알 수 있다. 따라서 정답은 (D)이다.

97. 9월 1일에 일어날 일을 묻는 문제이다. Janet Lee ~ has arranged a get-together on September 1이라며 Janet Lee가 9월 1일에 열릴 모임을 마련했다고 하였다. 따라서 정답은 (C)이다.

문제 풀이 전략

1. 지문을 듣기 전에 반드시 질문과 보기를 먼저 읽어야 합니다.

① Part 4의 디렉션을 들려줄 때 71번부터 73번까지의 질문과 보기를 읽으면, 이후 계속해서 지문을 듣기 전에 질문과 보기를 미리 읽을 수 있습니다.

② 질문을 읽을 때에는 질문 유형을 파악한 후, 해당 유형에 따라 어느 부분을 들을지와 어떤 내용을 들을지 듣기 전략을 세웁니다. 시각 자료가 출제된 담화의 경우, 시각 자료를 함께 확인하면서 시각 자료의 종류와 그 내용을 파악합니다.

③ 보기를 읽을 때에는 각 보기를 다르게 구별해주는 어휘를 선택적으로 읽어야 합니다. 특별히 보기가 문장일 경우, 주어가 모두 다르면 주어를, 주어가 모두 같으면 동사 또는 목적어 등의 중요 어휘를 키워드로 결정합니다.

2. 지문을 들으면서 동시에 정답을 선택합니다.

① 질문과 보기를 읽으며 세운 듣기 전략을 토대로, 지문을 들으면서 동시에 각 문제의 정답을 곧바로 선택합니다.

② 지문의 음성이 끝날 때에는 세 문제의 정답 선택도 완료되어 있어야 합니다.

③ 지문의 음성이 끝난 후 관련된 3개의 질문을 읽어줄 때 다음 지문과 관련된 3개의 질문과 보기를 재빨리 읽으면서 듣기 전략을 다시 세워야 합니다.

④ 만약 지문이 다 끝났는데도 정답을 선택하지 못했다면 가장 정답인 것 같은 보기를 선택하고, 곧바로 다음 지문에 해당하는 질문과 보기를 읽기 시작하는 것이 오답률을 줄이는 현명한 방법입니다.

3. 지문의 초반은 반드시 들어야 합니다.

① 지문에서 초반에 언급된 내용 중 80% 이상이 문제로 출제되므로 지문의 초반을 반드시 들어야 합니다.

② 특별히 지문의 주제/목적 문제나 화자/청자 및 담화 장소 문제처럼 전체 지문 관련 문제에 대한 정답의 단서는 대부분 지문의 초반에 언급됩니다.

③ 초반을 듣지 못하고 놓칠 경우 더 이상 관련된 내용이 언급되지 않아 정답 선택이 어려워질 수 있으므로 주의해야 합니다.

수준별 맞춤 학습 플랜

TEST 01을 마친 후 자신의 환산 점수에 맞는 학습 플랜을 선택하고 매일매일 박스에 체크하며 공부합니다. 각 TEST를 마친 후, 다양한 자료를 활용하여 각 테스트를 꼼꼼하게 리뷰합니다.

* 각 테스트를 마친 후, 해당 테스트의 점수를 교재 앞쪽에 있는 [토익 Listening 목표 달성기]에 기록하여 자신의 점수 변화를 확인할 수 있습니다.

400점 이상
2주 완성 학습 플랜

· 2주 동안 매일 테스트 1회분을 교재 뒤의 Answer Sheet(p.229)을 활용하여 실전처럼 풀어본 후 꼼꼼하게 리뷰합니다.
· 리뷰 시, 틀렸던 문제를 다시 듣고 풀어본 후, 교재 뒤의 **스크립트**를 활용하여 들리지 않았던 부분까지 완벽히 이해합니다.
· 해커스토익(Hackers.co.kr)에서 무료로 제공되는 **지문 및 문제 해석**으로 틀린 지문과 문제의 의미를 확실하게 이해합니다.
· 해커스인강(HackersIngang.com)에서 무료로 제공되는 **단어암기장 및 단어암기 MP3**로 각 TEST의 핵심 어휘 중 모르는 어휘만 체크하여 암기합니다.

	Day 1	Day 2	Day 3	Day 4	Day 5
Week 1	☐ Test 01 풀기 및 리뷰	☐ Test 02 풀기 및 리뷰	☐ Test 03 풀기 및 리뷰	☐ Test 04 풀기 및 리뷰	☐ Test 05 풀기 및 리뷰
Week 2	☐ Test 06 풀기 및 리뷰	☐ Test 07 풀기 및 리뷰	☐ Test 08 풀기 및 리뷰	☐ Test 09 풀기 및 리뷰	☐ Test 10 풀기 및 리뷰

※ ≪해커스 토익 실전 1000제 1 Listening 해설집≫(별매)으로 리뷰하기
· 자신이 틀렸던 문제와 난이도 최상 문제를 다시 한번 풀어보고 완벽하게 이해합니다.
· 틀린 문제는 정답 및 오답 해설을 보며 오답이 왜 오답인지 그 이유까지 확실하게 파악합니다.

300~395점
3주 완성 학습 플랜

· 3주 동안 첫째 날, 둘째 날에 테스트 1회분씩을 풀어본 후 꼼꼼하게 리뷰하고, 셋째 날에는 2회분에 대한 심화 학습을 합니다.
· 리뷰 시, 틀렸던 문제를 다시 듣고 풀어본 후, 교재 뒤의 **스크립트**를 활용하여 들리지 않았던 부분까지 완벽히 이해합니다.
· 심화 학습 시, 리뷰했던 내용을 복습하고 대화/지문의 핵심 어휘를 정리하고 암기합니다.
· 해커스토익(Hackers.co.kr)에서 무료로 제공되는 **지문 및 문제 해석**으로 틀린 지문과 문제의 의미를 확실하게 이해합니다.
· 해커스인강(HackersIngang.com)에서 무료로 제공되는 **단어암기장 및 단어암기 MP3**로 각 TEST의 핵심 어휘를 암기합니다.

	Day 1	Day 2	Day 3	Day 4	Day 5
Week 1	☐ Test 01 풀기 및 리뷰	☐ Test 02 풀기 및 리뷰	☐ Test 01&02 심화 학습	☐ Test 03 풀기 및 리뷰	☐ Test 04 풀기 및 리뷰
Week 2	☐ Test 03&04 심화 학습	☐ Test 05 풀기 및 리뷰	☐ Test 06 풀기 및 리뷰	☐ Test 05&06 심화 학습	☐ Test 07 풀기 및 리뷰
Week 3	☐ Test 08 풀기 및 리뷰	☐ Test 07&08 심화 학습	☐ Test 09 풀기 및 리뷰	☐ Test 10 풀기 및 리뷰	☐ Test 09&10 심화 학습

※ ≪해커스 토익 실전 1000제 1 Listening 해설집≫(별매)으로 리뷰하기
· 자신이 틀렸던 문제와 난이도 중 이상의 문제를 다시 한번 풀어보고 완벽하게 이해합니다.
· 틀린 문제는 정답 및 오답 해설을 보며 오답이 왜 오답인지 그 이유까지 확실하게 파악합니다.
· 모든 문제마다 표시된 문제 유형을 보며 자신이 자주 틀리는 문제 유형이 무엇인지 파악하고 보완합니다.
· 대화/지문에 보라색으로 표시된 정답의 단서를 보고 정답을 선택해보며 문제 풀이 노하우를 파악합니다.

295점 이하
4주 완성 학습 플랜

· 4주 동안 이틀에 걸쳐 테스트 1회분을 풀고 꼼꼼하게 리뷰합니다.
· 리뷰 시, 모든 문제를 다시 듣고 풀어본 후, 교재 뒤쪽의 **스크립트**를 활용하여 들리지 않았던 부분까지 완벽하게 이해합니다.
· 해커스토익(Hackers.co.kr)에서 무료로 제공되는 **지문 및 문제 해석**으로 모든 지문과 문제의 의미를 완벽하게 이해합니다.
· 해커스인강(HackersIngang.com)에서 무료로 제공되는 **단어암기장 및 단어암기 MP3**로 각 TEST의 핵심 어휘를 암기합니다.

	Day 1	Day 2	Day 3	Day 4	Day 5
Week 1	☐ Test 01 풀기	☐ Test 01 리뷰	☐ Test 02 풀기	☐ Test 02 리뷰	☐ Test 03 풀기
Week 2	☐ Test 03 리뷰	☐ Test 04 풀기	☐ Test 04 리뷰	☐ Test 05 풀기	☐ Test 05 리뷰
Week 3	☐ Test 06 풀기	☐ Test 06 리뷰	☐ Test 07 풀기	☐ Test 07 리뷰	☐ Test 08 풀기
Week 4	☐ Test 08 리뷰	☐ Test 09 풀기	☐ Test 09 리뷰	☐ Test 10 풀기	☐ Test 10 리뷰

※ 《**해커스 토익 실전 1000제 1 Listening 해설집**》(별매)**으로 리뷰하기**
· 자신이 틀렸던 문제와 난이도 중 이상의 문제를 다시 한번 풀어보고 완벽하게 이해합니다.
· 틀린 문제는 정답 및 오답 해설을 보며 오답이 왜 오답인지 그 이유까지 확실하게 파악합니다.
· 모든 문제마다 표시된 문제 유형을 보며 자신이 자주 틀리는 문제 유형이 무엇인지 파악하고 보완합니다.
· 대화/지문에 보라색으로 표시된 정답의 단서를 보고 정답을 선택해보며 문제 풀이 노하우를 파악합니다.
· Part 3·4의 중요한 바꾸어 표현하기를 정리하고 암기합니다.

해커스와 함께라면 여러분의 목표를 더 빠르게 달성할 수 있습니다!
자신의 점수에 맞춰 아래 해커스 교재로 함께 학습하시면 더욱 빠르게 여러분이 목표한 바를 달성할 수 있습니다.

400점 이상	300~395점	295점 이하
《해커스 토익 Listening》	《해커스 토익 750+ LC》	《해커스 토익 스타트 Listening》

▌TEST 01

PART 1
PART 2
PART 3
PART 4
Self 체크 리스트

잠깐! 테스트 전 확인사항

1. 휴대 전화의 전원을 끄셨나요? □ 예
2. Answer Sheet, 연필, 지우개를 준비하셨나요? □ 예
3. MP3를 들을 준비가 되셨나요? □ 예

모든 준비가 완료되었으면 목표 점수를 떠올린 후 테스트를 시작합니다.
TEST 01을 통해 본인의 실력을 평가해 본 후, 본인에게 맞는 학습 플랜(p.20~21)으로 본 교재를 효율적으로 학습해 보세요.

🎧 TEST 01.mp3
실전용·복습용 문제풀이 MP3 무료 다운로드 및 스트리밍 바로듣기 (HackersIngang.com)
* 실제 시험장의 소음까지 재현해 낸 고사장 소음/매미 버전 MP3, 영국식·호주식 발음 집중 MP3, 고속 버전 MP3까지
  구매하면 실전에 더욱 완벽히 대비할 수 있습니다.

무료MP3 바로듣기

LISTENING TEST

In this section, you must demonstrate your ability to understand spoken English. This section is divided into four parts and will take approximately 45 minutes to complete. Do not mark the answers in your test book. Use the answer sheet that is provided separately.

PART 1

Directions: For each question, you will listen to four short statements about a picture in your test book. These statements will not be printed and will only be spoken one time. Select the statement that best describes what is happening in the picture and mark the corresponding letter (A), (B), (C), or (D) on the answer sheet.

Sample Answer

The statement that best describes the picture is (B), "The man is sitting at the desk." So, you should mark letter (B) on the answer sheet.

1.

2.

GO ON TO THE NEXT PAGE ▶

3.

4.

5.

6.

GO ON TO THE NEXT PAGE

PART 2

Directions: For each question, you will listen to a statement or question followed by three possible responses spoken in English. They will not be printed and will only be spoken one time. Select the best response and mark the corresponding letter (A), (B), or (C) on your answer sheet.

7. Mark your answer on your answer sheet.

8. Mark your answer on your answer sheet.

9. Mark your answer on your answer sheet.

10. Mark your answer on your answer sheet.

11. Mark your answer on your answer sheet.

12. Mark your answer on your answer sheet.

13. Mark your answer on your answer sheet.

14. Mark your answer on your answer sheet.

15. Mark your answer on your answer sheet.

16. Mark your answer on your answer sheet.

17. Mark your answer on your answer sheet.

18. Mark your answer on your answer sheet.

19. Mark your answer on your answer sheet.

20. Mark your answer on your answer sheet.

21. Mark your answer on your answer sheet.

22. Mark your answer on your answer sheet.

23. Mark your answer on your answer sheet.

24. Mark your answer on your answer sheet.

25. Mark your answer on your answer sheet.

26. Mark your answer on your answer sheet.

27. Mark your answer on your answer sheet.

28. Mark your answer on your answer sheet.

29. Mark your answer on your answer sheet.

30. Mark your answer on your answer sheet.

31. Mark your answer on your answer sheet.

PART 3

Directions: In this part, you will listen to several conversations between two or more speakers. These conversations will not be printed and will only be spoken one time. For each conversation, you will be asked to answer three questions. Select the best response and mark the corresponding letter (A), (B), (C), or (D) on your answer sheet.

32. What is the conversation mainly about?
    (A) Lowering an expense
    (B) Selecting a location
    (C) Repairing a machine
    (D) Moving to a new office

33. What is the man concerned about?
    (A) Employees take breaks too often.
    (B) The solar panels are not efficient.
    (C) A site is unsuitable for an installation.
    (D) Air conditioners may not work properly.

34. What does the woman suggest doing?
    (A) Installing fans in all of the offices
    (B) Upgrading the air conditioning system
    (C) Moving existing equipment to an empty
        space
    (D) Replacing the building's roof

35. Why is the woman calling?
    (A) To pay her bill at a later date
    (B) To change ownership of an account
    (C) To upgrade her cable subscription
    (D) To add another address to a cable plan

36. What does the woman say about her cable plan?
    (A) It includes a penalty for breaking the
        contract.
    (B) It has been operating for a year.
    (C) It has become too expensive.
    (D) It can be used on multiple devices.

37. What does the woman say she will do next?
    (A) Speak to her roommate
    (B) Cancel her transfer
    (C) E-mail some information
    (D) Look up a number

38. What will take place on January 3?
    (A) A shareholder meeting
    (B) An annual dinner
    (C) A training seminar
    (D) A retirement celebration

39. Why does Harold apologize?
    (A) He has a dietary restriction.
    (B) He cannot accept an offer.
    (C) He forgot to make a reservation.
    (D) He has not submitted a document.

40. What does the woman ask the men to do?
    (A) Contact a nutritionist
    (B) Look over a plan
    (C) Make some copies
    (D) Place an order

41. Where do the speakers most likely work?
    (A) At an accounting firm
    (B) At an advertising agency
    (C) At a food manufacturer
    (D) At a print shop

42. What does the woman mean when she says, "I'm going to fill out and submit my quarterly employee survey"?
    (A) She does not need help with a task at
        the moment.
    (B) She would like to ask a question later.
    (C) She is headed to another meeting in a
        few minutes.
    (D) She cannot discuss a project now.

43. What does the woman say she will do tomorrow?
    (A) Visit the man's office
    (B) Write a reference letter
    (C) Explain some guidelines
    (D) Turn in a form

GO ON TO THE NEXT PAGE

44. What are the speakers mainly discussing?

(A) A seasonal discount
(B) A new food menu
(C) A potential promotion
(D) A business expansion

45. What does the man suggest?

(A) Announcing some plans
(B) Searching for real estate
(C) Expanding a delivery area
(D) Promoting an opportunity

46. According to the woman, what will happen next month?

(A) An executive will visit.
(B) Some staff will be trained.
(C) A headquarters will be relocated.
(D) Some merchandise will arrive.

47. What do the men agree to do?

(A) Discontinue remote work
(B) Adjust business hours
(C) Hire part-time staff
(D) Move to a smaller office

48. What information does the woman provide?

(A) A monthly cost of a property
(B) The size of an office
(C) The name of a business
(D) A facility's hours of operation

49. What will the men most likely do later today?

(A) Take a tour of a facility
(B) Contact a real estate agent
(C) Print a rental contract
(D) Change a company policy

50. What problem does the man mention?

(A) He needs to fix a lock.
(B) He damaged his keys.
(C) He broke his leg.
(D) He misplaced an item.

51. Who most likely is the woman?

(A) A building manager
(B) A locksmith
(C) A shop owner
(D) A neighbor

52. What does the woman like about Nick's Hardware Store?

(A) It is open seven days a week.
(B) It is quicker than other stores.
(C) It is located on 19th Street.
(D) It is the oldest in town.

53. Where do the speakers work?

(A) At a dining establishment
(B) At a construction site
(C) At a retail outlet
(D) At a manufacturing plant

54. What did the woman do a few minutes ago?

(A) Posted a notice
(B) Assisted a customer
(C) Moved a product display
(D) Read some messages

55. Why does the man say, "There are only nine here"?

(A) To express concern
(B) To confirm some details
(C) To explain a decision
(D) To offer some help

56. What was dropped off at a venue?

(A) Some dishware
(B) Some outfits
(C) Some decorations
(D) Some equipment

57. What does the man suggest the woman do?

(A) Show guests to tables
(B) Refer to a printout
(C) Choose a song
(D) Hang some signs

58. What does the man say he needs to do?

(A) Arrange some flowers
(B) Revise a menu
(C) Review sample photographs
(D) Share some information

---

59. What problem does the man mention?

(A) A gift shop has closed.
(B) Some files are inaccurate.
(C) A service might be too expensive.
(D) Some taxes have gone up.

60. Why does the woman recommend hiring an online firm?

(A) To reduce a tax payment
(B) To increase returns on investments
(C) To produce professional reports
(D) To limit a cost

61. What will the woman probably do next?

(A) Cancel an appointment
(B) Collect some estimates
(C) Create a job listing
(D) Contact some coworkers

	Kenwood - $589
	Ridgeport - $649
	Wellington - $699
	New Hampton - $759

62. Why does the man want to buy some furniture?

(A) He moved to a larger home.
(B) He opened a new business.
(C) He heard about a sale.
(D) He damaged his current sofa.

63. Look at the graphic. How much will the man pay?

(A) $589
(B) $649
(C) $699
(D) $759

64. What does the man qualify for?

(A) Complimentary shipping
(B) A size upgrade
(C) Free cushions
(D) A trial membership

GO ON TO THE NEXT PAGE

Jet Airways

Boston ➜ Barcelona

Flight: DF465
Date: April 12
Row: 23
Seat: B
Gate: 10

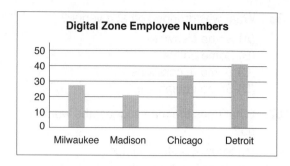

Digital Zone Employee Numbers

65. Why is the man traveling to Barcelona?

(A) To visit family
(B) To meet clients
(C) To conduct an interview
(D) To attend a conference

66. Look at the graphic. Which number will be changed?

(A) 465
(B) 12
(C) 23
(D) 10

67. What will the man probably do next?

(A) Wait in a different line
(B) Review a display board
(C) Check some luggage
(D) Find some identification

68. Who is Kenrick Jackson?

(A) A store manager
(B) A personal assistant
(C) A company president
(D) A human resources director

69. Look at the graphic. Where will a position become available?

(A) Milwaukee
(B) Madison
(C) Chicago
(D) Detroit

70. What does the woman offer to do?

(A) Talk to an employee
(B) Print out a form
(C) Assist with a document
(D) Write a recommendation

PART 4

Directions: In this part, you will listen to several short talks by a single speaker. These talks will not be printed and will only be spoken one time. For each talk, you will be asked to answer three questions. Select the best response and mark the corresponding letter (A), (B), (C), or (D) on your answer sheet.

71. Who is Neil Grady?

(A) A home owner
(B) An institute director
(C) An architect
(D) A tour guide

72. What does the speaker encourage the listeners to do?

(A) Click an icon to get more information
(B) Wait until the end to ask questions
(C) View the plans for the house
(D) Read the history of a family

73. What is mentioned about the Wilson Home?

(A) It will finish construction soon.
(B) It has a library on the second floor.
(C) It is open only part of the year.
(D) It has been worked on by many people.

74. Who are the listeners?

(A) Training managers
(B) Recently hired staff
(C) Emergency medical technicians
(D) Security guards

75. What will the listeners most likely do this morning?

(A) Review safety procedures
(B) Practice first-aid techniques
(C) Take a brief break
(D) Receive a pamphlet

76. What will be given at the end of the day?

(A) A ticket
(B) A coupon
(C) A certificate
(D) A prescription

77. Who most likely are the listeners?

(A) Job applicants
(B) Staff members
(C) Event organizers
(D) Store managers

78. What does the speaker want to do by November 27?

(A) Hold a meeting
(B) Attend a job fair
(C) Hire some new employees
(D) Write a proposal

79. What does the speaker want to happen in the company?

(A) The extension of a deadline
(B) The creation of a department
(C) The expansion of the client list
(D) The opening of a new branch

80. What is being announced?

(A) A flight postponement
(B) A terminal change
(C) A seating update
(D) A route modification

81. What does the speaker mean when she says, "I know you have taken your seats already"?

(A) The trip will take longer than planned.
(B) The listeners should fasten their seatbelts.
(C) The aircraft has malfunctioned.
(D) The listeners will be disrupted.

82. What does the speaker suggest the listeners do?

(A) Contact a travel agency
(B) Redeem a coupon
(C) Move to another gate
(D) Book another flight

GO ON TO THE NEXT PAGE

83. What does the speaker say about an event?

(A) It will feature a musical performance.
(B) It will be repeated in international locations.
(C) It will take less time than expected.
(D) It will include online viewers.

84. According to the speaker, what did Ms. Tucker recently do?

(A) Appeared in a commercial
(B) Earned a degree in engineering
(C) Transferred to another country
(D) Became a chief executive officer

85. What will one of the listeners receive?

(A) An event invitation
(B) A visitor's pass
(C) A free mobile device
(D) A monthly subscription

---

86. Why does the speaker say, "It's created from biodegradable and recycled materials"?

(A) To emphasize a commitment to the environment
(B) To recognize the efforts of product designers
(C) To explain why a manufacturing process takes time
(D) To clarify the information on a label

87. What does the company sell?

(A) Medical equipment
(B) Beauty products
(C) Clothing
(D) Agricultural supplies

88. What is supposed to happen in April?

(A) Some free samples will be distributed.
(B) A marketing campaign will commence.
(C) An online store will sell some items.
(D) A new package design will be revealed.

---

89. According to the speaker, what is available for free?

(A) Some park activities
(B) Public transportation
(C) Museum admissions
(D) Some streaming content

90. What is scheduled until September?

(A) Some farmer's markets
(B) Some city fairs
(C) Some morning workouts
(D) Some landscaping upgrades

91. What can be found online?

(A) Tips on improving fitness
(B) The location of a yoga studio
(C) A park's opening schedule
(D) Information about performances

---

92. What will take place on Saturday?

(A) A tasting event
(B) A baking class
(C) A monthly sale
(D) A fundraising gala

93. What does the speaker imply when she says, "the cake you asked about has multiple layers"?

(A) The product needs special packaging.
(B) Some preparations will take more time.
(C) Some design revisions will have to be made.
(D) The selected option is expensive.

94. Why should the listener talk to Genevieve?

(A) To ask for a sample
(B) To file a complaint
(C) To request a discount
(D) To inquire about personalization

Activity	Guide
Kayaking Tour	Kyle Hill
Parasailing	Jerome Weber
Scuba Diving	Dennis Maron
Jetboat Adventure	Billy Garcia

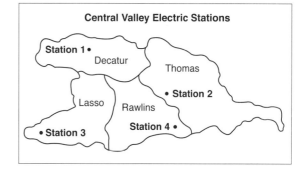

95. What does the speaker say about Carson Island Resort?

(A) It offers some activities for free.
(B) It is fully booked for the weekend.
(C) It ordered some new equipment.
(D) It is only accessible by boat.

96. What does the speaker recommend that the listeners do?

(A) Do some warmup exercises
(B) Wear appropriate clothing
(C) Bring some snacks on a trip
(D) Follow safety procedures

97. Look at the graphic. Who most likely is the speaker?

(A) Kyle Hill
(B) Jerome Weber
(C) Dennis Maron
(D) Billy Garcia

98. Who most likely is the speaker?

(A) A customer service representative
(B) A factory supervisor
(C) A county official
(D) A certified electrician

99. Look at the graphic. Which branch is restoring the service?

(A) Station 1
(B) Station 2
(C) Station 3
(D) Station 4

100. According to the speaker, why should the listener call back?

(A) To complain about noise
(B) To provide some contact information
(C) To pay an overdue utility fee
(D) To report an unresolved problem

정답 p.164 / 점수 환산표 p.167 / 스크립트 p.168 / 무료 해석 바로 보기(정답 및 정답 음성 포함)

▌정답 음성(QR)이나 정답(p.164)을 이용해 채점하시기 바랍니다. 정답 음성에서 Boy는 (B)를, David는 (D)를 나타냅니다.
▌점수 환산표(p.167)를 이용하여 본인의 점수를 확인하고, 그에 따른 학습 플랜을 p.20~21에서 선택한 후 실천해 보세요.
▌다음 페이지에 있는 Self 체크 리스트를 통해 자신의 문제 풀이 방식과 태도를 점검해 보세요.

Self 체크 리스트

TEST 01은 무사히 잘 마치셨죠?
이제 다음의 Self 체크 리스트를 통해 자신의 테스트 진행 내용을 점검해 볼까요?

1. 나는 테스트가 진행되는 동안 한 번도 중도에 멈추지 않았다.

   ☐ 예   ☐ 아니오

   아니오에 답한 경우, 이유는 무엇인가요?

2. 나는 답안지 표기까지 성실하게 모두 마무리하였다.

   ☐ 예   ☐ 아니오

   아니오에 답한 경우, 이유는 무엇인가요?

3. 나는 Part 2의 25문항을 푸는 동안 완전히 테스트에 집중하였다.

   ☐ 예   ☐ 아니오

   아니오에 답한 경우, 이유는 무엇인가요?

4. 나는 Part 3를 풀 때 음성이 들리기 전에 해당 질문과 보기를 모두 먼저 읽었다.

   ☐ 예   ☐ 아니오

   아니오에 답한 경우, 이유는 무엇인가요?

5. 나는 Part 4를 풀 때 음성이 들리기 전에 해당 질문과 보기를 모두 먼저 읽었다.

   ☐ 예   ☐ 아니오

   아니오에 답한 경우, 이유는 무엇인가요?

6. 개선해야 할 점 또는 나를 위한 충고를 적어보세요.

* 교재의 첫 장으로 돌아가서 자신이 적은 목표 점수를 확인하면서 목표에 대한 의지를 다지기 바랍니다. 개선해야 할 점은 반드시 다음 테스트에
  실천해야 합니다. 그것이 가장 중요하며, 그래야만 발전할 수 있습니다.

TEST 02

PART 1
PART 2
PART 3
PART 4
Self 체크 리스트

잠깐! 테스트 전 확인사항

1. 휴대 전화의 전원을 끄셨나요? □ 예
2. Answer Sheet, 연필, 지우개를 준비하셨나요? □ 예
3. MP3를 들을 준비가 되셨나요? □ 예

모든 준비가 완료되었으면 목표 점수를 떠올린 후 테스트를 시작합니다.

🎧 TEST 02.mp3

실전용·복습용 문제풀이 MP3 무료 다운로드 및 스트리밍 바로듣기 (HackersIngang.com)
* 실제 시험장의 소음까지 재현해 낸 고사장 소음/매미 버전 MP3, 영국식·호주식 발음 집중 MP3, 고속 버전 MP3까지
 구매하면 실전에 더욱 완벽히 대비할 수 있습니다.

무료MP3 바로듣기

LISTENING TEST

In this section, you must demonstrate your ability to understand spoken English. This section is divided into four parts and will take approximately 45 minutes to complete. Do not mark the answers in your test book. Use the answer sheet that is provided separately.

PART 1

Directions: For each question, you will listen to four short statements about a picture in your test book. These statements will not be printed and will only be spoken one time. Select the statement that best describes what is happening in the picture and mark the corresponding letter (A), (B), (C), or (D) on the answer sheet.

Sample Answer

The statement that best describes the picture is (B), "The man is sitting at the desk." So, you should mark letter (B) on the answer sheet.

1.

2.

GO ON TO THE NEXT PAGE ➤

3.

4.

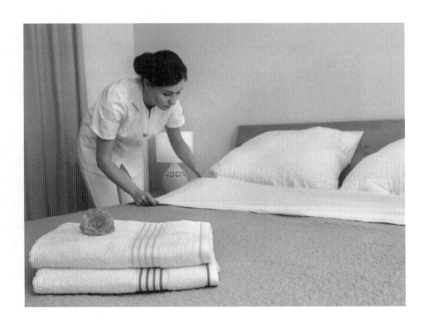

5.

6.

GO ON TO THE NEXT PAGE

PART 2

Directions: For each question, you will listen to a statement or question followed by three possible responses spoken in English. They will not be printed and will only be spoken one time. Select the best response and mark the corresponding letter (A), (B), or (C) on your answer sheet.

7. Mark your answer on your answer sheet.

8. Mark your answer on your answer sheet.

9. Mark your answer on your answer sheet.

10. Mark your answer on your answer sheet.

11. Mark your answer on your answer sheet.

12. Mark your answer on your answer sheet.

13. Mark your answer on your answer sheet.

14. Mark your answer on your answer sheet.

15. Mark your answer on your answer sheet.

16. Mark your answer on your answer sheet.

17. Mark your answer on your answer sheet.

18. Mark your answer on your answer sheet.

19. Mark your answer on your answer sheet.

20. Mark your answer on your answer sheet.

21. Mark your answer on your answer sheet.

22. Mark your answer on your answer sheet.

23. Mark your answer on your answer sheet.

24. Mark your answer on your answer sheet.

25. Mark your answer on your answer sheet.

26. Mark your answer on your answer sheet.

27. Mark your answer on your answer sheet.

28. Mark your answer on your answer sheet.

29. Mark your answer on your answer sheet.

30. Mark your answer on your answer sheet.

31. Mark your answer on your answer sheet.

PART 3

Directions: In this part, you will listen to several conversations between two or more speakers. These conversations will not be printed and will only be spoken one time. For each conversation, you will be asked to answer three questions. Select the best response and mark the corresponding letter (A), (B), (C), or (D) on your answer sheet.

32. What problem does the man mention?
    (A) A package was sent to the wrong place.
    (B) A letter contains inaccurate details.
    (C) A courier arrived at a destination late.
    (D) An order is going to be changed.

33. What does the woman inquire about?
    (A) Whether the man wants a quote
    (B) When the man received an item
    (C) Whether the man recognized some information
    (D) Where the man currently works

34. What does the woman say she will do?
    (A) Send out a worker
    (B) Waive a fee
    (C) Look up an address
    (D) Inform a sender

35. Where is the conversation most likely taking place?
    (A) In a hotel
    (B) In a staffing agency
    (C) In a pharmacy
    (D) In a research center

36. What task will Steve carry out?
    (A) Leading an orientation session
    (B) Giving a facility tour
    (C) Assembling a research team
    (D) Retrieving medicine samples

37. What do the men agree to do?
    (A) Share some study results
    (B) Meet in the afternoon
    (C) Introduce new employees
    (D) Work overtime hours

38. Why is the man calling?
    (A) To request an extension
    (B) To confirm a facility's hours
    (C) To check an item's availability
    (D) To cancel an appointment

39. Why does the woman say, "that publication is part of our rare book collection"?
    (A) To recommend another publication
    (B) To ask for extra caution
    (C) To justify a product's high cost
    (D) To point out a problem

40. What will the woman probably do next?
    (A) Locate some reading material
    (B) Verify a book title
    (C) Change a reservation
    (D) Transfer a call

41. What type of business does the woman probably work for?
    (A) An art supply shop
    (B) A photography studio
    (C) A hardware store
    (D) An interior design firm

42. What does the man show the woman?
    (A) A picture of a home
    (B) A membership card
    (C) A blueprint
    (D) A list of purchased items

43. According to the woman, how can the man obtain a discount?
    (A) By using a special coupon
    (B) By completing a survey
    (C) By presenting a receipt
    (D) By joining a store program

GO ON TO THE NEXT PAGE

44. What are the speakers mainly discussing?

(A) A seasonal sale
(B) A business launch
(C) A company inventory
(D) A temporary product

45. What does the man imply when he says, "I've never done anything like that before"?

(A) He is unsure about a proposed service.
(B) He wants to change the person in charge.
(C) He needs assistance with a task.
(D) He is unqualified for a job.

46. What is mentioned about Mr. Martin?

(A) He is the department manager.
(B) He will attend a meeting.
(C) He was recently promoted.
(D) He will be delivering a presentation.

---

47. What does the woman want to do?

(A) Find additional roommates
(B) Rent a house
(C) Sell some property
(D) View some real estate

48. What happened this morning?

(A) An offer was rejected.
(B) An appointment was made.
(C) An agent was hired.
(D) A document was printed.

49. What did the agent provide information about?

(A) Insurance rates
(B) Local businesses
(C) Monthly fees
(D) Employment opportunities

---

50. Where is the conversation taking place?

(A) At a tailoring shop
(B) At a dry-cleaning business
(C) At a postal office
(D) At a clothing store

51. What problem does the man identify?

(A) An item has been damaged.
(B) Some personnel took a sick day.
(C) Some equipment is malfunctioning.
(D) A bill is incorrect.

52. What will the woman probably do next?

(A) Request a refund
(B) Provide an address
(C) Examine a receipt
(D) Make a payment

---

53. Why does the woman need assistance?

(A) A phone isn't turning on.
(B) A product manual is missing.
(C) A screen is broken.
(D) A button is stuck.

54. What does the man ask about?

(A) Which product was selected
(B) When a purchase was made
(C) How a fee was paid
(D) Why an item was returned

55. According to the man, what will the woman receive?

(A) A full refund
(B) A free accessory
(C) A software upgrade
(D) A new device

---

56. Where most likely is the conversation taking place?

(A) At a ticket counter
(B) In a storage facility
(C) In an elevator
(D) At a security desk

57. What does the man say about his driver's license?

(A) It is a temporary replacement.
(B) It was left at home.
(C) It is going to expire soon.
(D) It was issued last year.

58. What will the man probably do next?

(A) Exchange a purchase
(B) Reschedule an appointment
(C) Show an access pass
(D) Fill out a document

---

59. Where do the speakers most likely work?

(A) At a department store
(B) At a marketing firm
(C) At a cosmetics company
(D) At a technology firm

60. What problem does the man mention?

(A) An online system was slow.
(B) A flight will be delayed.
(C) An offer has been refused.
(D) A document is outdated.

61. According to the man, what did Janice Miller do?

(A) Requested a status report
(B) Uploaded some files
(C) Altered some designs
(D) E-mailed a department head

Room 101	Break Room	Room 102	Printer Room	Elevators
Room 104	Mail Room	Room 103	Conference Room	Staircase

62. What is scheduled to take place tomorrow afternoon?

(A) The submission of a layout
(B) The distribution of a notice
(C) The inspection of an elevator
(D) The relocation of an office

63. Look at the graphic. Which room does the woman choose?

(A) Room 101
(B) Room 102
(C) Room 103
(D) Room 104

64. What does the man recommend?

(A) Rearranging a desk
(B) Replacing some shades
(C) Turning off some lights
(D) Installing window coverings

GO ON TO THE NEXT PAGE

Save Maldon Nature Preserve
Charity Concert
Saturday, June 13

7 P.M. – Transpire
8 P.M. – Blue Diamonds
9 P.M. – North Pines
10 P.M. – Watershed

Shelf 5	Memory cards	Memory cards	Memory cards
Shelf 4	Lenses		Lenses
Shelf 3	Tripods	Tripods	Tripods
Shelf 2	Flashes		Flashes
Shelf 1	Cameras		Cameras

65. What did the woman do yesterday?

(A) Contacted some guests
(B) Attended a rehearsal
(C) Canceled some plans
(D) Finalized a booking

66. What does the man say about Helmsley Park?

(A) It has a limited parking.
(B) It has a performance platform.
(C) It is temporarily closed.
(D) It requires a deposit.

67. Look at the graphic. Which band will not perform at the charity concert?

(A) Transpire
(B) Blue Diamonds
(C) North Pines
(D) Watershed

68. Why do the speakers need to reorganize a section of the store?

(A) A shipment will be delivered.
(B) An inspection will be conducted.
(C) A display will be removed.
(D) A sale will be held.

69. Look at the graphic. Where does the man want to put the cameras?

(A) On Shelf 2
(B) On Shelf 3
(C) On Shelf 4
(D) On Shelf 5

70. What does the man say he will give the woman?

(A) Order forms
(B) Customer information
(C) Camera accessories
(D) Promotional materials

PART 4

Directions: In this part, you will listen to several short talks by a single speaker. These talks will not be printed and will only be spoken one time. For each talk, you will be asked to answer three questions. Select the best response and mark the corresponding letter (A), (B), (C), or (D) on your answer sheet.

71. What are the listeners asked to do?

(A) Pick up their boarding passes
(B) Arrange bags in a specific way
(C) Tell attendants about meal preferences
(D) Go to another gate

72. According to the speaker, what will volunteers receive?

(A) Loyalty program points
(B) Free Internet access
(C) A coupon for food
(D) A seat upgrade

73. What does the speaker mention about passengers from economy class?

(A) They can get onto an aircraft.
(B) They have to check in their baggage.
(C) They must confirm their seat before boarding.
(D) They will have to pay for special amenities.

74. According to the speaker, what is Mr. Rothman famous for?

(A) Producing a fitness video
(B) Giving advice to celebrities
(C) Developing a health plan
(D) Writing a book about diets

75. What will Mr. Rothman probably discuss?

(A) A way to get more vitamins
(B) A method for eliminating fat
(C) Some workout tips
(D) Some exercise benefits

76. What will the listeners probably hear next?

(A) A song
(B) A speech
(C) A traffic report
(D) An advertisement

77. Where does the speaker most likely work?

(A) At a library
(B) At an education center
(C) At a bookstore
(D) At a publishing company

78. What does the speaker ask the listener to do?

(A) Submit a document
(B) Visit an office
(C) Respond to an e-mail
(D) Postpone a meeting

79. What does the speaker imply when she says, "we are flexible"?

(A) A meeting time can be changed.
(B) A staff is ready to offer help.
(C) A problem has many solutions.
(D) A document delivery may be delayed.

80. Where does the speaker most likely work?

(A) At a travel agency
(B) At a catering company
(C) At an accommodation facility
(D) At a sport arena

81. What does the speaker ask the listeners to do?

(A) Promote a special offer
(B) Join an employee program
(C) Continue recruiting members
(D) Submit leave requests

82. What are the listeners uncertain about?

(A) A vacation policy
(B) Overtime compensation
(C) A schedule change
(D) Salary increases

GO ON TO THE NEXT PAGE

83. Who most likely is the speaker?

(A) A realtor
(B) A painter
(C) A customer service representative
(D) A product designer

84. What does the speaker mean when she says, "I plan to head out after I get off the phone"?

(A) A customer wants to view samples.
(B) Additional measurements must be taken.
(C) Another product will be purchased.
(D) A project was completed early.

85. What will the speaker probably do tomorrow?

(A) Come back to a job site
(B) Contact her supervisor
(C) Visit a nearby store
(D) Hire a painting crew

86. What is the speaker mainly discussing?

(A) A clothing trend
(B) A textile firm
(C) A new procedure
(D) A new material

87. What does the speaker say about consumers?

(A) They could reduce their energy consumption.
(B) They look for natural ingredients.
(C) They are too busy to wash their clothes.
(D) They prefer environmentally friendly products.

88. What will the speaker probably do next?

(A) Distribute garment samples
(B) Install a lighting fixture
(C) Demonstrate a technology
(D) Show a video

89. What does the speaker want the listener to do?

(A) Train some employees
(B) Participate in a competition
(C) Promote a company
(D) Join a sports team

90. Why does the speaker say, "You won a gold medal at the Olympics last month"?

(A) To explain a change in a schedule
(B) To introduce an upcoming match
(C) To honor an accomplishment
(D) To give a reason for a request

91. What will happen next week?

(A) A new store will open.
(B) A spokesperson will be hired.
(C) A celebrity will receive an award.
(D) A business event will be held.

92. What will take place on Wednesday?

(A) A career fair
(B) An educational talk
(C) A book signing
(D) A charity fund-raiser

93. Why will an event be held at the Selby Auditorium?

(A) It offers an affordable rate.
(B) It has an excellent sound system.
(C) It can accommodate a big audience.
(D) It is close to an association's headquarters.

94. How can an event be attended for free?

(A) By completing a survey
(B) By doing volunteer work
(C) By arriving at a venue early
(D) By verifying a membership

Books by Lisa Duval Available on PageFlipper.com

Tomorrow's Export Market	★★★☆☆
Where the Jobs Have Gone	★★★★☆
Evaluating Globalization	★★☆☆☆
The Biggest Tech Boom	★★★★★

AIDQUEST Non-Profit Conference		
Topic	**Speaker**	**Time**
Fundraising	Carl Hendrickson	9 A.M.
Utilizing social media	Melody Ray	11 A.M.
Volunteer organizing	Miyuki Watanabe	1 P.M.
Government assistance	Evan Silverton	2 P.M.

95. What type of event is most likely taking place?

(A) A training session
(B) A book launch
(C) A financial convention
(D) A job fair

96. Look at the graphic. Which of Lisa Duval's books was released most recently?

(A) *Tomorrow's Export Market*
(B) *Where the Jobs Have Gone*
(C) *Evaluating Globalization*
(D) *The Biggest Tech Boom*

97. According to the speaker, what topic will be discussed?

(A) Recycling programs
(B) Urban design
(C) Organically grown food
(D) Renewable energy

98. Look at the graphic. Who is the message for?

(A) Carl Hendrickson
(B) Melody Ray
(C) Miyuki Watanabe
(D) Evan Silverton

99. Why does the speaker want to meet with the listener?

(A) To prepare a presentation
(B) To talk about a convention
(C) To discuss a job offer
(D) To congratulate a colleague

100. What does the speaker say he must do next Monday?

(A) Attend a company picnic
(B) Respond to an advisor
(C) Meet with a potential client
(D) Stop by a college campus

▮ 정답 음성(QR)이나 정답(p.164)을 이용해 채점하시기 바랍니다. 정답 음성에서 Boy는 (B)를, David는 (D)를 나타냅니다.
▮ 다음 페이지에 있는 Self 체크 리스트를 통해 자신의 문제 풀이 방식과 태도를 점검해 보세요.

Self 체크 리스트

TEST 02는 무사히 잘 마치셨죠?
이제 다음의 Self 체크 리스트를 통해 자신의 테스트 진행 내용을 점검해 볼까요?

1. 나는 테스트가 진행되는 동안 한 번도 중도에 멈추지 않았다.

   ☐ 예   ☐ 아니오

   아니오에 답한 경우, 이유는 무엇인가요?

2. 나는 답안지 표기까지 성실하게 모두 마무리하였다.

   ☐ 예   ☐ 아니오

   아니오에 답한 경우, 이유는 무엇인가요?

3. 나는 Part 2의 25문항을 푸는 동안 완전히 테스트에 집중하였다.

   ☐ 예   ☐ 아니오

   아니오에 답한 경우, 이유는 무엇인가요?

4. 나는 Part 3를 풀 때 음성이 들리기 전에 해당 질문과 보기를 모두 먼저 읽었다.

   ☐ 예   ☐ 아니오

   아니오에 답한 경우, 이유는 무엇인가요?

5. 나는 Part 4를 풀 때 음성이 들리기 전에 해당 질문과 보기를 모두 먼저 읽었다.

   ☐ 예   ☐ 아니오

   아니오에 답한 경우, 이유는 무엇인가요?

6. 개선해야 할 점 또는 나를 위한 충고를 적어보세요.

* 교재의 첫 장으로 돌아가서 자신이 적은 목표 점수를 확인하면서 목표에 대한 의지를 다지기 바랍니다. 개선해야 할 점은 반드시 다음 테스트에 실천해야 합니다. 그것이 가장 중요하며, 그래야만 발전할 수 있습니다.

█ TEST 03

PART 1
PART 2
PART 3
PART 4
Self 체크 리스트

잠깐! 테스트 전 확인사항

1. 휴대 전화의 전원을 끄셨나요? □ 예
2. Answer Sheet, 연필, 지우개를 준비하셨나요? □ 예
3. MP3를 들을 준비가 되셨나요? □ 예

모든 준비가 완료되었으면 목표 점수를 떠올린 후 테스트를 시작합니다.

🎧 TEST 03.mp3
실전용·복습용 문제풀이 MP3 무료 다운로드 및 스트리밍 바로듣기 (HackersIngang.com)
* 실제 시험장의 소음까지 재현해 낸 고사장 소음/매미 버전 MP3, 영국식·호주식 발음 집중 MP3, 고속 버전 MP3까지
  구매하면 실전에 더욱 완벽히 대비할 수 있습니다.

무료MP3 바로듣기

LISTENING TEST

In this section, you must demonstrate your ability to understand spoken English. This section is divided into four parts and will take approximately 45 minutes to complete. Do not mark the answers in your test book. Use the answer sheet that is provided separately.

PART 1

Directions: For each question, you will listen to four short statements about a picture in your test book. These statements will not be printed and will only be spoken one time. Select the statement that best describes what is happening in the picture and mark the corresponding letter (A), (B), (C), or (D) on the answer sheet.

Sample Answer

The statement that best describes the picture is (B), "The man is sitting at the desk." So, you should mark letter (B) on the answer sheet.

1.

2.

GO ON TO THE NEXT PAGE

3.

4.

5.

6.

GO ON TO THE NEXT PAGE

PART 2

Directions: For each question, you will listen to a statement or question followed by three possible responses spoken in English. They will not be printed and will only be spoken one time. Select the best response and mark the corresponding letter (A), (B), or (C) on your answer sheet.

7. Mark your answer on your answer sheet.

8. Mark your answer on your answer sheet.

9. Mark your answer on your answer sheet.

10. Mark your answer on your answer sheet.

11. Mark your answer on your answer sheet.

12. Mark your answer on your answer sheet.

13. Mark your answer on your answer sheet.

14. Mark your answer on your answer sheet.

15. Mark your answer on your answer sheet.

16. Mark your answer on your answer sheet.

17. Mark your answer on your answer sheet.

18. Mark your answer on your answer sheet.

19. Mark your answer on your answer sheet.

20. Mark your answer on your answer sheet.

21. Mark your answer on your answer sheet.

22. Mark your answer on your answer sheet.

23. Mark your answer on your answer sheet.

24. Mark your answer on your answer sheet.

25. Mark your answer on your answer sheet.

26. Mark your answer on your answer sheet.

27. Mark your answer on your answer sheet.

28. Mark your answer on your answer sheet.

29. Mark your answer on your answer sheet.

30. Mark your answer on your answer sheet.

31. Mark your answer on your answer sheet.

PART 3

Directions: In this part, you will listen to several conversations between two or more speakers. These conversations will not be printed and will only be spoken one time. For each conversation, you will be asked to answer three questions. Select the best response and mark the corresponding letter (A), (B), (C), or (D) on your answer sheet.

32. Why will the woman go to Mexico?
    (A) For a job interview
    (B) For a vacation
    (C) For a business trip
    (D) For a ceremony

33. What problem does the woman mention?
    (A) Her reimbursement request was denied.
    (B) A product needs to be repaired.
    (C) Her trip has been postponed.
    (D) A service is expensive.

34. What will the woman most likely do this evening?
    (A) Visit a business
    (B) Cancel a contract
    (C) Update an itinerary
    (D) Pay a bill

35. Why does the man need a permit?
    (A) He bought a car last month.
    (B) He was informed about a policy change.
    (C) He lives near a subway station.
    (D) He moved into a new residence.

36. Who is Mr. Hong?
    (A) A building manager
    (B) A department head
    (C) A corporate shareholder
    (D) A company president

37. According to the woman, what are staff prohibited from doing?
    (A) Taking unauthorized breaks
    (B) Parking in certain spots
    (C) Using a pass for multiple cars
    (D) Contacting clients directly

38. What is Shannon in charge of?
    (A) Negotiating a contract
    (B) Scheduling a repair
    (C) Filling an order
    (D) Reviewing a process

39. What does the woman mean when she says, "Three other employees were just added to her team"?
    (A) A project will get started soon.
    (B) A manager has approved a request.
    (C) A company decided to hire more staff.
    (D) A task will be completed on time.

40. Why is the man relieved?
    (A) Some work has been reassigned.
    (B) A document has been finished.
    (C) Some negotiations have ended.
    (D) A project schedule has been changed.

41. Where do the women work?
    (A) At a grocery store
    (B) At a city government office
    (C) At a real estate agency
    (D) At a construction company

42. What is the man planning to do?
    (A) Open a store
    (B) Sell a farm
    (C) Grow fruit
    (D) Purchase a business

43. What will the man most likely do next?
    (A) Look at a map
    (B) Redesign a property
    (C) Meet a client
    (D) Make a phone call

GO ON TO THE NEXT PAGE

44. What problem does the man mention?

(A) A sign has been taken down.
(B) A delivery has been delayed.
(C) An appliance is malfunctioning.
(D) A staff member is absent.

45. Why does the woman say, "That technician was here to inspect our fire sprinkler system"?

(A) To explain the need for overtime work
(B) To agree with a colleague
(C) To explain additional costs
(D) To correct a misunderstanding

46. What does the man ask the woman to do?

(A) Set up an appointment
(B) Empty out a refrigerator
(C) Check a schedule online
(D) Test a sprinkler system

---

47. What problem does the man mention?

(A) He was charged the wrong amount.
(B) He did not select the right product.
(C) He did not provide the correct information.
(D) He was given inaccurate instructions.

48. What does the woman ask for?

(A) An identification card
(B) An application form
(C) A business address
(D) A tracking number

49. What does the woman say the man must do?

(A) Have a package properly weighed
(B) Send a message to a friend
(C) Visit a post office Web site
(D) Wait for a parcel to be sent back

---

50. What most likely is the man's job?

(A) Fitness instructor
(B) Delivery person
(C) Interior decorator
(D) Sales associate

51. What does the man say about the EZ Keep?

(A) It is recommended by an expert.
(B) It works using a remote control.
(C) It is exclusively available online.
(D) It comes with free accessories.

52. What will the man probably do next?

(A) Contact another branch
(B) Compare some items
(C) Show a product
(D) Look up a price

---

53. What does the man say about his flight?

(A) It includes a stopover.
(B) It is going to be delayed by an hour.
(C) It is fully booked.
(D) It will depart in the afternoon.

54. Why are the speakers going to San Jose?

(A) To review a hotel
(B) To take part in a session
(C) To inspect an office
(D) To do some sightseeing

55. What does the woman suggest?

(A) Arranging a wake-up call
(B) Speaking to a front desk clerk
(C) Meeting in the lobby
(D) Moving to another hotel

---

56. What does the woman ask the man to do?

(A) Clean out an office
(B) Install some devices
(C) Read some instructions
(D) Train a coworker

57. What department will the new employees most likely work in?

(A) Accounting
(B) Marketing
(C) Human resources
(D) Information technology

58. What will the man probably do next?

(A) Visit a colleague
(B) Unload a package
(C) Return a shipment
(D) Assist an intern

---

59. Where most likely are the speakers?

(A) In a classroom
(B) In a bookstore
(C) In a library
(D) In an auditorium

60. What is mentioned about *Forgotten Time*?

(A) It is currently unavailable.
(B) It was sold at discount.
(C) It was recently published.
(D) It is set in Seattle.

61. What does the woman offer to do?

(A) Process a return
(B) Extend a loan
(C) Cancel a payment
(D) Reprint a receipt

Inventory List	
Item #3851	
Red Pullover Sweater	
Size	**Units in Stock**
Extra Small	6
Small	11
Medium	9
Large	15

62. According to the woman, what should be shared with staff?

(A) A password to an account
(B) Samples of merchandise
(C) A key to a storage room
(D) Copies of a document

63. Why does the man apologize?

(A) He failed to respond to a message.
(B) He misplaced some lists.
(C) He misunderstood directions.
(D) He forgot about an appointment.

64. Look at the graphic. Which size should the man reorder?

(A) Extra small
(B) Small
(C) Medium
(D) Large

GO ON TO THE NEXT PAGE

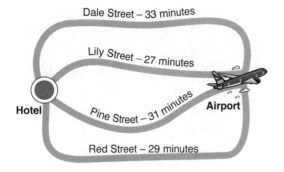

Dale Street – 33 minutes

Lily Street – 27 minutes

Hotel

Pine Street – 31 minutes

Red Street – 29 minutes

Airport

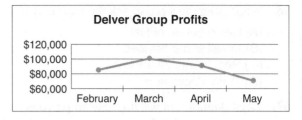

Delver Group Profits

$120,000
$100,000
$80,000
$60,000

February   March   April   May

65. What is mentioned about the woman?

(A) She is an experienced employee.
(B) She must travel tomorrow.
(C) She works at an airport.
(D) She plans to stay at a hotel.

66. What information does the woman ask about?

(A) A flight time
(B) An airline name
(C) A terminal number
(D) A departure gate

67. Look at the graphic. Which route is the woman going to take?

(A) Dale Street
(B) Lily Street
(C) Pine Street
(D) Red Street

68. What is the conversation mainly about?

(A) A consulting fee
(B) An upcoming meeting
(C) An urgent report
(D) A promotional event

69. Look at the graphic. When did Delver Group expand overseas?

(A) In February
(B) In March
(C) In April
(D) In May

70. What does the woman want to discuss in an e-mail?

(A) Customer feedback
(B) Business advice
(C) Expansion locations
(D) Company policies

Directions: In this part, you will listen to several short talks by a single speaker. These talks will not be printed and will only be spoken one time. For each talk, you will be asked to answer three questions. Select the best response and mark the corresponding letter (A), (B), (C), or (D) on your answer sheet.

71. What is the speaker's occupation?

(A) Government official
(B) Professional writer
(C) Real estate agent
(D) Financial consultant

72. What will the speaker discuss first?

(A) The risks of some investments
(B) The goals of a company
(C) The price of a service
(D) The benefits of savings accounts

73. What does the speaker say she will show the listeners?

(A) A brochure
(B) Some photographs
(C) A schedule
(D) Some diagrams

74. Where does the listener work?

(A) At a shipping company
(B) At a manufacturing plant
(C) At a television station
(D) At a repair shop

75. What does the speaker say about a television?

(A) It is the incorrect size.
(B) It was sent to an office.
(C) It can be customized.
(D) It has been damaged.

76. What does the speaker mean when he says, "it is being held this Saturday"?

(A) A refund does not need to be issued.
(B) A complaint must be resolved soon.
(C) A warranty should be extended.
(D) An event date has been changed.

77. Who are the listeners?

(A) Restaurant investors
(B) Business owners
(C) New employees
(D) Workshop leaders

78. What does the speaker ask the listeners to do?

(A) Offer assistance to incoming workers
(B) Arrange appointments with a supervisor
(C) Read through a training manual
(D) Write about a past work experience

79. What will probably take place in 15 minutes?

(A) A video screening
(B) A group discussion
(C) A registration period
(D) A lunch break

80. What is the speaker inquiring about?

(A) Whether a client is in town
(B) How much an upgrade will cost
(C) If he can use a vehicle
(D) When a trip will end

81. Why is the speaker traveling to Portland?

(A) To arrange an event
(B) To visit a friend
(C) To attend a conference
(D) To tour a college campus

82. What does the speaker ask the listener to do?

(A) Make a decision known
(B) Contact a rental company
(C) Return a car before Sunday
(D) Drive to Portland

GO ON TO THE NEXT PAGE

83. What is the announcement mainly about?

(A) A grand opening
(B) A branch expansion
(C) A product launch
(D) A sales event

84. What does the speaker suggest customers do?

(A) Become a member
(B) Purchase a gift card
(C) Download a flyer
(D) Check out reviews

85. What does the speaker say the listeners can do online?

(A) Review recent purchases
(B) Take advantage of deals
(C) Read about an upcoming line
(D) Request product exchanges

---

86. Where most likely are the listeners?

(A) At a tourist information office
(B) At a local museum
(C) At a private residence
(D) At an art school

87. Why does the speaker say, "that stands as a record"?

(A) To praise an administrator's career
(B) To explain a business strategy
(C) To describe a piece of artwork
(D) To draw attention to a donation

88. What will the listeners probably do next?

(A) Talk with some students
(B) Head to an auditorium
(C) Look at an exhibition
(D) Pay for facility passes

---

89. What does the speaker suggest the listeners do?

(A) Try out some running gear
(B) Raise funds for a registration fee
(C) Cheer on coworkers
(D) Stop by a booth

90. Why does the speaker feel optimistic?

(A) A lot of people have shown up.
(B) An additional product was donated.
(C) A weather forecast is favorable.
(D) An event was well publicized.

91. How can the listeners receive a sweatshirt?

(A) By buying an admission ticket
(B) By talking to an event organizer
(C) By sponsoring a colleague
(D) By taking part in a race

---

92. What does the speaker say happened in May?

(A) Some funding was awarded.
(B) Some focus groups were held.
(C) A library branch was closed.
(D) An online database was deleted.

93. Why does the speaker say, "Many people report using them two or three times weekly"?

(A) To give some usage directions
(B) To change some information
(C) To justify a decision
(D) To explain a schedule

94. What are the listeners asked to do?

(A) Sign up for a service
(B) Conduct some research
(C) Create a budget proposal
(D) Test out a new system

Length of Subscription	Discount
One month	$50
Three months	$100
Six months	$200
One Year	$400

95. What kind of business is Increda?

(A) A courier business
(B) A game developer
(C) A food service
(D) A publishing company

96. Look at the graphic. How much of a discount did the speaker receive?

(A) $50
(B) $100
(C) $200
(D) $400

97. What is mentioned about the sequel to *Fireflies*?

(A) It is not highly rated.
(B) It is not available yet.
(C) It is free to play.
(D) It is a puzzle game.

SAVE BIG on Quick Refresh!

10% off travel-sized bottles
15% off regular-sized bottles
20% off deluxe-sized bottles
25% off economy-sized bottles

Valid at all CityMart stores
Expires January 10

98. What is being advertised?

(A) A soft drink
(B) A diet pill
(C) A pain medicine
(D) A cleaning liquid

99. Look at the graphic. Which deal is offered for a recently launched bottle?

(A) 10% off
(B) 15% off
(C) 20% off
(D) 25% off

100. What does the speaker say about CityMart?

(A) It offers free shipping.
(B) It sells products through a Web site.
(C) It operates branches nationwide.
(D) It opened stores in another country.

정답 p.164 / 점수 환산표 p.167 / 스크립트 p.180 / 무료 해석 바로 보기(정답 및 정답 음성 포함)

■ 정답 음성(QR)이나 정답(p.164)을 이용해 채점하시기 바랍니다. 정답 음성에서 Boy는 (B)를, David는 (D)를 나타냅니다.
■ 다음 페이지에 있는 Self 체크 리스트를 통해 자신의 문제 풀이 방식과 태도를 점검해 보세요.

Self 체크 리스트

TEST 03는 무사히 잘 마치셨죠?
이제 다음의 Self 체크 리스트를 통해 자신의 테스트 진행 내용을 점검해 볼까요?

1. 나는 테스트가 진행되는 동안 한 번도 중도에 멈추지 않았다.

   ☐ 예   ☐ 아니오

   아니오에 답한 경우, 이유는 무엇인가요?

2. 나는 답안지 표기까지 성실하게 모두 마무리하였다.

   ☐ 예   ☐ 아니오

   아니오에 답한 경우, 이유는 무엇인가요?

3. 나는 Part 2의 25문항을 푸는 동안 완전히 테스트에 집중하였다.

   ☐ 예   ☐ 아니오

   아니오에 답한 경우, 이유는 무엇인가요?

4. 나는 Part 3를 풀 때 음성이 들리기 전에 해당 질문과 보기를 모두 먼저 읽었다.

   ☐ 예   ☐ 아니오

   아니오에 답한 경우, 이유는 무엇인가요?

5. 나는 Part 4를 풀 때 음성이 들리기 전에 해당 질문과 보기를 모두 먼저 읽었다.

   ☐ 예   ☐ 아니오

   아니오에 답한 경우, 이유는 무엇인가요?

6. 개선해야 할 점 또는 나를 위한 충고를 적어보세요.

* 교재의 첫 장으로 돌아가서 자신이 적은 목표 점수를 확인하면서 목표에 대한 의지를 다지기 바랍니다. 개선해야 할 점은 반드시 다음 테스트에 실천해야 합니다. 그것이 가장 중요하며, 그래야만 발전할 수 있습니다.

▌TEST 04

PART 1
PART 2
PART 3
PART 4
Self 체크 리스트

잠깐! 테스트 전 확인사항

1. 휴대 전화의 전원을 끄셨나요? □ 예
2. Answer Sheet, 연필, 지우개를 준비하셨나요? □ 예
3. MP3를 들을 준비가 되셨나요? □ 예

모든 준비가 완료되었으면 목표 점수를 떠올린 후 테스트를 시작합니다.

🎧 **TEST 04.mp3**

실전용·복습용 문제풀이 MP3 무료 다운로드 및 스트리밍 바로듣기 (HackersIngang.com)
* 실제 시험장의 소음까지 재현해 낸 고사장 소음/매미 버전 MP3, 영국식·호주식 발음 집중 MP3, 고속 버전 MP3까지
  구매하면 실전에 더욱 완벽히 대비할 수 있습니다.

무료MP3 바로듣기

LISTENING TEST

In this section, you must demonstrate your ability to understand spoken English. This section is divided into four parts and will take approximately 45 minutes to complete. Do not mark the answers in your test book. Use the answer sheet that is provided separately.

PART 1

Directions: For each question, you will listen to four short statements about a picture in your test book. These statements will not be printed and will only be spoken one time. Select the statement that best describes what is happening in the picture and mark the corresponding letter (A), (B), (C), or (D) on the answer sheet.

Sample Answer

The statement that best describes the picture is (B), "The man is sitting at the desk." So, you should mark letter (B) on the answer sheet.

1.

2.

GO ON TO THE NEXT PAGE

3.

4.

5.

6.

GO ON TO THE NEXT PAGE

PART 2

Directions: For each question, you will listen to a statement or question followed by three possible responses spoken in English. They will not be printed and will only be spoken one time. Select the best response and mark the corresponding letter (A), (B), or (C) on your answer sheet.

7. Mark your answer on your answer sheet.

8. Mark your answer on your answer sheet.

9. Mark your answer on your answer sheet.

10. Mark your answer on your answer sheet.

11. Mark your answer on your answer sheet.

12. Mark your answer on your answer sheet.

13. Mark your answer on your answer sheet.

14. Mark your answer on your answer sheet.

15. Mark your answer on your answer sheet.

16. Mark your answer on your answer sheet.

17. Mark your answer on your answer sheet.

18. Mark your answer on your answer sheet.

19. Mark your answer on your answer sheet.

20. Mark your answer on your answer sheet.

21. Mark your answer on your answer sheet.

22. Mark your answer on your answer sheet.

23. Mark your answer on your answer sheet.

24. Mark your answer on your answer sheet.

25. Mark your answer on your answer sheet.

26. Mark your answer on your answer sheet.

27. Mark your answer on your answer sheet.

28. Mark your answer on your answer sheet.

29. Mark your answer on your answer sheet.

30. Mark your answer on your answer sheet.

31. Mark your answer on your answer sheet.

Directions: In this part, you will listen to several conversations between two or more speakers. These conversations will not be printed and will only be spoken one time. For each conversation, you will be asked to answer three questions. Select the best response and mark the corresponding letter (A), (B), (C), or (D) on your answer sheet.

32. What did the man recently do?

(A) Accepted a funding offer
(B) Spoke with a bank employee
(C) Met with a potential customer
(D) Revised an operational budget

33. What is mentioned about Rebecca Holt?

(A) She is currently seeking employment.
(B) She has made a proposal.
(C) She used to work with the man.
(D) She agreed to a request.

34. What task is given to the man?

(A) Calculating some expenses
(B) Giving a presentation
(C) Arranging a meeting
(D) Reviewing some paperwork

35. What are the speakers preparing for?

(A) A software upgrade
(B) A training session
(C) A business expansion
(D) A recruiting effort

36. What is the problem?

(A) A team member is late.
(B) Some guests cannot attend a meeting.
(C) A deadline is not realistic.
(D) Some devices are malfunctioning.

37. What does the woman suggest?

(A) Changing a location
(B) Sharing an idea
(C) Posting a schedule
(D) Assisting a coworker

38. Where most likely are the speakers?

(A) At a culinary school
(B) At a restaurant
(C) At a television studio
(D) At a convention center

39. What does the man want the woman to do?

(A) Give a demonstration
(B) Review a potential menu
(C) Pick up some ingredients
(D) Judge a cooking competition

40. What does the woman say she will do?

(A) Hire a chef
(B) Taste some dishes
(C) Visit a store
(D) Share some information

41. What does the man want the woman to help with?

(A) Scheduling a negotiation
(B) Checking an announcement
(C) Sending some e-mails
(D) Cleaning up a workspace

42. Who does the man plan to e-mail?

(A) A magazine owner
(B) Some office managers
(C) An event organizer
(D) Some online writers

43. What does the woman imply when she says, "Clarissa went into her office a few minutes ago"?

(A) Clarissa was not informed about a meeting.
(B) Clarissa is not going on a trip.
(C) Clarissa can give some feedback.
(D) Clarissa is busy with some work.

GO ON TO THE NEXT PAGE

44. Why did the woman visit the office?

(A) For a facility tour
(B) For a job interview
(C) For a contract signing
(D) For a staff party

45. What does the woman say about Harding Development?

(A) It has hired a manager.
(B) It has few staff members.
(C) It has completed a project.
(D) It has several branches.

46. What does the woman say she received?

(A) A recommendation letter
(B) An international award
(C) An educational grant
(D) An annual bonus

---

47. Why does the woman apologize to the man?

(A) A defective product was sent.
(B) A refund policy was changed.
(C) A promotion has ended.
(D) A refrigerator is out of stock.

48. What will the man receive by e-mail?

(A) A set of pictures
(B) An instruction manual
(C) A discount coupon
(D) An application form

49. What is the man considering doing?

(A) Stopping by a product showroom
(B) Buying another appliance
(C) Going home earlier than usual
(D) Requesting a store catalog

---

50. What industry do the speakers most likely work in?

(A) Publishing
(B) Technology
(C) Marketing
(D) Entertainment

51. What did the man do during his lunch break?

(A) Read about a recent conference
(B) Listened to a business podcast
(C) Spoke with a company executive
(D) Went out to a local restaurant

52. Why does the man say, "It gets 500,000 downloads a month"?

(A) To highlight the popularity of a show
(B) To indicate a project's timeline
(C) To suggest upgrading a network system
(D) To recommend a change in content

---

53. Why did the man visit a store yesterday?

(A) To have a device repaired
(B) To buy a replacement part
(C) To seek out expert advice
(D) To compare some new models

54. According to the woman, what step is necessary?

(A) Removing a piece of plastic
(B) Unplugging a printer
(C) Downloading some software
(D) Inserting enough paper

55. What does the woman ask the man to do?

(A) Call another department
(B) Check some other cartridges
(C) Press a button on a printer
(D) Submit a formal complaint

---

56. What will happen on Saturday?

    (A) A team will make an announcement.
    (B) An athlete will appear at an event.
    (C) A basketball tournament will be held.
    (D) A sports documentary will be screened.

57. Why does the woman apologize?

    (A) She is unsure about a start time.
    (B) She is unable to join the man.
    (C) She cannot provide a ride.
    (D) She did not purchase tickets.

58. What does the woman suggest?

    (A) Using an application
    (B) Renting a vehicle
    (C) Taking public transportation
    (D) Looking up a schedule

59. What does the man say a business can do?

    (A) Complete a job in one day
    (B) Clean a specific fabric
    (C) Negotiate prices
    (D) Offer a customer a refund

60. What type of event does the woman intend to go to tomorrow?

    (A) A wedding ceremony
    (B) A corporate convention
    (C) A job interview
    (D) A formal dinner

61. What problem does the man mention?

    (A) A company is short-staffed.
    (B) An item is out of stock.
    (C) A machine is not working.
    (D) A voucher is not valid.

Project Management Process

Stage 1		Stage 2		Stage 3		Stage 4
Review budget	→	Submit proposal	→	Choose candidates	→	Assign tasks

62. What does the woman ask the man to send her?

    (A) A financial report
    (B) An employee evaluation
    (C) A project proposal
    (D) An application manual

63. Look at the graphic. Which stage will happen tomorrow?

    (A) Stage 1
    (B) Stage 2
    (C) Stage 3
    (D) Stage 4

64. What does the man suggest?

    (A) Installing new software
    (B) Assessing work experience
    (C) Meeting with a candidate
    (D) Removing a job posting

GO ON TO THE NEXT PAGE

TechnoForce Directory	
Floor 4	Research and Development
Floor 3	Accounting
Floor 2	Human Resources
Floor 1	Marketing

65. What is mentioned about Mr. Rogers?

(A) He had to reschedule a meeting.
(B) He did not respond to a voice mail.
(C) He will conduct an interview.
(D) He is not currently in his office.

66. Look at the graphic. Which floor will the woman visit?

(A) Floor 4
(B) Floor 3
(C) Floor 2
(D) Floor 1

67. What will the woman receive?

(A) A building floor plan
(B) A parking pass
(C) A registration form
(D) A temporary access card

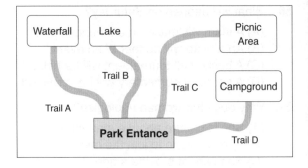

68. What is mentioned about the race?

(A) It will involve many students.
(B) It will raise money for an organization.
(C) It will take place in the morning.
(D) It will include several companies.

69. Look at the graphic. Which trail will runners most likely follow?

(A) Trail A
(B) Trail B
(C) Trail C
(D) Trail D

70. Why must the man contact Ms. Harris soon?

(A) A donation has not been received.
(B) A park trail was unexpectedly closed.
(C) A firm will not be able to sponsor an event.
(D) A registration period is about to end.

Directions: In this part, you will listen to several short talks by a single speaker. These talks will not be printed and will only be spoken one time. For each talk, you will be asked to answer three questions. Select the best response and mark the corresponding letter (A), (B), (C), or (D) on your answer sheet.

71. What are the listeners instructed to do?

(A) Go to a meeting area
(B) E-mail a coworker
(C) Join a videoconference
(D) Try on a clothing item

72. What does the speaker mention about Branson Uniform representatives?

(A) They can help determine a correct fit.
(B) They can look up a past purchase.
(C) They can apply a company discount.
(D) They can make a color choice.

73. What does the speaker say the company will do?

(A) Cancel an order
(B) Pay for some merchandise
(C) Change a uniform style
(D) Hire additional personnel

74. Who is the speaker?

(A) A professor
(B) An author
(C) An editor
(D) A librarian

75. Why is Mr. Short unable to attend an event?

(A) His assistant made a scheduling error.
(B) His train has been delayed by an hour.
(C) He is attending to a personal matter.
(D) He resides in another country.

76. Why has Mr. Short received an award?

(A) For donating his time to a school
(B) For founding an organization
(C) For serving as a longtime employee
(D) For creating children's books

77. What is the speaker mainly discussing?

(A) A school renovation
(B) Some road construction
(C) A community festival
(D) Some severe weather

78. What does the speaker mean when he says, "It's doubtful at this point"?

(A) Classes will not likely be held.
(B) City safety plans may not be revised.
(C) Repairs probably will not begin soon.
(D) A route might not reopen today.

79. Why should the listeners visit a Web site?

(A) To report some feedback
(B) To get additional updates
(C) To download a traffic map
(D) To sign up for alerts

80. What aspect of the machine does the dial control?

(A) Its volume
(B) Its height
(C) Its temperature
(D) Its speed

81. Who should the listeners contact if an issue arises?

(A) A floor supervisor
(B) A mechanical engineer
(C) A front desk worker
(D) A human resources manager

82. What are the listeners instructed to do at the end of a shift?

(A) Switch off a piece of equipment
(B) Provide information to a technician
(C) Conduct a safety inspection of a site
(D) Replace any damaged parts

GO ON TO THE NEXT PAGE

83. What is the topic of the talk?

(A) The concerns of some clients
(B) The purpose of a charity fund-raiser
(C) The founding of an organization
(D) The significance of a gathering

84. Who most likely are the listeners?

(A) Serving staff
(B) Event planners
(C) Business advisors
(D) Elected officials

85. Why should the listeners pay attention to requests?

(A) To encourage more donations
(B) To finish a task early
(C) To make a good impression
(D) To promote a new venue

---

86. What does the speaker say about Pomerta Incorporated?

(A) It is looking for new investors.
(B) It runs an online shopping site.
(C) It is experiencing technical problems.
(D) It has a meeting every year.

87. Why does the speaker say, "We only have an hour"?

(A) To encourage attendees to show up early
(B) To explain why prior preparations were made
(C) To show why an event is being held virtually
(D) To indicate a schedule change

88. What will the listeners do next?

(A) Move to a meeting location
(B) Listen to some financial details
(C) Select an award winner
(D) Open a new store

---

89. What type of event is being held?

(A) A sports competition
(B) A shareholder meeting
(C) A community gathering
(D) A commercial exhibition

90. What does the speaker mean when she says, "over 1,000 people are expected to take part"?

(A) A larger space will be needed.
(B) A prize has attracted a lot of interest.
(C) A corporate project has been expanded.
(D) A lecture series was well publicized.

91. What does the speaker suggest the listeners do?

(A) Pick up a coupon
(B) Watch a demonstration
(C) Wear a name tag
(D) Find an available seat

---

92. According to the speaker, what did Martin Keillor do yesterday?

(A) Led a group discussion
(B) Met with an inspector
(C) Copied some files
(D) Sent an e-mail

93. What is the speaker worried about?

(A) A facility cannot be renovated.
(B) A doorway has been blocked.
(C) A document has gone missing.
(D) A parking space is inaccessible.

94. Why will the listeners go to the main floor?

(A) To conduct a safety drill
(B) To retrieve some plastic bins
(C) To throw out some paper
(D) To pick up a shipment

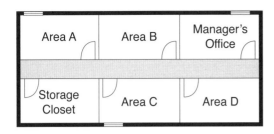

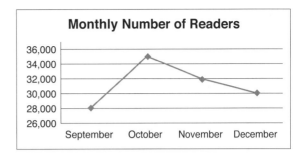

95. According to the speaker, what is set up in the lobby?

(A) Some photographs
(B) Some furniture
(C) Some awards
(D) Some refreshments

96. What does the speaker say about *The Nashville Gazette*?

(A) It was founded by a local resident.
(B) It has been in operation for 20 years.
(C) It recently updated its computer systems.
(D) It employs thousands of staff members.

97. Look at the graphic. Where are the printers located?

(A) In Area A
(B) In Area B
(C) In Area C
(D) In Area D

98. Look at the graphic. When did the TV commercial air?

(A) In September
(B) In October
(C) In November
(D) In December

99. What does the company plan to do?

(A) Seek advice from specialists
(B) Unveil new advertisements
(C) Release a special issue
(D) Reconsider a pricing policy

100. According to the speaker, what will be offered to some customers in January?

(A) A full refund
(B) A subscription renewal
(C) An issue of a magazine
(D) A price reduction

정답 p.164 / 점수 환산표 p.167 / 스크립트 p.186 / 무료 해석 바로 보기(정답 및 정답 음성 포함)

Self 체크 리스트

TEST 04는 무사히 잘 마치셨죠?
이제 다음의 Self 체크 리스트를 통해 자신의 테스트 진행 내용을 점검해 볼까요?

1. 나는 테스트가 진행되는 동안 한 번도 중도에 멈추지 않았다.

   ☐ 예　　　　　　　☐ 아니오

   아니오에 답한 경우, 이유는 무엇인가요?

2. 나는 답안지 표기까지 성실하게 모두 마무리하였다.

   ☐ 예　　　　　　　☐ 아니오

   아니오에 답한 경우, 이유는 무엇인가요?

3. 나는 Part 2의 25문항을 푸는 동안 완전히 테스트에 집중하였다.

   ☐ 예　　　　　　　☐ 아니오

   아니오에 답한 경우, 이유는 무엇인가요?

4. 나는 Part 3를 풀 때 음성이 들리기 전에 해당 질문과 보기를 모두 먼저 읽었다.

   ☐ 예　　　　　　　☐ 아니오

   아니오에 답한 경우, 이유는 무엇인가요?

5. 나는 Part 4를 풀 때 음성이 들리기 전에 해당 질문과 보기를 모두 먼저 읽었다.

   ☐ 예　　　　　　　☐ 아니오

   아니오에 답한 경우, 이유는 무엇인가요?

6. 개선해야 할 점 또는 나를 위한 충고를 적어보세요.

* 교재의 첫 장으로 돌아가서 자신이 적은 목표 점수를 확인하면서 목표에 대한 의지를 다지기 바랍니다. 개선해야 할 점은 반드시 다음 테스트에
  실천해야 합니다. 그것이 가장 중요하며, 그래야만 발전할 수 있습니다.

▌TEST 05

PART 1
PART 2
PART 3
PART 4
Self 체크 리스트

잠깐! 테스트 전 확인사항
1. 휴대 전화의 전원을 끄셨나요? □ 예
2. Answer Sheet, 연필, 지우개를 준비하셨나요? □ 예
3. MP3를 들을 준비가 되셨나요? □ 예

모든 준비가 완료되었으면 목표 점수를 떠올린 후 테스트를 시작합니다.

🎧 TEST 05.mp3

실전용·복습용 문제풀이 MP3 무료 다운로드 및 스트리밍 바로듣기 (HackersIngang.com)
* 실제 시험장의 소음까지 재현해 낸 고사장 소음/매미 버전 MP3, 영국식·호주식 발음 집중 MP3, 고속 버전 MP3까지
  구매하면 실전에 더욱 완벽히 대비할 수 있습니다.

무료MP3 바로듣기

LISTENING TEST

In this section, you must demonstrate your ability to understand spoken English. This section is divided into four parts and will take approximately 45 minutes to complete. Do not mark the answers in your test book. Use the answer sheet that is provided separately.

PART 1

Directions: For each question, you will listen to four short statements about a picture in your test book. These statements will not be printed and will only be spoken one time. Select the statement that best describes what is happening in the picture and mark the corresponding letter (A), (B), (C), or (D) on the answer sheet.

Sample Answer

The statement that best describes the picture is (B), "The man is sitting at the desk." So, you should mark letter (B) on the answer sheet.

1.

2.

GO ON TO THE NEXT PAGE →

3.

4.

5.

6.

GO ON TO THE NEXT PAGE

PART 2

Directions: For each question, you will listen to a statement or question followed by three possible responses spoken in English. They will not be printed and will only be spoken one time. Select the best response and mark the corresponding letter (A), (B), or (C) on your answer sheet.

7. Mark your answer on your answer sheet.

8. Mark your answer on your answer sheet.

9. Mark your answer on your answer sheet.

10. Mark your answer on your answer sheet.

11. Mark your answer on your answer sheet.

12. Mark your answer on your answer sheet.

13. Mark your answer on your answer sheet.

14. Mark your answer on your answer sheet.

15. Mark your answer on your answer sheet.

16. Mark your answer on your answer sheet.

17. Mark your answer on your answer sheet.

18. Mark your answer on your answer sheet.

19. Mark your answer on your answer sheet.

20. Mark your answer on your answer sheet.

21. Mark your answer on your answer sheet.

22. Mark your answer on your answer sheet.

23. Mark your answer on your answer sheet.

24. Mark your answer on your answer sheet.

25. Mark your answer on your answer sheet.

26. Mark your answer on your answer sheet.

27. Mark your answer on your answer sheet.

28. Mark your answer on your answer sheet.

29. Mark your answer on your answer sheet.

30. Mark your answer on your answer sheet.

31. Mark your answer on your answer sheet.

PART 3

Directions: In this part, you will listen to several conversations between two or more speakers. These conversations will not be printed and will only be spoken one time. For each conversation, you will be asked to answer three questions. Select the best response and mark the corresponding letter (A), (B), (C), or (D) on your answer sheet.

32. What problem does the man mention?

(A) A password is incorrect.
(B) A business has been closed.
(C) A screen is malfunctioning.
(D) A receipt was lost.

33. What does the woman recommend doing?

(A) Trying another device
(B) Pressing a button
(C) Calling a technician
(D) Waiting in line

34. What does the woman offer the man?

(A) A flyer
(B) A voucher
(C) A calendar
(D) An invitation card

35. What does the man say about PointAlert products?

(A) They are very expensive.
(B) They are out of stock.
(C) They are advertised online.
(D) They are being discounted.

36. What changed last month?

(A) An application requirement
(B) A sales promotion
(C) A membership program
(D) A business location

37. What will the woman most likely do next?

(A) Make a purchase
(B) Replace a battery
(C) Download a program
(D) Call a branch

38. Where does the woman most likely work?

(A) At a music store
(B) At a theater
(C) At a recording studio
(D) At a concert venue

39. What is causing the delay?

(A) The malfunctioning of some speakers
(B) The late arrival of a performer
(C) The long rehearsal of a band
(D) The repair of some lighting

40. What will the men probably do next?

(A) Request a refund
(B) Message an acquaintance
(C) Return to their seats
(D) Purchase their tickets

41. What are the speakers mainly discussing?

(A) Parking options
(B) Room rates
(C) Payment methods
(D) Travel plans

42. What does the man suggest?

(A) Unpacking some bags
(B) Signing up for an activity
(C) Doing activities separately
(D) Posing for a photograph

43. What will Jen probably do next?

(A) Ask for directions
(B) Check in to a hotel
(C) Go to a park
(D) Provide recommendations

GO ON TO THE NEXT PAGE

44. What are the speakers mainly discussing?

(A) Training some employees
(B) Booking a flight
(C) Planning an event
(D) Raising some funds

45. What is a feature of the restaurant?

(A) It is close to the office.
(B) It serves good food.
(C) It offers private spaces.
(D) It has been renovated.

46. Why does the woman say, "We're attending a budget meeting that day"?

(A) To make a complaint
(B) To explain a request
(C) To respond to an inquiry
(D) To decline an invitation

---

47. What will the man's company do?

(A) Launch a product
(B) Open a branch
(C) Cancel an order
(D) Support a competition

48. What does the woman offer to do?

(A) Speed up a process
(B) Check a system
(C) Provide a refund
(D) Show a sample

49. What will most likely happen next?

(A) A package will be delivered.
(B) A payment will be made.
(C) A service will be canceled.
(D) An image will be sent.

---

50. What type of business does the man most likely work for?

(A) A fitness center
(B) A staffing agency
(C) A moving company
(D) An advertising firm

51. What does the man say about the gym?

(A) It will host an event.
(B) It has been inspected.
(C) It will reopen soon.
(D) It has some new machines.

52. What will the man probably do next?

(A) Make some inquiries
(B) Complete some paperwork
(C) Demonstrate a product
(D) Distribute a pamphlet

---

53. What are the speakers mainly discussing?

(A) Automated devices
(B) A Web site's design
(C) Training workshops
(D) A customer review

54. What does the woman expect to happen?

(A) Customers will complain.
(B) Staff will be replaced.
(C) Revenue will increase.
(D) Installations will be delayed.

55. What did the woman do an hour ago?

(A) Paid a delivery person
(B) Contacted a worker
(C) Checked a text message
(D) Conducted an interview

---

56. Who is Brenda Frost?

(A) A hair stylist
(B) A personal assistant
(C) An accountant
(D) A property owner

57. Why does the woman say, "We've established a large client base in the neighborhood."?

(A) To confirm that a decision was reached
(B) To explain why she agrees with an opinion
(C) To show how she achieved a goal
(D) To indicate that a plan is unacceptable

58. What does the woman say she will do this afternoon?

(A) Make a phone call
(B) Address a complaint
(C) Change a work schedule
(D) Adjust a budget

---

59. What is the man's area of expertise?

(A) Real estate
(B) Advertising
(C) Radio broadcasting
(D) Finance

60. What does the woman ask the man to do?

(A) Interview a guest
(B) Share some advice
(C) Announce some commercials
(D) Sign a contract

61. What will most likely happen next?

(A) The next show will be introduced.
(B) A traffic report will be broadcast.
(C) Some calls will be taken.
(D) A prize will be given away.

Bus Number	Information
180	Express to Grayfield Station
195	Express to Windsor Station
199	Local to Windsor Station
210	Local to Grayfield Station

62. What did the woman recently do?

(A) Renewed a bus pass
(B) Relocated to a new area
(C) Published a travel book
(D) Made a career change

63. Look at the graphic. Which bus will the woman most likely take?

(A) 180
(B) 195
(C) 199
(D) 210

64. Where will the woman go at noon?

(A) To a bus company
(B) To a pharmacy
(C) To a train station
(D) To a dental clinic

GO ON TO THE NEXT PAGE

**Styx Photo Editing Software
User Manual**

Table of Contents

65. Who most likely is the woman?

(A) A repairperson
(B) A graphic designer
(C) A gallery owner
(D) A sales representative

66. Look at the graphic. Which section should the man refer to?

(A) Installation
(B) Tools
(C) Techniques
(D) Exporting

67. Why does the woman suggest reviewing some content?

(A) To find an image
(B) To prepare for a test
(C) To resolve a complaint
(D) To improve a presentation

Customer Survey on Mobile Telephone Plan
(Average ratings)

	Excellent	Good	Poor	Very Poor
Quality of calls		○		
Monthly rates	○			
Choice of calling plans				○
Customer service			○	

68. What does the man say he will do this week?

(A) Hand in a report
(B) Achieve a sales target
(C) Attend a gathering
(D) Purchase a new phone

69. Look at the graphic. Which category was the woman surprised about?

(A) Quality of calls
(B) Monthly rates
(C) Choice of calling plans
(D) Customer service

70. What does the woman say about Warren Jordan?

(A) He received a license recently.
(B) He provided some assistance previously.
(C) He plans to hire some new staff.
(D) He is concerned about a contract.

PART 4

Directions: In this part, you will listen to several short talks by a single speaker. These talks will not be printed and will only be spoken one time. For each talk, you will be asked to answer three questions. Select the best response and mark the corresponding letter (A), (B), (C), or (D) on your answer sheet.

71. What type of business does the speaker work for?

(A) A delivery service
(B) A printing company
(C) An office supply store
(D) A paper manufacturer

72. What problem does the speaker mention?

(A) A warehouse is understaffed.
(B) A vendor is no longer in business.
(C) Some color options have changed.
(D) Some shipments have been delayed.

73. Why is the listener asked to return the call?

(A) To discuss available products
(B) To confirm an e-mail address
(C) To provide payment details
(D) To review a return policy

74. Why does the speaker say, "So it wasn't safe to walk around"?

(A) To make a complaint
(B) To justify a detour
(C) To request a repair
(D) To explain a delay

75. What will happen next week?

(A) A construction project will be completed.
(B) Some community classes will be canceled.
(C) Some schedules will be posted online.
(D) A pool will be cleaned.

76. What does the speaker tell the listeners to do?

(A) Pass along some ideas
(B) Improve a Web site
(C) Show a membership card
(D) Sign up for a tour

77. What type of product is being advertised?

(A) A digital camera
(B) An energy-efficient laptop
(C) A phone accessory
(D) A portable speaker

78. What feature makes the product unique?

(A) A carrying case
(B) A removable battery
(C) A touchscreen display
(D) A solar panel

79. Why should the listeners visit a Web site?

(A) To read some reviews
(B) To order a special model
(C) To request express delivery
(D) To download a coupon

80. What will some customer service representatives most likely do in June?

(A) Begin working at a different time
(B) Move to a new office
(C) Take part in a session
(D) Inform clients about a policy

81. What does the speaker mean when he says, "anything longer than this is not acceptable"?

(A) Online chat programs will be adopted.
(B) Additional staff will be hired.
(C) Employees must become more efficient.
(D) Shorter breaks must be introduced.

82. What does the speaker say he will do?

(A) Choose a worker for a duty
(B) Sign a legal document
(C) Evaluate some applicants
(D) Provide some training

GO ON TO THE NEXT PAGE

83. According to the speaker, what can the listeners do at the information desk?

(A) Pick up a pamphlet
(B) View a match list
(C) Ask about some prizes
(D) Speak to some judges

84. Why is Mary O'Reilly unable to attend the tournament?

(A) She does not feel well.
(B) She missed a flight.
(C) She is hosting a fund-raiser.
(D) She is getting ready for a match.

85. What will be broadcast on WXTC Radio?

(A) Celebrity interviews
(B) Award recipient names
(C) Additional program changes
(D) Details about a competition

---

86. What is the radio broadcast mainly about?

(A) The success of an author
(B) Different formats of publications
(C) Special events at a bookstore
(D) A newly developed device

87. What does the speaker mention about Gail Boyd?

(A) She made a past appearance on the show.
(B) She gives informational talks at schools.
(C) She will be arriving later than planned.
(D) She founded her own company.

88. What will happen next?

(A) A guest will describe her work experience.
(B) A book excerpt will be read.
(C) A writer will discuss her novel.
(D) A special report will be aired.

---

89. What type of gathering is the listener organizing?

(A) A retirement party
(B) An awards banquet
(C) A corporate picnic
(D) A wedding ceremony

90. What did the speaker do this morning?

(A) Sent out a revised cost estimate
(B) Contacted a venue manager
(C) Added people to a guest list
(D) Spoke with a chef about a menu

91. Why does the speaker say, "There were 300 people at an event we catered yesterday"?

(A) To make a correction
(B) To provide a discount
(C) To explain a request
(D) To offer assurance

---

92. Where most likely are the listeners?

(A) At a farm
(B) At a food processing plant
(C) At a café
(D) At a research facility

93. What does the speaker say he will discuss?

(A) The origins of some ingredients
(B) The uses of some machinery
(C) The purpose of a project
(D) The size of an organization

94. What will the listeners be able to do at the end of the tour?

(A) View an instructional video
(B) Meet a business owner
(C) Make a purchase
(D) Try a sample

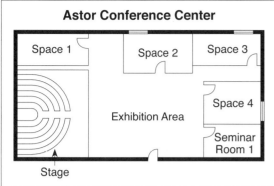

Astor Conference Center

Space 1

Space 2

Space 3

Space 4

Exhibition Area

Seminar Room 1

Stage

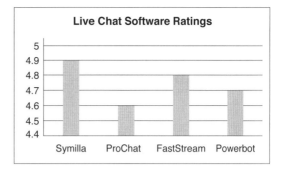

Live Chat Software Ratings

Symilla   ProChat   FastStream   Powerbot

95. According to the speaker, what did Amanda do?

(A) Met with some customers
(B) Decorated some conference halls
(C) Summarized some preparations
(D) Confirmed a reservation

96. What is mentioned about the speaker's company?

(A) It operates internationally.
(B) It will partner with another firm.
(C) It launched a new Web site.
(D) It is sponsoring a conference.

97. Look at the graphic. Where will the magazine rack be placed this year?

(A) In Space 1
(B) In Space 2
(C) In Space 3
(D) In Space 4

98. Why is the speaker calling?

(A) To report a technical problem
(B) To rearrange a meeting
(C) To follow up on a request
(D) To discuss a customer complaint

99. Look at the graphic. Which program does the speaker recommend?

(A) Symilla
(B) ProChat
(C) FastStream
(D) Powerbot

100. What does the speaker offer to do?

(A) Pay for a service
(B) Give a demonstration
(C) Instruct some staff
(D) Contact a manufacturer

정답 p.165 / 점수 환산표 p.167 / 스크립트 p.192 / 무료 해석 바로 보기(정답 및 정답 음성 포함)

▮ 정답 음성(QR)이나 정답(p.165)을 이용해 채점하시기 바랍니다. 정답 음성에서 Boy는 (B)를, David는 (D)를 나타냅니다.
▮ 다음 페이지에 있는 Self 체크 리스트를 통해 자신의 문제 풀이 방식과 태도를 점검해 보세요.

Self 체크 리스트

TEST 05는 무사히 잘 마치셨죠?
이제 다음의 Self 체크 리스트를 통해 자신의 테스트 진행 내용을 점검해 볼까요?

1. 나는 테스트가 진행되는 동안 한 번도 중도에 멈추지 않았다.

   ☐ 예   ☐ 아니오

   아니오에 답한 경우, 이유는 무엇인가요?

2. 나는 답안지 표기까지 성실하게 모두 마무리하였다.

   ☐ 예   ☐ 아니오

   아니오에 답한 경우, 이유는 무엇인가요?

3. 나는 Part 2의 25문항을 푸는 동안 완전히 테스트에 집중하였다.

   ☐ 예   ☐ 아니오

   아니오에 답한 경우, 이유는 무엇인가요?

4. 나는 Part 3를 풀 때 음성이 들리기 전에 해당 질문과 보기를 모두 먼저 읽었다.

   ☐ 예   ☐ 아니오

   아니오에 답한 경우, 이유는 무엇인가요?

5. 나는 Part 4를 풀 때 음성이 들리기 전에 해당 질문과 보기를 모두 먼저 읽었다.

   ☐ 예   ☐ 아니오

   아니오에 답한 경우, 이유는 무엇인가요?

6. 개선해야 할 점 또는 나를 위한 충고를 적어보세요.

* 교재의 첫 장으로 돌아가서 자신이 적은 목표 점수를 확인하면서 목표에 대한 의지를 다지기 바랍니다. 개선해야 할 점은 반드시 다음 테스트에 실천해야 합니다. 그것이 가장 중요하며, 그래야만 발전할 수 있습니다.

TEST 06

PART 1
PART 2
PART 3
PART 4
Self 체크 리스트

잠깐! 테스트 전 확인사항
1. 휴대 전화의 전원을 끄셨나요? □ 예
2. Answer Sheet, 연필, 지우개를 준비하셨나요? □ 예
3. MP3를 들을 준비가 되셨나요? □ 예

모든 준비가 완료되었으면 목표 점수를 떠올린 후 테스트를 시작합니다.

🎧 TEST 06.mp3
실전용·복습용 문제풀이 MP3 무료 다운로드 및 스트리밍 바로듣기 (HackersIngang.com)
* 실제 시험장의 소음까지 재현해 낸 고사장 소음/매미 버전 MP3, 영국식·호주식 발음 집중 MP3, 고속 버전 MP3까지 구매하면 실전에 더욱 완벽히 대비할 수 있습니다.

무료MP3 바로듣기

LISTENING TEST

In this section, you must demonstrate your ability to understand spoken English. This section is divided into four parts and will take approximately 45 minutes to complete. Do not mark the answers in your test book. Use the answer sheet that is provided separately.

PART 1

Directions: For each question, you will listen to four short statements about a picture in your test book. These statements will not be printed and will only be spoken one time. Select the statement that best describes what is happening in the picture and mark the corresponding letter (A), (B), (C), or (D) on the answer sheet.

Sample Answer
Ⓐ ● Ⓒ Ⓓ

The statement that best describes the picture is (B), "The man is sitting at the desk." So, you should mark letter (B) on the answer sheet.

1.

2.

GO ON TO THE NEXT PAGE

3.

4.

5.

6.

GO ON TO THE NEXT PAGE

PART 2

Directions: For each question, you will listen to a statement or question followed by three possible responses spoken in English. They will not be printed and will only be spoken one time. Select the best response and mark the corresponding letter (A), (B), or (C) on your answer sheet.

7. Mark your answer on your answer sheet.

8. Mark your answer on your answer sheet.

9. Mark your answer on your answer sheet.

10. Mark your answer on your answer sheet.

11. Mark your answer on your answer sheet.

12. Mark your answer on your answer sheet.

13. Mark your answer on your answer sheet.

14. Mark your answer on your answer sheet.

15. Mark your answer on your answer sheet.

16. Mark your answer on your answer sheet.

17. Mark your answer on your answer sheet.

18. Mark your answer on your answer sheet.

19. Mark your answer on your answer sheet.

20. Mark your answer on your answer sheet.

21. Mark your answer on your answer sheet.

22. Mark your answer on your answer sheet.

23. Mark your answer on your answer sheet.

24. Mark your answer on your answer sheet.

25. Mark your answer on your answer sheet.

26. Mark your answer on your answer sheet.

27. Mark your answer on your answer sheet.

28. Mark your answer on your answer sheet.

29. Mark your answer on your answer sheet.

30. Mark your answer on your answer sheet.

31. Mark your answer on your answer sheet.

PART 3

Directions: In this part, you will listen to several conversations between two or more speakers. These conversations will not be printed and will only be spoken one time. For each conversation, you will be asked to answer three questions. Select the best response and mark the corresponding letter (A), (B), (C), or (D) on your answer sheet.

32. What did the woman help the man with?
- (A) An interview
- (B) An experiment
- (C) A survey
- (D) A document

33. Why does the woman say she will call a business?
- (A) To confirm the location
- (B) To find out their opening hours
- (C) To make a reservation
- (D) To complain about the service

34. What does the woman suggest?
- (A) Placing a takeout order
- (B) Meeting in a lobby
- (C) Inviting some other colleagues
- (D) Hiring a different caterer

35. Where most likely do the speakers work?
- (A) At a restaurant
- (B) At a farm
- (C) At a supermarket
- (D) At a factory

36. Why does the man apologize?
- (A) He cannot attend a meeting.
- (B) He is not going to deliver some products.
- (C) He has not replied to a message.
- (D) He did not complete a task.

37. What does the woman say about Stephen?
- (A) He will provide assistance.
- (B) He will bring some equipment.
- (C) He is busy at the moment.
- (D) He recently started a job.

38. According to the man, what did his friend do?
- (A) Canceled an order
- (B) Called about a garment
- (C) Completed a repair
- (D) Purchased an item

39. What is mentioned about a shipment?
- (A) It recently arrived.
- (B) It came from overseas.
- (C) It includes some footwear.
- (D) It is stored in a warehouse.

40. What will Amy do next?
- (A) Scan a coupon
- (B) Check some inventory
- (C) Process a return
- (D) Help another customer

41. What took place last month?
- (A) An industry trade show
- (B) A product launch
- (C) A customer survey
- (D) A shareholder meeting

42. What does the woman mention about the X31?
- (A) It is being offered at a discount.
- (B) It is considered outdated by users.
- (C) It has multiple design issues.
- (D) It has a high-quality display.

43. Why does the man say, "The X32 is going to be smaller than the X31"?
- (A) To give reassurance
- (B) To express concern
- (C) To encourage testing of a device
- (D) To reject a request

GO ON TO THE NEXT PAGE

44. Who most likely is the man?

(A) A secretary
(B) A plumber
(C) A city official
(D) A building owner

45. What situation does the man say is unfortunate?

(A) Some projects have been canceled.
(B) Some supplies are running low.
(C) Some instructions are inaccurate.
(D) Some offers were declined.

46. What does the man say he will do?

(A) Make a list of necessary items
(B) Approve a construction permit
(C) Return some unused parts
(D) Send someone on an errand

---

47. Who most likely is the woman?

(A) A contractor
(B) A chef
(C) An inspector
(D) An investor

48. What has the man forgotten to put out?

(A) Updated menus
(B) Eating utensils
(C) Comment boxes
(D) Fire extinguishers

49. According to the woman, what will the man receive next week?

(A) An operating license
(B) An electronic appliance
(C) A price estimate
(D) A safety manual

---

50. Who most likely is the man?

(A) An interior designer
(B) A store clerk
(C) A tour guide
(D) A gallery director

51. What does the woman suggest doing?

(A) Comparing some estimates
(B) Creating an event flyer
(C) Offering a photo opportunity
(D) Moving some displays

52. What does the man say some participants might receive?

(A) Complimentary tickets
(B) A promotional poster
(C) An audio guide
(D) Printed photographs

---

53. What are the speakers mainly discussing?

(A) The acquisition of a business
(B) The reason for a deadline extension
(C) The status of presentation preparations
(D) The benefits of an investment opportunity

54. What does the woman say she needs to do?

(A) Respond to some e-mails
(B) Incorporate some images
(C) Assess some proposals
(D) Finalize some reservations

55. What are the men worried about?

(A) A script needs to be shortened.
(B) An executive cannot attend a talk.
(C) A meeting should be moved to a later time.
(D) A speech requires more research.

---

56. What problem does the woman mention?

(A) An itinerary needs to be modified.
(B) A company is temporarily closed.
(C) A store ran out of some items.
(D) An event has lost a sponsor.

57. What does the woman ask the man to do?

(A) Revise a contact list
(B) Notify the participants
(C) Draft a purchase agreement
(D) Pick up some groceries

58. What will most likely happen next?

(A) The merger will be delayed.
(B) Some e-mail addresses will be collected.
(C) A Web site will be updated.
(D) Text messages will be sent.

---

59. What did the man recently do?

(A) Traveled to another city
(B) Approved a new project
(C) Reviewed a report
(D) Requested some help

60. What does the man mean when he says, "A taxi will be here in 15 minutes"?

(A) A phone call can be made.
(B) A schedule is inaccurate.
(C) A reservation should be updated.
(D) A meeting must be held later.

61. According to the woman, what has been left in an office?

(A) Some luggage
(B) Some tickets
(C) An ID badge
(D) A garment

Order Form	
Item	**Quantity**
Folders	10 packs
Printer paper	8 packs
Black ink cartridges	5
Color ink cartridges	4

62. What does the woman inquire about?

(A) How much a product cost
(B) Whether a purchase was made
(C) Why some supplies are needed
(D) When a delivery will arrive

63. Look at the graphic. Which quantity must be changed?

(A) 10
(B) 8
(C) 5
(D) 4

64. What will the man probably do next?

(A) Talk with a supervisor
(B) Deliver some supplies
(C) Visit a storeroom
(D) Print a document

GO ON TO THE NEXT PAGE

Eastwood Public Library ①	②	Elmwood Park 🌳🌳🌳		

Map elements:
- Cannondale Street
- Raymond Lane
- Post Office 📪
- Conference Center ③
- Bayview Hotel ④
- Gas Station

MAY				
Monday	**Tuesday**	**Wednesday**	**Thursday**	**Friday**
15	16 Buyer Appreciation Day	17	18 New Model Arriving	19
22	23 Customer Service Workshop	24	25	26 End of Season Sale

65. Why is the man running late?

(A) He missed a bus.
(B) He got stuck in traffic.
(C) He was assisting a customer.
(D) He was preparing some pamphlets.

66. What does the woman ask the man to bring?

(A) Some documents
(B) Some signs
(C) Some timetables
(D) Some office supplies

67. Look at the graphic. Where will the man get off the bus?

(A) At Stop 1
(B) At Stop 2
(C) At Stop 3
(D) At Stop 4

68. Where does the woman most likely work?

(A) At a car dealership
(B) At an electric company
(C) At a gas station
(D) At an auto parts store

69. Look at the graphic. When will the man visit?

(A) On May 16
(B) On May 18
(C) On May 23
(D) On May 26

70. What will the woman do next?

(A) Meet a colleague
(B) Update a directory
(C) Prepare a product
(D) Postpone an appointment

PART 4

Directions: In this part, you will listen to several short talks by a single speaker. These talks will not be printed and will only be spoken one time. For each talk, you will be asked to answer three questions. Select the best response and mark the corresponding letter (A), (B), (C), or (D) on your answer sheet.

71. What will take place on the weekend?
    (A) A grand opening
    (B) A product sale
    (C) A service launch
    (D) A store cleaning

72. How can the listeners get a voucher?
    (A) By enrolling in an online club
    (B) By going to a particular branch
    (C) By purchasing a specific brand
    (D) By completing a survey

73. Why should the listeners visit the Willis Tires Web site?
    (A) To locate a business
    (B) To receive special offers
    (C) To enter a contest
    (D) To schedule a repair

74. What does the speaker say about the Turner Expo?
    (A) It has been held for 20 years.
    (B) It is sponsored by a city.
    (C) It invites industry leaders.
    (D) It sells children's products.

75. Where does the speaker work?
    (A) At a local hotel
    (B) At a landscaping company
    (C) At a university
    (D) At a wildlife park

76. What do the listeners most likely have in common?
    (A) An interest in gardening
    (B) A job in pest control
    (C) A college degree
    (D) A knowledge of chemicals

77. What does the speaker's company produce?
    (A) Water bottles
    (B) Custom snack kits
    (C) Beverage mixes
    (D) Individual meals

78. What did the company recently do?
    (A) Hired a marketing specialist
    (B) Conducted a consumer poll
    (C) Recalled a beverage
    (D) Established a waiting list

79. What will happen after the meeting?
    (A) A supervisor will be notified.
    (B) A survey result will be verified.
    (C) A reservation list will be changed.
    (D) A study will be publicized.

80. What is the announcement mainly about?
    (A) Expectations for new hires
    (B) Updates to a software system
    (C) Improvements to a workplace
    (D) Problems with a remote work system

81. Why does the speaker say, "I've had to wait 30 minutes for an answer"?
    (A) To suggest a change in a policy
    (B) To report a customer complaint
    (C) To ask the listeners to be more patient
    (D) To criticize some listeners' performance

82. What does the speaker instruct the listeners to do?
    (A) Attend a meeting
    (B) Install a program
    (C) Read some guidelines
    (D) Sign a form

GO ON TO THE NEXT PAGE

83. Why is the facility closed?

(A) It is after opening hours.
(B) It is holding a private event.
(C) It is installing a new exhibit.
(D) It is renovating an office.

84. According to the speaker, what will take place at the museum in August?

(A) An artist will visit.
(B) A new wing will be opened.
(C) An exhibit will be hosted.
(D) A lecture series be held.

85. Who is eligible for free entrance?

(A) People under 19 years old
(B) Participants in a program
(C) Visitors from out of town
(D) Museum membership holders

---

86. According to the speaker, what has happened recently?

(A) A company hired a new bookkeeper.
(B) A program received favorable reviews.
(C) The number of self-employed people increased.
(D) The software was sold at a discounted price.

87. What is a feature of FastTrack software?

(A) Invoice creation
(B) Shipment management
(C) Payment processing
(D) Task scheduling

88. Why does the speaker say, "Most users can complete their forms in a few hours"?

(A) To suggest the addition of a new option
(B) To endorse a company's product
(C) To explain that a process is lengthy
(D) To show that an item is highly rated

---

89. What is the report mainly about?

(A) A photography expo
(B) A weather condition
(C) A natural event
(D) A camping trip

90. What were some viewers excited about?

(A) Receiving a souvenir
(B) Experiencing short waiting lines
(C) Displaying their pictures
(D) Earning a free pass

91. Why would visitors have to buy a permit?

(A) To access a park for a day trip
(B) To be able to park a vehicle
(C) To take a tour of a preserve
(D) To spend a night in a park

---

92. What kind of services does the speaker provide?

(A) Hotel accommodations
(B) Floral arrangements
(C) Jewelry designs
(D) Catering services

93. What does the speaker say will happen in August?

(A) A design will be finished.
(B) An order will be placed.
(C) A business will be closed.
(D) A ceremony will be held.

94. What does the speaker imply when she says, "They are only available for the next two months"?

(A) The listener should act quickly.
(B) A schedule needs to be changed.
(C) Spaces on the beach are limited.
(D) A package is very popular.

Item 1 Item 2

Item 3 Item 4

Town Hall Meeting Agenda	
Date	**Topic**
May 2	Zoning and Land Use
May 7	School District Calendar
May 9	Water Conservation
May 13	Applying for Building Permits

95. What is the main topic of this talk?

(A) Proposed accessory lines
(B) Workplace clothing regulations
(C) Problems with product shipments
(D) Recent accidents in a factory

96. Look at the graphic. Which of the following items must be removed?

(A) Item 1
(B) Item 2
(C) Item 3
(D) Item 4

97. What does the speaker emphasize about the company?

(A) It is using an advanced device.
(B) It has an excellent safety record.
(C) It is hiring many new employees.
(D) It has equipment that can cause injuries.

98. Look at the graphic. When did the town hall meeting take place?

(A) On May 2
(B) On May 7
(C) On May 9
(D) On May 13

99. According to the speaker, what will be banned under the new rules?

(A) Installing new driveways
(B) Adding plants to private lawns
(C) Washing streets in commercial areas
(D) Cleaning cars at residences

100. Who most likely is Tom Loughlin?

(A) A local politician
(B) A real estate agent
(C) An expert plumber
(D) A news reporter

정답 p.165 / 점수 환산표 p.167 / 스크립트 p.198 / 무료 해석 바로 보기(정답 및 정답 음성 포함)

▌정답 음성(QR)이나 정답(p.165)을 이용해 채점하시기 바랍니다. 정답 음성에서 Boy는 (B)를, David는 (D)를 나타냅니다.
▌다음 페이지에 있는 Self 체크 리스트를 통해 자신의 문제 풀이 방식과 태도를 점검해 보세요.

TEST 06 PART 4 **105**

Self 체크 리스트

TEST 06는 무사히 잘 마치셨죠?
이제 다음의 Self 체크 리스트를 통해 자신의 테스트 진행 내용을 점검해 볼까요?

1. 나는 테스트가 진행되는 동안 한 번도 중도에 멈추지 않았다.

   ☐ 예   ☐ 아니오

   아니오에 답한 경우, 이유는 무엇인가요?

2. 나는 답안지 표기까지 성실하게 모두 마무리하였다.

   ☐ 예   ☐ 아니오

   아니오에 답한 경우, 이유는 무엇인가요?

3. 나는 Part 2의 25문항을 푸는 동안 완전히 테스트에 집중하였다.

   ☐ 예   ☐ 아니오

   아니오에 답한 경우, 이유는 무엇인가요?

4. 나는 Part 3를 풀 때 음성이 들리기 전에 해당 질문과 보기를 모두 먼저 읽었다.

   ☐ 예   ☐ 아니오

   아니오에 답한 경우, 이유는 무엇인가요?

5. 나는 Part 4를 풀 때 음성이 들리기 전에 해당 질문과 보기를 모두 먼저 읽었다.

   ☐ 예   ☐ 아니오

   아니오에 답한 경우, 이유는 무엇인가요?

6. 개선해야 할 점 또는 나를 위한 충고를 적어보세요.

* 교재의 첫 장으로 돌아가서 자신이 적은 목표 점수를 확인하면서 목표에 대한 의지를 다지기 바랍니다. 개선해야 할 점은 반드시 다음 테스트에
  실천해야 합니다. 그것이 가장 중요하며, 그래야만 발전할 수 있습니다.

▌TEST 07

PART 1
PART 2
PART 3
PART 4
Self 체크 리스트

잠깐! 테스트 전 확인사항
1. 휴대 전화의 전원을 끄셨나요? ☐ 예
2. Answer Sheet, 연필, 지우개를 준비하셨나요? ☐ 예
3. MP3를 들을 준비가 되셨나요? ☐ 예

모든 준비가 완료되었으면 목표 점수를 떠올린 후 테스트를 시작합니다.

🎧 TEST 07.mp3
실전용·복습용 문제풀이 MP3 무료 다운로드 및 스트리밍 바로듣기 (HackersIngang.com)
* 실제 시험장의 소음까지 재현해 낸 고사장 소음/매미 버전 MP3, 영국식·호주식 발음 집중 MP3, 고속 버전 MP3까지
  구매하면 실전에 더욱 완벽히 대비할 수 있습니다.

무료MP3 바로듣기

LISTENING TEST

In this section, you must demonstrate your ability to understand spoken English. This section is divided into four parts and will take approximately 45 minutes to complete. Do not mark the answers in your test book. Use the answer sheet that is provided separately.

PART 1

Directions: For each question, you will listen to four short statements about a picture in your test book. These statements will not be printed and will only be spoken one time. Select the statement that best describes what is happening in the picture and mark the corresponding letter (A), (B), (C), or (D) on the answer sheet.

Sample Answer

The statement that best describes the picture is (B), "The man is sitting at the desk." So, you should mark letter (B) on the answer sheet.

1.

2.

GO ON TO THE NEXT PAGE

3.

4.

5.

6.

GO ON TO THE NEXT PAGE

PART 2

Directions: For each question, you will listen to a statement or question followed by three possible responses spoken in English. They will not be printed and will only be spoken one time. Select the best response and mark the corresponding letter (A), (B), or (C) on your answer sheet.

7. Mark your answer on your answer sheet.

8. Mark your answer on your answer sheet.

9. Mark your answer on your answer sheet.

10. Mark your answer on your answer sheet.

11. Mark your answer on your answer sheet.

12. Mark your answer on your answer sheet.

13. Mark your answer on your answer sheet.

14. Mark your answer on your answer sheet.

15. Mark your answer on your answer sheet.

16. Mark your answer on your answer sheet.

17. Mark your answer on your answer sheet.

18. Mark your answer on your answer sheet.

19. Mark your answer on your answer sheet.

20. Mark your answer on your answer sheet.

21. Mark your answer on your answer sheet.

22. Mark your answer on your answer sheet.

23. Mark your answer on your answer sheet.

24. Mark your answer on your answer sheet.

25. Mark your answer on your answer sheet.

26. Mark your answer on your answer sheet.

27. Mark your answer on your answer sheet.

28. Mark your answer on your answer sheet.

29. Mark your answer on your answer sheet.

30. Mark your answer on your answer sheet.

31. Mark your answer on your answer sheet.

PART 3

Directions: In this part, you will listen to several conversations between two or more speakers. These conversations will not be printed and will only be spoken one time. For each conversation, you will be asked to answer three questions. Select the best response and mark the corresponding letter (A), (B), (C), or (D) on your answer sheet.

32. What does the woman say an article is about?

(A) International trade laws
(B) Stock market performance
(C) Overseas production
(D) Marketing methods

33. What does the man mention about competitors?

(A) They launched some products.
(B) They conducted customer surveys.
(C) They might introduce new design plans.
(D) They might reduce prices.

34. What does the woman suggest doing?

(A) Holding a press conference
(B) Creating a campaign
(C) Postponing a gathering
(D) Finding a new distributor

35. What are the speakers mainly discussing?

(A) A network problem
(B) A Web site design
(C) A software release
(D) A supply shortage

36. What does the woman say her supervisor is doing now?

(A) Ordering a replacement device
(B) Speaking with a department head
(C) Requesting a product upgrade
(D) E-mailing a service center

37. What does the man say he will do?

(A) Head to a manager's office
(B) Restart a computer
(C) Propose a change
(D) Complete some repairs

38. According to the man, what happened recently?

(A) An establishment was opened.
(B) A promotion expired.
(C) A worker resigned.
(D) A prize was given away.

39. What problem does the man mention?

(A) A product line is not selling well.
(B) A customer has made a complaint.
(C) An ingredient is no longer fresh.
(D) A branch manager has not returned.

40. What does the man say he will do?

(A) Refill a display case with sandwiches
(B) Extend the operating hours of a business
(C) Install an additional cash register
(D) Ask an employee to distribute samples

41. Where do the speakers most likely work?

(A) At a gardening store
(B) At a fire station
(C) At a train station
(D) At an apartment complex

42. What does the woman mention about Justin?

(A) He has asked for assistance.
(B) He requires more training.
(C) He will make an announcement.
(D) He recently moved an item.

43. What does Justin offer to do?

(A) Share an idea with a manager
(B) Hang up another hose
(C) Lead coworkers to a location
(D) Make room for some goods

GO ON TO THE NEXT PAGE

44. Where is the conversation most likely taking place?

(A) At a tourist information center
(B) At a clothing retail outlet
(C) At a language academy
(D) At a manufacturing plant

45. What does the woman suggest?

(A) Requesting some help
(B) Changing a speech
(C) Hiring a guide
(D) Reviewing some research

46. What will the man most likely do in 30 minutes?

(A) Restock some clothing
(B) Participate in a meeting
(C) Read over an application
(D) Speak to a client

47. Who most likely are the speakers?

(A) Safety inspectors
(B) Laboratory workers
(C) Clothing designers
(D) Store clerks

48. What problem does the woman mention?

(A) A deadline is tight.
(B) A branch has moved.
(C) A worker is late.
(D) A warranty has expired.

49. What does the woman give the man?

(A) A new uniform
(B) A closet key
(C) A credit card
(D) An area map

50. What does the man say about Ms. Fleming?

(A) She will be leaving a company.
(B) She will oversee a division expansion.
(C) She will modify an accounting policy.
(D) She will study the cause of a sales decline.

51. What did the man speak about with the CEO?

(A) An evaluation
(B) A promotion
(C) An orientation
(D) A celebration

52. What does the man mean when he says, "I'm quite comfortable where I am"?

(A) A conference room will not be used.
(B) A workspace will not be moved.
(C) A position will be turned down.
(D) A housing search will be canceled.

53. Where is the conversation most likely taking place?

(A) At a bookstore
(B) At an electronics store
(C) At a bank
(D) At a subway station

54. What does the man ask for?

(A) A train route
(B) An item description
(C) A business address
(D) A telephone number

55. Why will the man send out an e-mail?

(A) To express gratitude
(B) To provide instructions
(C) To explain an error
(D) To inquire about a change

56. Why does the man say, "They kept changing their price"?

(A) He has a more affordable option.
(B) He needs to verify some prices.
(C) He thinks that the situation is urgent.
(D) He wants the woman to reconsider a service.

57. What happened last week?

(A) A programmer was hired.
(B) A restaurant closed down.
(C) An application malfunctioned.
(D) A system was updated.

58. What will the woman most likely do next?

(A) Post an advertisement online
(B) Review a document
(C) Search for potential candidates
(D) Contact a coworker for help

---

59. Where does the man most likely work?

(A) In a supermarket
(B) In a café
(C) In a warehouse
(D) In a bakery

60. What information does Beth provide?

(A) The location of an office
(B) The time of an event
(C) The name of a manager
(D) The amount of a charge

61. What does the man offer to do for an extra fee?

(A) Expedite an order
(B) Change a service
(C) Upgrade a product
(D) Deliver an item

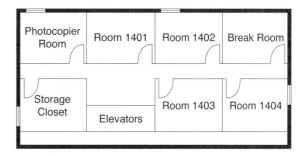

62. What problem does the man mention?

(A) Some participants have not arrived.
(B) Some equipment was not installed.
(C) A room is occupied.
(D) An elevator is out of order.

63. Who most likely is the man?

(A) A senior manager
(B) A new employee
(C) A technician
(D) A receptionist

64. Look at the graphic. Where is a meeting being held?

(A) In Room 1401
(B) In Room 1402
(C) In Room 1403
(D) In Room 1404

GO ON TO THE NEXT PAGE

	Stage	

Section 1	Section 2
□ ■ □ ■ ■	■ ■ ■ ■ ■
■ ■ ■ ■ □	■ ■ □ □ ■

Section 3	Section 4
■ ■ ■ □ □	□ □ □ ■ ■
■ ■ ■ ■ ■	■ ■ ■ ■ ■

□ empty seat

Class	Day
Oil Painting	Thursday
Figure Drawing	Friday
Watercolors	Saturday
Sculpting	Sunday

65. What is mentioned about *Coral Sea*?

(A) Its first performance is on Saturday.
(B) It was written by a local playwright.
(C) It is playing only on the weekend.
(D) Its leading actor will retire next year.

66. Look at the graphic. Where will the man most likely sit?

(A) In Section 1
(B) In Section 2
(C) In Section 3
(D) In Section 4

67. What does the man request?

(A) A seating chart
(B) A show program
(C) A proof of purchase
(D) A confirmation number

68. Look at the graphic. Which day will the woman take a class?

(A) Thursday
(B) Friday
(C) Saturday
(D) Sunday

69. Why is it difficult to register for a class?

(A) It takes place only once.
(B) A classroom is small.
(C) The teacher is famous.
(D) Many artists have taken it.

70. What does the woman ask the man about?

(A) A payment method
(B) The length of a lesson
(C) A cancellation policy
(D) The size of a class

PART 4

Directions: In this part, you will listen to several short talks by a single speaker. These talks will not be printed and will only be spoken one time. For each talk, you will be asked to answer three questions. Select the best response and mark the corresponding letter (A), (B), (C), or (D) on your answer sheet.

71. Where is the talk taking place?

(A) At a grocery store
(B) At a restaurant
(C) In a banquet hall
(D) In an office

72. What is mentioned about Michael Trager?

(A) He was recently hired.
(B) He sampled different products.
(C) He did not receive training.
(D) He does not like some decorations.

73. According to the speaker, what will happen on October 23?

(A) A business owner will visit.
(B) A facility will be temporarily closed.
(C) Staff members will be surveyed.
(D) New offerings will be made available.

74. Why is the speaker calling?

(A) To verify personal information
(B) To change a work schedule
(C) To apologize for an accident
(D) To respond to an inquiry

75. What does the speaker say the listener must do?

(A) Pay for a special service
(B) Send out another e-mail
(C) Visit a business in person
(D) Have a prescription renewed

76. Who most likely is Vincent Mitchel?

(A) A safety inspector
(B) A medical doctor
(C) A delivery person
(D) A store supervisor

77. What is the topic of the lecture?

(A) Graphic design
(B) Drawing techniques
(C) Ancient history
(D) Modern art

78. What will most likely happen in the first session?

(A) A professor will speak.
(B) A demonstration will be given.
(C) A brochure will be passed out.
(D) A documentary will be shown.

79. What does the speaker imply when he says, "Dr. Sorenson usually doesn't take part in these"?

(A) A planned event may be canceled.
(B) The listeners should take advantage of a situation.
(C) The listeners should check a schedule.
(D) Questions will be answered by e-mail.

80. What will some listeners do next week?

(A) Promote some bicycles
(B) Test out new merchandise
(C) Take part in a fundraiser
(D) Rearrange some desks

81. What did Marcelle do yesterday?

(A) Revised a guest list
(B) Finalized some plans
(C) Collected some fees
(D) Passed out some clothing

82. Why does the speaker say, "please note that there are only a few left in the small size"?

(A) To urge employees to hurry
(B) To apologize for limited options
(C) To warn that shirts will be tight
(D) To request a larger size

GO ON TO THE NEXT PAGE

83. What is the announcement mainly about?

(A) A sports competition
(B) A celebrity spokesperson
(C) A business partnership
(D) A new soft drink

84. What did the speaker do this morning?

(A) Formalized a contract
(B) Met with soccer players
(C) Visited a sports arena
(D) Negotiated different rates

85. What does the speaker say a company will be able to do?

(A) Enter an international market
(B) Hold a press conference
(C) Increase its number of online subscribers
(D) Use a symbol for promotional purposes

---

86. What is the broadcast mainly about?

(A) Upcoming local elections
(B) A scholarship program
(C) Library membership benefits
(D) A community investment

87. What does the speaker say about Sherry Keenam?

(A) She filled out an application.
(B) She accepted a proposal.
(C) She came up with an idea.
(D) She is going to retire.

88. How can the listeners learn more about a project?

(A) By calling an agency
(B) By listening to some reports
(C) By going to a Web site
(D) By attending some meetings

---

89. What problem is mentioned?

(A) Sales for a line have dropped.
(B) A battery will not charge properly.
(C) Car models received bad press.
(D) A recall must be carried out.

90. What does the speaker imply when he says, "The impact is expected to be considerable"?

(A) A factory will bring in additional workers.
(B) A business will benefit from a merger.
(C) A schedule change will go into effect today.
(D) A production strategy will save money.

91. What will be sent out next week?

(A) A catalog
(B) A sales forecast
(C) A product
(D) A radio commercial

---

92. What will the speaker discuss first?

(A) Reasons for using training manuals
(B) Ways for making a workplace pleasant
(C) Methods for recruiting personnel
(D) Benefits of working fewer hours

93. What does the speaker mention about some group exercises?

(A) They are no longer open for registration.
(B) They will take place in an auditorium.
(C) They had to be delayed by an hour.
(D) They are aimed at improving trust.

94. What does the speaker ask the listeners to do?

(A) Find a free seat
(B) Introduce themselves
(C) Refer to a handout
(D) Break up into pairs

Monday	Tuesday	Wednesday	Thursday
Meeting with Professor Parker	Convention Lecture	Awards Banquet	Writing Workshop

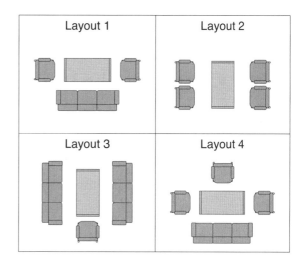

95. Look at the graphic. When does the speaker want to schedule a book signing?

(A) On Monday
(B) On Tuesday
(C) On Wednesday
(D) On Thursday

96. What is located near the bookstore?

(A) A convention center
(B) A hotel
(C) An airport
(D) A company headquarters

97. What does the speaker offer to do?

(A) Call a bookstore
(B) Send an itinerary
(C) Provide accommodation
(D) Arrange transportation

98. What did the listener do last week?

(A) Decorated a lobby
(B) Attended a meeting
(C) Purchased some items
(D) Provided some samples

99. Why did the speaker contact Marvin Griggs?

(A) To explain a delay
(B) To ask about a deadline
(C) To request a change
(D) To get an opinion

100. Look at the graphic. Which option does the speaker prefer?

(A) Layout 1
(B) Layout 2
(C) Layout 3
(D) Layout 4

정답 p.165 / 점수 환산표 p.167 / 스크립트 p.204 / 무료 해석 바로 보기(정답 및 정답 음성 포함)

▌정답 음성(QR)이나 정답(p.165)을 이용해 채점하시기 바랍니다. 정답 음성에서 Boy는 (B)를, David는 (D)를 나타냅니다.
▌다음 페이지에 있는 Self 체크 리스트를 통해 자신의 문제 풀이 방식과 태도를 점검해 보세요.

Self 체크 리스트

TEST 07은 무사히 잘 마치셨죠?
이제 다음의 Self 체크 리스트를 통해 자신의 테스트 진행 내용을 점검해 볼까요?

1. 나는 테스트가 진행되는 동안 한 번도 중도에 멈추지 않았다.

   ☐ 예   ☐ 아니오

   아니오에 답한 경우, 이유는 무엇인가요?

2. 나는 답안지 표기까지 성실하게 모두 마무리하였다.

   ☐ 예   ☐ 아니오

   아니오에 답한 경우, 이유는 무엇인가요?

3. 나는 Part 2의 25문항을 푸는 동안 완전히 테스트에 집중하였다.

   ☐ 예   ☐ 아니오

   아니오에 답한 경우, 이유는 무엇인가요?

4. 나는 Part 3를 풀 때 음성이 들리기 전에 해당 질문과 보기를 모두 먼저 읽었다.

   ☐ 예   ☐ 아니오

   아니오에 답한 경우, 이유는 무엇인가요?

5. 나는 Part 4를 풀 때 음성이 들리기 전에 해당 질문과 보기를 모두 먼저 읽었다.

   ☐ 예   ☐ 아니오

   아니오에 답한 경우, 이유는 무엇인가요?

6. 개선해야 할 점 또는 나를 위한 충고를 적어보세요.

* 교재의 첫 장으로 돌아가서 자신이 적은 목표 점수를 확인하면서 목표에 대한 의지를 다지기 바랍니다. 개선해야 할 점은 반드시 다음 테스트에 실천해야 합니다. 그것이 가장 중요하며, 그래야만 발전할 수 있습니다.

TEST 08

PARID 1
PART 2
PART 3
PART 4
Self 체크 리스트

잠깐! 테스트 전 확인사항

1. 휴대 전화의 전원을 끄셨나요? □ 예
2. Answer Sheet, 연필, 지우개를 준비하셨나요? □ 예
3. MP3를 들을 준비가 되셨나요? □ 예

모든 준비가 완료되었으면 목표 점수를 떠올린 후 테스트를 시작합니다.

🎧 TEST 08.mp3

실전용·복습용 문제풀이 MP3 무료 다운로드 및 스트리밍 바로듣기 (HackersIngang.com)
* 실제 시험장의 소음까지 재현해 낸 고사장 소음/매미 버전 MP3, 영국식·호주식 발음 집중 MP3, 고속 버전 MP3까지 구매하면 실전에 더욱 완벽히 대비할 수 있습니다.

무료MP3 바로듣기

LISTENING TEST

In this section, you must demonstrate your ability to understand spoken English. This section is divided into four parts and will take approximately 45 minutes to complete. Do not mark the answers in your test book. Use the answer sheet that is provided separately.

PART 1

Directions: For each question, you will listen to four short statements about a picture in your test book. These statements will not be printed and will only be spoken one time. Select the statement that best describes what is happening in the picture and mark the corresponding letter (A), (B), (C), or (D) on the answer sheet.

Sample Answer

The statement that best describes the picture is (B), "The man is sitting at the desk." So, you should mark letter (B) on the answer sheet.

1.

2.

GO ON TO THE NEXT PAGE

3.

4.

5.

6.

GO ON TO THE NEXT PAGE ➤

PART 2

Directions: For each question, you will listen to a statement or question followed by three possible responses spoken in English. They will not be printed and will only be spoken one time. Select the best response and mark the corresponding letter (A), (B), or (C) on your answer sheet.

7. Mark your answer on your answer sheet.

8. Mark your answer on your answer sheet.

9. Mark your answer on your answer sheet.

10. Mark your answer on your answer sheet.

11. Mark your answer on your answer sheet.

12. Mark your answer on your answer sheet.

13. Mark your answer on your answer sheet.

14. Mark your answer on your answer sheet.

15. Mark your answer on your answer sheet.

16. Mark your answer on your answer sheet.

17. Mark your answer on your answer sheet.

18. Mark your answer on your answer sheet.

19. Mark your answer on your answer sheet.

20. Mark your answer on your answer sheet.

21. Mark your answer on your answer sheet.

22. Mark your answer on your answer sheet.

23. Mark your answer on your answer sheet.

24. Mark your answer on your answer sheet.

25. Mark your answer on your answer sheet.

26. Mark your answer on your answer sheet.

27. Mark your answer on your answer sheet.

28. Mark your answer on your answer sheet.

29. Mark your answer on your answer sheet.

30. Mark your answer on your answer sheet.

31. Mark your answer on your answer sheet.

Directions: In this part, you will listen to several conversations between two or more speakers. These conversations will not be printed and will only be spoken one time. For each conversation, you will be asked to answer three questions. Select the best response and mark the corresponding letter (A), (B), (C), or (D) on your answer sheet.

32. What does the woman want to promote?

(A) A Web site
(B) Some footwear
(C) A local charity
(D) Some new policies

33. What is mentioned about the radio commercials?

(A) They were not approved by a director.
(B) They featured a popular celebrity.
(C) They were expensive to produce.
(D) They did not reach the right listeners.

34. What does the man suggest?

(A) Uploading an attachment
(B) Seeking another opinion
(C) Preparing for a future launch
(D) Rearranging some displays

35. What are the speakers mainly discussing?

(A) A building remodeling
(B) A computer program
(C) An upcoming event
(D) A weekly schedule

36. Why is the man concerned?

(A) Some information does not match.
(B) A Web site is difficult to navigate.
(C) A document has been lost.
(D) Some library staff have not arrived.

37. What does the man say he will do next?

(A) Call a caterer
(B) Notify a supervisor
(C) Visit a library
(D) Organize some files

38. Who most likely is the woman?

(A) A delivery person
(B) A shop owner
(C) A tourist
(D) A travel agent

39. What does the man offer to do?

(A) Provide a map
(B) Cover a shipping fee
(C) Package an item
(D) Recommend a restaurant

40. What does the man say about loyalty points?

(A) They can be used as payment.
(B) They expire within one year.
(C) They are earned online only.
(D) They work at multiple stores.

41. Where most likely do the speakers work?

(A) At a manufacturing plant
(B) At a shopping center
(C) At a government office
(D) At a photography studio

42. What problem is mentioned?

(A) Some software has errors.
(B) A complaint was made.
(C) Some shoots were canceled.
(D) A business is understaffed.

43. What will the man most likely do before noon?

(A) Take additional pictures
(B) Respond to a message
(C) Edit some pictures
(D) Send out an invoice

GO ON TO THE NEXT PAGE

44. What did the woman recently do?

(A) Attended a party
(B) Purchased a sweater
(C) Opened a business
(D) Sent a package

45. What does the man imply when he says, "It's just something I heard, though"?

(A) He may be incorrect about some information.
(B) He has never been to the flea market.
(C) He directly spoke with a customer.
(D) He recently listened to a commercial.

46. What does the man suggest doing?

(A) Selling items online
(B) Looking for another location
(C) Buying some jewelry
(D) Speaking to a friend

---

47. Why does the man want to update his kitchen?

(A) Some appliances are outdated.
(B) A floor is unsafe.
(C) Some tiles have faded.
(D) A property is going to be sold.

48. What does the man say about HomeRefresh?

(A) Its services are expensive.
(B) Its contract is complicated.
(C) Its employees are friendly.
(D) Its location is inconvenient.

49. What will probably happen next?

(A) A budget will be discussed.
(B) A discount will be applied.
(C) An appointment will be arranged.
(D) A message will be sent.

---

50. Who is Henry Goodrich?

(A) A company president
(B) A board member
(C) An investor
(D) A restaurant owner

51. What does the woman say about Chiang Rai Grill?

(A) It is highly recommended.
(B) It has a private room.
(C) It has several branches.
(D) It takes reservations online.

52. Why does the woman want to contact Mr. Goodrich?

(A) To invite him to come to the office
(B) To find out when his flight arrives
(C) To check which dates he is available
(D) To see if he likes certain foods

---

53. According to the woman, what does Ms. Bailey need?

(A) A conference agenda
(B) Electronic equipment
(C) An audio recording
(D) Presentation handouts

54. What does the woman mean when she says, "I'm sure we can handle that"?

(A) A technician will be hired.
(B) An event will be successful.
(C) A presentation can be shortened.
(D) An expense can be covered.

55. What does the man say he must do?

(A) Revise a request
(B) Download a document
(C) Tour an event hall
(D) Consult with a team

---

56. Where most likely is the conversation taking place?

(A) At a consultancy headquarters
(B) At a conference venue
(C) At a retail store
(D) At a post office

57. What does the man ask the woman to do?

(A) Move some items
(B) Lock a room
(C) Organize some supplies
(D) Place an order

58. What is mentioned about the list?

(A) It was recently thrown away.
(B) It has to be reprinted.
(C) It has been relocated.
(D) It has been updated.

---

59. Why is the woman calling?

(A) To report a delay
(B) To inquire about a property
(C) To request a service
(D) To file a complaint

60. According to the woman, what will happen this evening?

(A) A vehicle will be purchased.
(B) Some repairs will be completed.
(C) A new worker will be trained.
(D) Some paint will be picked up.

61. Who is Angela Dawson?

(A) An office manager
(B) A professional painter
(C) An automotive mechanic
(D) An administrative assistant

Jackson Street		
Bartow Manufacturing	Parking Lot A	Parking Lot B
Riverside Street		
Pizza Palace	Parking Lot C	Parking Lot D

62. According to the woman, what will happen on Thursday?

(A) A project will be finalized.
(B) Some staff will carpool.
(C) A parade will be held.
(D) Some lights will be set up.

63. Look at the graphic. Where should employees park on Thursday?

(A) Parking Lot A
(B) Parking Lot B
(C) Parking Lot C
(D) Parking Lot D

64. What will workers have to do to receive free parking?

(A) Display a coupon
(B) Submit transaction records
(C) Reserve a space
(D) Adhere to a time limit

GO ON TO THE NEXT PAGE

PulseTrain Multivitamin	
Type	Daily Value
Vitamin A	40%
Vitamin B	55%
Vitamin C	70%
Vitamin D	85%

65. What does the woman say she will do this afternoon?

(A) Attend a business event
(B) Update a schedule
(C) Become a gym member
(D) Stop by a clinic

66. Look at the graphic. Which vitamin is the woman lacking?

(A) Vitamin A
(B) Vitamin B
(C) Vitamin C
(D) Vitamin D

67. What does the man offer the woman?

(A) A medical prescription
(B) A pamphlet
(C) A sample
(D) A membership card

Weston Climate Change Lecture Series				
	Room 101	Room 102	Room 103	Room 104
8 A.M.			Reducing Food Waste	
9 A.M.	Renewable Energy			Cars Are the Problem
10 A.M.		Sea Levels and Cities		Weather and Its Changes

68. What will the woman notify the audience about?

(A) A seating shortage
(B) A technical malfunction
(C) A miscommunication
(D) A schedule change

69. Look at the graphic. Where will Andrea Parker most likely give a talk?

(A) In Room 101
(B) In Room 102
(C) In Room 103
(D) In Room 104

70. Why does the man apologize?

(A) An inaccurate program was printed.
(B) A team will be short on staff.
(C) A time slot is no longer available.
(D) A registration form is missing.

PART 4

Directions: In this part, you will listen to several short talks by a single speaker. These talks will not be printed and will only be spoken one time. For each talk, you will be asked to answer three questions. Select the best response and mark the corresponding letter (A), (B), (C), or (D) on your answer sheet.

71. What is the radio broadcast mainly about?

(A) A traffic disruption
(B) A building expansion
(C) A medical grant
(D) An education campaign

72. What will happen next week?

(A) A facility will resume operations.
(B) A press conference will take place.
(C) An executive position will be filled.
(D) A monument will be unveiled.

73. What is Roselyn Geddy going to discuss?

(A) Public health issues
(B) Membership requirements
(C) Plans for a celebration
(D) Increases in taxes

---

74. What did the speaker talk to Ms. Carver about?

(A) Some schedules
(B) Some research
(C) Some expectations
(D) Some concerns

75. What will the production focus on?

(A) Safety procedures
(B) Workplace communication
(C) Scientific discoveries
(D) Laboratory equipment

76. What are the listeners instructed to do next?

(A) Review some educational materials
(B) Put on a piece of clothing
(C) Rehearse lines from a script
(D) Repair some machinery

77. Where do the listeners most likely work?

(A) At a financial institution
(B) At a government agency
(C) At a computer manufacturer
(D) At a publishing company

78. What does the speaker imply when he says, "today is Tuesday"?

(A) There is little time to prepare.
(B) A contract needs to be signed.
(C) There will be a product launch soon.
(D) A shipment had arrived late.

79. What does the speaker hope to do?

(A) Upgrade some software
(B) Address a client's complaints
(C) Arrange an initial meeting
(D) Form a business relationship

---

80. What is being unveiled?

(A) A community center
(B) A monument
(C) A painting
(D) An orchestra hall

81. According to the speaker, what did Janice Longoria do?

(A) Trained with a well-known musician
(B) Volunteered her time
(C) Gave a speech to a crowd
(D) Created a piece of art

82. What is mentioned about the city council?

(A) It declared a special holiday.
(B) It welcomed a new member.
(C) It covered an expense.
(D) It made a recommendation.

GO ON TO THE NEXT PAGE

83. What is being advertised?

(A) An e-book reader
(B) A portable printer
(C) An audio device
(D) A television

84. What does the speaker mean when she says, "Techtime Magazine gave it their highest rating"?

(A) She wants people to write a review.
(B) She is concerned that some goods will sell out quickly.
(C) She believes that an item is very affordable.
(D) She is certain that a product will be satisfying.

85. According to the speaker, why should the listeners visit a store?

(A) To preorder merchandise
(B) To request a free upgrade
(C) To take advantage of a sale
(D) To test a product

86. What does the speaker say he will do?

(A) Hand out workshop schedules
(B) Present a slideshow
(C) Conduct additional studies
(D) Explain some posters

87. What does the speaker say about Hashtag Goods?

(A) It is famous for its cleaning products.
(B) It has overseas factories.
(C) It has hired a new president.
(D) It is a large retail company.

88. What is a video about?

(A) International industry trade shows
(B) Award-winning advertising campaigns
(C) Marketing techniques from different countries
(D) Sports teams from around the world

89. Who most likely is the listener?

(A) A product designer
(B) A sales associate
(C) A travel agent
(D) A technical worker

90. What does the speaker ask the listener to do?

(A) Call a manager
(B) Order a new device
(C) Reschedule a meeting
(D) Visit a workspace

91. What does the speaker say she must do in Madrid?

(A) Negotiate some contracts
(B) Deliver a package
(C) Send meeting details
(D) Attend a seminar

92. Who are the listeners?

(A) Tour guides
(B) Museum staff
(C) Gallery curators
(D) City officials

93. What are the listeners instructed to do?

(A) Print out some pamphlets
(B) Direct guests to a lobby
(C) Show up at a site early
(D) Wear a name tag for an event

94. Why does the speaker say, "They are coming for the first time"?

(A) There will be a large group.
(B) There will be a lot of questions.
(C) A map will be needed.
(D) A tour may take longer than planned.

Order Number	Expected Delivery Date (Updated)
8832019	September 5
8823901	September 10
8800929	September 15
8811118	September 25

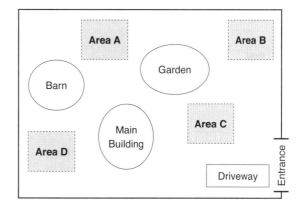

95. What problem does the speaker mention?

(A) A billing statement is inaccurate.
(B) A Web site recently malfunctioned.
(C) A piece of apparel was damaged.
(D) A delivery truck is stuck in traffic.

96. Look at the graphic. What is the listener's order number?

(A) 8832019
(B) 8823901
(C) 8800929
(D) 8811118

97. According to the speaker, what will the listener have to do?

(A) Provide a different address
(B) Sign for a parcel
(C) Pay a shipping fee
(D) Return some merchandise

98. Who most likely is the speaker?

(A) A park ranger
(B) A developer
(C) A farmer
(D) A landscape designer

99. Look at the graphic. Where will the magnolia trees be planted?

(A) Area A
(B) Area B
(C) Area C
(D) Area D

100. What is the listener asked to do?

(A) Change a location
(B) Notify an assistant
(C) Select an alternative
(D) Schedule a visit

정답 p.165 / 점수 환산표 p.167 / 스크립트 p.210 / 무료 해석 바로 보기(정답 및 정답 음성 포함)

▮정답 음성(QR)이나 정답(p.165)을 이용해 채점하시기 바랍니다. 정답 음성에서 Boy는 (B)를, David는 (D)를 나타냅니다.
▮다음 페이지에 있는 Self 체크 리스트를 통해 자신의 문제 풀이 방식과 태도를 점검해 보세요.

Self 체크 리스트

TEST 08은 무사히 잘 마치셨죠?
이제 다음의 Self 체크 리스트를 통해 자신의 테스트 진행 내용을 점검해 볼까요?

1. 나는 테스트가 진행되는 동안 한 번도 중도에 멈추지 않았다.

　□ 예　　　　　　　□ 아니오

　아니오에 답한 경우, 이유는 무엇인가요?

2. 나는 답안지 표기까지 성실하게 모두 마무리하였다.

　□ 예　　　　　　　□ 아니오

　아니오에 답한 경우, 이유는 무엇인가요?

3. 나는 Part 2의 25문항을 푸는 동안 완전히 테스트에 집중하였다.

　□ 예　　　　　　　□ 아니오

　아니오에 답한 경우, 이유는 무엇인가요?

4. 나는 Part 3를 풀 때 음성이 들리기 전에 해당 질문과 보기를 모두 먼저 읽었다.

　□ 예　　　　　　　□ 아니오

　아니오에 답한 경우, 이유는 무엇인가요?

5. 나는 Part 4를 풀 때 음성이 들리기 전에 해당 질문과 보기를 모두 먼저 읽었다.

　□ 예　　　　　　　□ 아니오

　아니오에 답한 경우, 이유는 무엇인가요?

6. 개선해야 할 점 또는 나를 위한 충고를 적어보세요.

* 교재의 첫 장으로 돌아가서 자신이 적은 목표 점수를 확인하면서 목표에 대한 의지를 다지기 바랍니다. 개선해야 할 점은 반드시 다음 테스트에
　실천해야 합니다. 그것이 가장 중요하며, 그래야만 발전할 수 있습니다.

▌TEST 09

PART **1**
PART **2**
PART **3**
PART **4**
Self 체크 리스트

잠깐! 테스트 전 확인사항

1. 휴대 전화의 전원을 끄셨나요? ☐ 예
2. Answer Sheet, 연필, 지우개를 준비하셨나요? ☐ 예
3. MP3를 들을 순비가 되셨나요? ☐ 예

모든 준비가 완료되었으면 목표 점수를 떠올린 후 테스트를 시작합니다.

🎧 TEST 09.mp3

실전용·복습용 문제풀이 MP3 무료 다운로드 및 스트리밍 바로듣기 (HackersIngang.com)

* 실제 시험장의 소음까지 재현해 낸 고사장 소음/매미 버전 MP3, 영국식·호주식 발음 집중 MP3, 고속 버전 MP3까지
   구매하면 실전에 더욱 완벽히 대비할 수 있습니다.

무료MP3 바로듣기

LISTENING TEST

In this section, you must demonstrate your ability to understand spoken English. This section is divided into four parts and will take approximately 45 minutes to complete. Do not mark the answers in your test book. Use the answer sheet that is provided separately.

PART 1

Directions: For each question, you will listen to four short statements about a picture in your test book. These statements will not be printed and will only be spoken one time. Select the statement that best describes what is happening in the picture and mark the corresponding letter (A), (B), (C), or (D) on the answer sheet.

Sample Answer

The statement that best describes the picture is (B), "The man is sitting at the desk." So, you should mark letter (B) on the answer sheet.

1.

2.

GO ON TO THE NEXT PAGE

3.

4.

5.

6.

GO ON TO THE NEXT PAGE ➤

PART 2

Directions: For each question, you will listen to a statement or question followed by three possible responses spoken in English. They will not be printed and will only be spoken one time. Select the best response and mark the corresponding letter (A), (B), or (C) on your answer sheet.

7. Mark your answer on your answer sheet.

8. Mark your answer on your answer sheet.

9. Mark your answer on your answer sheet.

10. Mark your answer on your answer sheet.

11. Mark your answer on your answer sheet.

12. Mark your answer on your answer sheet.

13. Mark your answer on your answer sheet.

14. Mark your answer on your answer sheet.

15. Mark your answer on your answer sheet.

16. Mark your answer on your answer sheet.

17. Mark your answer on your answer sheet.

18. Mark your answer on your answer sheet.

19. Mark your answer on your answer sheet.

20. Mark your answer on your answer sheet.

21. Mark your answer on your answer sheet.

22. Mark your answer on your answer sheet.

23. Mark your answer on your answer sheet.

24. Mark your answer on your answer sheet.

25. Mark your answer on your answer sheet.

26. Mark your answer on your answer sheet.

27. Mark your answer on your answer sheet.

28. Mark your answer on your answer sheet.

29. Mark your answer on your answer sheet.

30. Mark your answer on your answer sheet.

31. Mark your answer on your answer sheet.

Directions: In this part, you will listen to several conversations between two or more speakers. These conversations will not be printed and will only be spoken one time. For each conversation, you will be asked to answer three questions. Select the best response and mark the corresponding letter (A), (B), (C), or (D) on your answer sheet.

32. Where is the conversation taking place?

(A) In a sports arena
(B) In a government office
(C) In a shopping mall
(D) In a public park

33. Why is the woman meeting with Mr. Baxter?

(A) To demonstrate a product
(B) To give a presentation
(C) To conduct an interview
(D) To join an organization

34. What will the woman most likely do next?

(A) Use an elevator
(B) Move some furniture
(C) Pick up a pamphlet
(D) Look at a directory

35. What was the woman asked to do?

(A) Suggest an employee for a position
(B) Visit a newly opened office
(C) Train a new project manager
(D) Organize a public relations campaign

36. What is mentioned about Polson Incorporated?

(A) It operates branches in several cities.
(B) It is planning to hire additional employees.
(C) It held a press conference recently.
(D) It was acquired by another company.

37. What will the woman most likely do next?

(A) Call some colleagues
(B) Attend a workshop
(C) Update some records
(D) Download a file

38. What is the man's problem?

(A) A remote control is missing.
(B) A connection cannot be made.
(C) A facility is fully booked.
(D) A Web site is difficult to use.

39. What does the woman mean when she says, "Did you check your printed receipt"?

(A) A charged amount is incorrect.
(B) Coupons are attached to a document.
(C) Required information is on the paper.
(D) Discounts are not provided.

40. What is mentioned about the business lounge?

(A) It is exclusively for guests.
(B) It is open 24 hours a day.
(C) It is closed for renovations.
(D) It provides free Internet access.

41. What type of event is most likely taking place?

(A) An awards ceremony
(B) A charity banquet
(C) A literature conference
(D) A staff orientation

42. What does the woman say she forgot to do?

(A) Send a donation
(B) Update some information
(C) Select a meal preference
(D) Sign up ahead of time

43. What does the man suggest doing?

(A) Returning to a desk
(B) Visiting some booths
(C) Finding a seat
(D) Storing some baggage

GO ON TO THE NEXT PAGE

44. What did the man try to do?

(A) Enroll in a workshop
(B) Find some contact information
(C) Reserve a facility visit
(D) Place a product order

45. What does the woman imply when she says, "Group of four, right"?

(A) A table is ready.
(B) A discount will be provided.
(C) A notification was received.
(D) A booking has been confirmed.

46. According to the woman, what does the man have to do?

(A) Show some identification
(B) Fill out some paperwork
(C) Bring a credit card
(D) Wear formal apparel

47. What are the speakers mainly discussing?

(A) A business trip
(B) Some equipment
(C) Some cloth
(D) A facility tour

48. What does the man say about the spring collection?

(A) It will be sold internationally.
(B) It needs to have floral designs.
(C) It will be released today.
(D) It includes a variety of fabrics.

49. What does the woman offer to do?

(A) Visit a shop
(B) Meet with some suppliers
(C) Cancel an order
(D) Request some samples

50. What is the conversation mainly about?

(A) Expanding a department
(B) Celebrating an anniversary
(C) Promoting an employee
(D) Changing a design

51. What does the woman tell Luke to do?

(A) Conduct some research
(B) Skip an upcoming meeting
(C) Postpone a discussion
(D) Give a demonstration

52. Who is Maria Sutherland?

(A) A new colleague
(B) A hiring director
(C) A travel agent
(D) A regular customer

53. What kind of business does the man most likely work for?

(A) A publishing house
(B) A security firm
(C) A furniture manufacturer
(D) A shipping company

54. What does the woman ask about?

(A) A price increase
(B) A delivery date
(C) An order process
(D) A store closing time

55. What does the man say he will do?

(A) Confirm some information
(B) Reschedule an appointment
(C) Make a correction
(D) Send out an e-mail

56. What is Lucy invited to do?

(A) Visit an exhibit
(B) Watch a film
(C) Go to a restaurant
(D) Attend a concert

57. Why must Lucy work late?

(A) To write an evaluation
(B) To plan a project
(C) To update a homepage
(D) To prepare for a meeting

58. What does the man suggest?

(A) Reserving tickets
(B) Traveling together
(C) Editing a report
(D) Reading a review

---

59. What problem does the man mention?

(A) Some equipment is malfunctioning.
(B) Some information is not available.
(C) Some staff made complaints.
(D) Some products are sold out.

60. What will the woman do later today?

(A) Complete a questionnaire
(B) Do some research
(C) Rearrange a workspace
(D) Copy a publication

61. What will Mr. Roland do?

(A) Find a lost item
(B) Check a database
(C) Consult with employees
(D) Assemble furniture

SALES RECEIPT	
Decorative Vase	$74.99
Bed Sheet	$19.95
Window Blind	$149.99
Table Cloth	$21.85
Total (Paid by Credit Card)	$266.78

62. Why is the woman returning an item?

(A) It is overpriced.
(B) It is damaged.
(C) It is the wrong color.
(D) It is an incorrect size.

63. Look at the graphic. How much will the woman be refunded?

(A) $74.99
(B) $19.95
(C) $149.99
(D) $21.85

64. What will the man probably do next?

(A) Inspect a product
(B) Reduce some prices
(C) Check a storage room
(D) Send a catalog

GO ON TO THE NEXT PAGE

Design 1	Design 2
Design 3	Design 4

Lewis Instruments Instructors	
Instrument	Teacher
Guitar	Matt Hope
Piano	Omar Yanis
Drums	Mavis Liston
Violin	Sue Johnson

65. What is a feature of the new notebook covers?

(A) They can be custom designed.
(B) They come in different sizes.
(C) They were created by famous artists.
(D) They have multiple colors.

66. Look at the graphic. Which design has been chosen as the first sample?

(A) Design 1
(B) Design 2
(C) Design 3
(D) Design 4

67. What problem does the woman mention?

(A) A delivery schedule is delayed.
(B) A promotion has already expired.
(C) A tool will not get enough attention.
(D) An accessory is not popular.

68. How did the man learn about a service?

(A) By speaking to a friend
(B) By reading a flyer
(C) By listening to the radio
(D) By visiting a Web site

69. Look at the graphic. Who will most likely instruct the man?

(A) Matt Hope
(B) Omar Yanis
(C) Mavis Liston
(D) Sue Johnson

70. What will the speakers probably do next?

(A) Try out some instruments
(B) Begin a training session
(C) Check a schedule
(D) Discuss the price of an item

Directions: In this part, you will listen to several short talks by a single speaker. These talks will not be printed and will only be spoken one time. For each talk, you will be asked to answer three questions. Select the best response and mark the corresponding letter (A), (B), (C), or (D) on your answer sheet.

71. Who most likely are the listeners?

(A) Potential investors
(B) Board members
(C) Accounting consultants
(D) Product designers

72. What does the speaker say will be discussed at 3 P.M.?

(A) New government regulations
(B) International markets
(C) Mobile phone applications
(D) Expansion plans

73. What will most likely happen next?

(A) Some devices will be installed.
(B) Participants will take a short break.
(C) Some materials will be passed out.
(D) Attendees will ask some questions.

74. Why is the speaker calling?

(A) To inquire about a deadline
(B) To answer questions about tickets
(C) To ask for a payment
(D) To arrange a meeting

75. What does the speaker mean when he says, "I'm guessing it'll just be half an hour or so"?

(A) A press conference will begin shortly.
(B) An appointment will not take long.
(C) A music rehearsal will not be extended.
(D) A conductor will be leaving soon.

76. What does the speaker ask the listener to do?

(A) Cancel a consultation
(B) Provide an answer
(C) Attend a concert
(D) Visit an office

77. What type of class is being advertised?

(A) Photography
(B) Piano
(C) Pottery
(D) Painting

78. What does the speaker say about Diego Bello?

(A) He trained with famous artists.
(B) He has participated in exhibits.
(C) He received a major prize.
(D) He was featured in a magazine.

79. According to the speaker, why should the listeners go to a Web site?

(A) To download a document
(B) To look at some pictures
(C) To read a course list
(D) To review special prices

80. Who most likely are the listeners?

(A) Accountants
(B) Technicians
(C) Software developers
(D) Advertising specialists

81. According to the speaker, what task was assigned to Mr. Nunes?

(A) Giving workers an office tour
(B) Explaining a computer program
(C) Correcting some recording errors
(D) Talking about a firm's history

82. What will the listeners do next?

(A) Install a program
(B) Sign a document
(C) Get a manual
(D) Register for a workshop

GO ON TO THE NEXT PAGE

83. Where most likely are the listeners?

(A) At a business launch
(B) At a convention
(C) At a corporate banquet
(D) At a fund-raiser

84. What does the speaker mean when she says, "They have been laid out on the table near the entrance"?

(A) Some handouts should be relocated.
(B) A booth is no longer available.
(C) Some materials can be picked up.
(D) A request has been carried out.

85. What does the speaker suggest the listeners do?

(A) View some auction items
(B) Socialize with others
(C) Take an event schedule
(D) Return to their seats

86. Why is the speaker calling?

(A) To turn down an invitation
(B) To greet a new resident
(C) To change a schedule
(D) To sign up for a group

87. What does the speaker have for the listener?

(A) A membership card
(B) A welcome basket
(C) A rental contract
(D) A registration sheet

88. What will most likely happen within the week?

(A) A meeting will take place.
(B) A coupon book will be mailed.
(C) A homeowner will move.
(D) A newsletter will be issued.

89. What event will take place in October?

(A) A trade fair
(B) An art contest
(C) A sports competition
(D) A regional festival

90. What is mentioned about the event?

(A) It will attract international visitors.
(B) It is going to feature local celebrities.
(C) It will have performances daily.
(D) It is going to be partially televised.

91. How can the listeners acquire tickets?

(A) By calling a phone number
(B) By entering a special drawing
(C) By ordering them online
(D) By buying them at a gate

92. Where do the listeners work?

(A) At a movie theater
(B) At a conference center
(C) At a retail outlet
(D) At a concert venue

93. Why does the speaker say, "smartphones are used in all sorts of ways"?

(A) To promote some device accessories
(B) To justify an admission procedure
(C) To recommend a paid service
(D) To explain a warranty benefit

94. What will the listeners do at a front desk?

(A) Watch a demonstration
(B) Register for training
(C) Meet new personnel
(D) Install some equipment

Gibson Mall	
Store	**Wing**
Kids Palace	North
Vincent Books	East
The Nook	South
Readtopia	West

Follow-up Customer Survey Results (Average Scores)	
Store location	★★★☆☆
Staff friendliness	★★★★☆
Interior design	★★☆☆☆
Service timeliness	★★☆☆☆

95. What was recently opened?

(A) A clothing outlet
(B) A bookstore
(C) A dining establishment
(D) An amusement park

96. What does the speaker say some customers will receive for free?

(A) An admission pass
(B) A menu item
(C) A book
(D) A souvenir

97. Look at the graphic. Where will a signing event take place?

(A) In the North Wing
(B) In the East Wing
(C) In the South Wing
(D) In the West Wing

98. Who is Dan McGee?

(A) A human resources worker
(B) An auto mechanic
(C) A corporate lawyer
(D) A marketing supervisor

99. Look at the graphic. Which category got the lowest score last year?

(A) Store location
(B) Staff friendliness
(C) Interior design
(D) Service timeliness

100. What will the listeners probably do next?

(A) Watch a presentation
(B) Come up with some ideas
(C) Return to their regular jobs
(D) Fill out another survey

❚ 정답 음성(QR)이나 정답(p.166)을 이용해 채점하시기 바랍니다. 정답 음성에서 Boy는 (B)를, David는 (D)를 나타냅니다.
❚ 다음 페이지에 있는 Self 체크 리스트를 통해 자신의 문제 풀이 방식과 태도를 점검해 보세요.

Self 체크 리스트

TEST 09은 무사히 잘 마치셨죠?
이제 다음의 Self 체크 리스트를 통해 자신의 테스트 진행 내용을 점검해 볼까요?

1. 나는 테스트가 진행되는 동안 한 번도 중도에 멈추지 않았다.

  □ 예　　　　　　　□ 아니오

  아니오에 답한 경우, 이유는 무엇인가요?

2. 나는 답안지 표기까지 성실하게 모두 마무리하였다.

  □ 예　　　　　　　□ 아니오

  아니오에 답한 경우, 이유는 무엇인가요?

3. 나는 Part 2의 25문항을 푸는 동안 완전히 테스트에 집중하였다.

  □ 예　　　　　　　□ 아니오

  아니오에 답한 경우, 이유는 무엇인가요?

4. 나는 Part 3를 풀 때 음성이 들리기 전에 해당 질문과 보기를 모두 먼저 읽었다.

  □ 예　　　　　　　□ 아니오

  아니오에 답한 경우, 이유는 무엇인가요?

5. 나는 Part 4를 풀 때 음성이 들리기 전에 해당 질문과 보기를 모두 먼저 읽었다.

  □ 예　　　　　　　□ 아니오

  아니오에 답한 경우, 이유는 무엇인가요?

6. 개선해야 할 점 또는 나를 위한 충고를 적어보세요.

* 교재의 첫 장으로 돌아가서 자신이 적은 목표 점수를 확인하면서 목표에 대한 의지를 다지기 바랍니다. 개선해야 할 점은 반드시 다음 테스트에 실천해야 합니다. 그것이 가장 중요하며, 그래야만 발전할 수 있습니다.

TEST 10

PART 1
PART 2
PART 3
PART 4
Self 체크 리스트

잠깐! 테스트 전 확인사항

1. 휴대 전화의 전원을 끄셨나요? □ 예
2. Answer Sheet, 연필, 지우개를 준비하셨나요? □ 예
3. MP3를 들을 준비가 되셨나요? □ 예

모든 준비가 완료되었으면 목표 점수를 떠올린 후 테스트를 시작합니다.

🎧 TEST 10.mp3

실전용·복습용 문제풀이 MP3 무료 다운로드 및 스트리밍 바로듣기 (HackersIngang.com)
* 실제 시험장의 소음까지 재현해 낸 고사장 소음/매미 버전 MP3, 영국식·호주식 발음 집중 MP3, 고속 버전 MP3까지
  구매하면 실전에 더욱 완벽히 대비할 수 있습니다.

무료MP3 바로듣기

LISTENING TEST

In this section, you must demonstrate your ability to understand spoken English. This section is divided into four parts and will take approximately 45 minutes to complete. Do not mark the answers in your test book. Use the answer sheet that is provided separately.

PART 1

Directions: For each question, you will listen to four short statements about a picture in your test book. These statements will not be printed and will only be spoken one time. Select the statement that best describes what is happening in the picture and mark the corresponding letter (A), (B), (C), or (D) on the answer sheet.

Sample Answer
Ⓐ ● Ⓒ Ⓓ

The statement that best describes the picture is (B), "The man is sitting at the desk." So, you should mark letter (B) on the answer sheet.

1.

2.

GO ON TO THE NEXT PAGE

3.

4.

5.

6.

GO ON TO THE NEXT PAGE

Directions: For each question, you will listen to a statement or question followed by three possible responses spoken in English. They will not be printed and will only be spoken one time. Select the best response and mark the corresponding letter (A), (B), or (C) on your answer sheet.

7. Mark your answer on your answer sheet.

8. Mark your answer on your answer sheet.

9. Mark your answer on your answer sheet.

10. Mark your answer on your answer sheet.

11. Mark your answer on your answer sheet.

12. Mark your answer on your answer sheet.

13. Mark your answer on your answer sheet.

14. Mark your answer on your answer sheet.

15. Mark your answer on your answer sheet.

16. Mark your answer on your answer sheet.

17. Mark your answer on your answer sheet.

18. Mark your answer on your answer sheet.

19. Mark your answer on your answer sheet.

20. Mark your answer on your answer sheet.

21. Mark your answer on your answer sheet.

22. Mark your answer on your answer sheet.

23. Mark your answer on your answer sheet.

24. Mark your answer on your answer sheet.

25. Mark your answer on your answer sheet.

26. Mark your answer on your answer sheet.

27. Mark your answer on your answer sheet.

28. Mark your answer on your answer sheet.

29. Mark your answer on your answer sheet.

30. Mark your answer on your answer sheet.

31. Mark your answer on your answer sheet.

PART 3

Directions: In this part, you will listen to several conversations between two or more speakers. These conversations will not be printed and will only be spoken one time. For each conversation, you will be asked to answer three questions. Select the best response and mark the corresponding letter (A), (B), (C), or (D) on your answer sheet.

32. Why will the man travel to Beijing?
(A) To meet with a client
(B) To attend a seminar
(C) To inspect a factory
(D) To do some sightseeing

33. What does the man suggest?
(A) Making a phone call
(B) Filling out a form
(C) Looking up a venue
(D) Visiting a Web site

34. What does the woman say about Eli Price?
(A) He did not read a publication.
(B) He recently released a book.
(C) He will edit a presentation.
(D) He cannot join a gathering.

35. What type of business do the speakers probably work for?
(A) An accounting firm
(B) A marketing company
(C) A clothing manufacturer
(D) A department store

36. According to the man, what did Nancy recently do?
(A) Completed an analysis
(B) Gave a demonstration
(C) Designed more apparel
(D) Contacted a representative

37. What does the man say about the training session?
(A) It will take place tomorrow.
(B) It will focus on a computer program.
(C) It will be recorded by a film crew.
(D) It will be moved to another room.

38. What is scheduled for Saturday?
(A) A warehouse sale
(B) A retirement dinner
(C) A fundraising event
(D) A medical appointment

39. What does the woman imply when she says, "Some doctors are volunteering"?
(A) Medical supplies are ready.
(B) Some volunteers have not been trained.
(C) The event includes a dangerous course.
(D) Hiring staff will not be necessary.

40. What does the man say he will do?
(A) Interview some personnel
(B) Go for a medical exam
(C) Look for volunteers
(D) Identify areas on a route

41. What type of business does the man probably work for?
(A) A moving company
(B) A furniture retailer
(C) An insurance provider
(D) A construction firm

42. What does the woman tell the man to do?
(A) Read an agreement
(B) Park a truck in a garage
(C) Place items on the floor
(D) Call a worker for help

43. What does the man say about the invoice?
(A) It can be sent electronically.
(B) It has been received already.
(C) It is enclosed in a box.
(D) It contains an error.

GO ON TO THE NEXT PAGE

44. What is the conversation mainly about?

(A) An office opening
(B) A marketing campaign
(C) An interview process
(D) A business trip

45. What does the man inquire about?

(A) A project deadline
(B) A building address
(C) A meeting location
(D) A facility supervisor

46. What does the man suggest that Kara do?

(A) Make an announcement
(B) Apply for a position
(C) Speak to an executive
(D) Review a résumé

---

47. What is the man's problem?

(A) An appliance is not available.
(B) A record is inaccurate.
(C) A shipment has not arrived.
(D) A product has malfunctioned.

48. Why does the man say, "I purchased a Gateway 350"?

(A) To check a price
(B) To request a form
(C) To make a correction
(D) To change an order

49. What does the woman say she can do?

(A) Pick up an item
(B) Process a refund
(C) Make an appointment
(D) Expedite a delivery

---

50. Why is the man calling?

(A) To book a trip
(B) To purchase a publication
(C) To learn about a product
(D) To request a meeting

51. What does the woman have planned on Friday?

(A) A business luncheon
(B) A press conference
(C) A book launch
(D) A personal trip

52. What does the woman agree to do?

(A) Subscribe to some magazines
(B) Participate in a photo shoot
(C) Donate some money
(D) Sign autographs for fans

---

53. What is the conversation mainly about?

(A) A service request
(B) A sports competition
(C) A uniform design
(D) A community center

54. According to the woman, what should people be able to do on a Web site?

(A) Watch some videos
(B) Order a uniform
(C) Reserve tickets
(D) Register for a workshop

55. What will happen next?

(A) A photo will be taken.
(B) A presentation will be given.
(C) A proposal will be reviewed.
(D) An estimate will be provided.

---

56. Where must some crates be taken?

(A) To a production plant
(B) To a loading dock
(C) To a storage building
(D) To a store showroom

57. What problem does the man mention?

(A) A vehicle is unavailable.
(B) A container has been misplaced.
(C) A building door is locked.
(D) A worker is late for a shift.

58. What does the man ask the woman to do?

(A) Unpack a shipment
(B) Examine some labels
(C) Check a staff schedule
(D) Hold a team meeting

59. What is mentioned about the ski resort?

(A) It is attracting too few customers.
(B) It will be temporarily closed down.
(C) It hosted a competition.
(D) It will open a new restaurant.

60. What does Connie suggest?

(A) Setting up a display
(B) Decreasing some rates
(C) Hiring more staff
(D) Meeting with a competitor

61. What will the man do this afternoon?

(A) Inspect a building site
(B) Sign some forms
(C) Share some ideas
(D) Clean up an area

→ Inbox
☐ **From:** Chau Nguyen   ⟫ **Subject:** Catering Meal
☐ **From:** Kayla Baker   ⟫ **Subject:** Banquet Hall Invoice
☐ **From:** Javier Valencia   ⟫ **Subject:** Beeman Guest List
☐ **From:** Andre Wood   ⟫ **Subject:** Lunch Meeting

62. What is the woman working on?

(A) Room decorations
(B) Event invitations
(C) Menu changes
(D) Seating arrangements

63. Look at the graphic. Who sent an e-mail half an hour ago?

(A) Chau Nguyen
(B) Kayla Baker
(C) Javier Valencia
(D) Andre Wood

64. According to the man, what happened last month?

(A) Venue reservations were modified.
(B) Catering choices were confirmed.
(C) A conference center was renovated.
(D) A guest list was posted online.

GO ON TO THE NEXT PAGE

Miller's Office Supplies
Paper Product Coupon

Buy	Receive
1 pack	5 percent off
2 packs	10 percent off
3 packs	15 percent off
4 packs	20 percent off

Bicycle World Inc.

Service Request Number: 2534

Part	Price
Tire	$105
Brake pads	$50
Chain	$35
Cable	$5
TOTAL DUE	**$195**

65. What does the man ask about?

(A) The price of a device
(B) The size of a printer
(C) The location of merchandise
(D) The duration of a promotion

66. What does the woman say about the PaperPro 300?

(A) It is a durable product.
(B) It is simple to use.
(C) It comes in several colors.
(D) It was featured in a magazine.

67. Look at the graphic. What discount will the man most likely receive?

(A) 5 percent off
(B) 10 percent off
(C) 15 percent off
(D) 20 percent off

68. What did the man do earlier today?

(A) Checked a bicycle tire
(B) Called a local repair shop
(C) Shopped for parts online
(D) Went for a bike ride

69. What problem does the woman mention?

(A) A request will take some time to fulfill.
(B) A store does not sell a certain brand.
(C) A credit card has been rejected.
(D) A component was not properly installed.

70. Look at the graphic. How much will be deducted from the total cost?

(A) $105
(B) $50
(C) $35
(D) $5

PART 4

Directions: In this part, you will listen to several short talks by a single speaker. These talks will not be printed and will only be spoken one time. For each talk, you will be asked to answer three questions. Select the best response and mark the corresponding letter (A), (B), (C), or (D) on your answer sheet.

71. What was found in a store?

    (A) A garment
    (B) A wallet
    (C) An umbrella
    (D) A wristwatch

72. What does the speaker mention about the information desk?

    (A) It is staffed by two people.
    (B) It is marked with a sign.
    (C) It is closing in five minutes.
    (D) It is near the dairy section.

73. What does the speaker say was recently introduced?

    (A) A delivery service
    (B) A security measure
    (C) A phone application
    (D) A rewards program

74. What type of business does the listener most likely work for?

    (A) A restaurant chain
    (B) A remodeling company
    (C) A real estate agency
    (D) A market research firm

75. What does the speaker like about the proposal?

    (A) The color
    (B) The size
    (C) The schedule
    (D) The price

76. What does the speaker mean when she says, "I live by myself"?

    (A) A request cannot be accommodated.
    (B) She wants another suggestion.
    (C) A room expansion is not necessary.
    (D) She is making the decisions herself.

77. Where most likely do the listeners work?

    (A) At a financial consulting agency
    (B) At a corporate law firm
    (C) At a public relations company
    (D) At an educational institution

78. What is mentioned about Mr. Pearce?

    (A) He founded the firm.
    (B) He is waiting in the break room.
    (C) He will be leaving the company.
    (D) He won an industry award.

79. According to the speaker, what will happen tomorrow?

    (A) Some staff will be transferred.
    (B) A break room will be closed off.
    (C) A training session will be held.
    (D) Some refreshments will be available.

80. According to the speaker, what has a team been working on?

    (A) A company symbol
    (B) Clothing designs
    (C) A business deal
    (D) Office renovations

81. What does the speaker say clients will be given?

    (A) Business brochures
    (B) Branded gifts
    (C) Updated contracts
    (D) Price estimates

82. Why does the speaker say, "The more, the better"?

    (A) To welcome personnel
    (B) To encourage suggestions
    (C) To accept an offer
    (D) To praise an achievement

GO ON TO THE NEXT PAGE

83. Who is the speaker going to interview?

(A) A zoo official
(B) A filmmaker
(C) A travel blogger
(D) A scientist

84. What does the speaker imply when she says, "I've got no reason to doubt them"?

(A) A project goal will be met.
(B) Some praise is justified.
(C) A campaign will be successful.
(D) Some concerns are valid.

85. What will the listeners most likely hear next?

(A) Details about an event
(B) Advertisements from sponsors
(C) Comments about a production
(D) Information from a reporter

---

86. What does the speaker inform the listener about?

(A) A loyalty program
(B) A service price
(C) A new stylist
(D) A schedule change

87. What is offered to the listener?

(A) A membership card
(B) A follow-up consultation
(C) A hair-care product
(D) A gift certificate

88. What does the speaker say is inaccessible?

(A) An elevator
(B) A parking lot
(C) A staircase
(D) A waiting area

---

89. Who most likely are the listeners?

(A) Electronics salespeople
(B) Computer programmers
(C) Product designers
(D) Media representatives

90. What does the speaker suggest?

(A) Posting about a product online
(B) Setting up some displays
(C) Correcting some malfunctions
(D) Becoming familiar with a device

91. What feature distinguishes the Koring Pro?

(A) It comes in multiple colors.
(B) It does not need a cord to function.
(C) It contains built-in speakers.
(D) It is compatible with previous models.

---

92. What is the report mainly about?

(A) A business opening
(B) A product release
(C) A health study
(D) A company acquisition

93. According to the speaker, what took place in the spring?

(A) A product trial
(B) An awareness campaign
(C) A seasonal promotion
(D) A national recall

94. Why was the preorder service halted?

(A) It proved to be too popular.
(B) It violated state regulations.
(C) It was not approved by a CEO.
(D) It cost a lot of money.

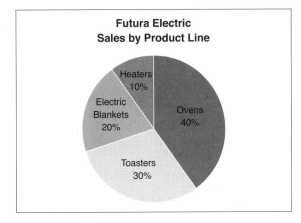

**Futura Electric
Sales by Product Line**

- Heaters 10%
- Electric Blankets 20%
- Ovens 40%
- Toasters 30%

Office	Phone number
Denver	555-2466
Seattle	555-9183
Tacoma	555-7833
Phoenix	555-3422

95. What does the speaker say he did this morning?

(A) He used a new appliance.
(B) He had a meeting with a competitor.
(C) He found out about a product release.
(D) He studied the company's total sales.

96. Look at the graphic. Which product category needs to be discussed?

(A) Ovens
(B) Toasters
(C) Electric Blankets
(D) Heaters

97. What does the speaker ask the listeners to do?

(A) Contact a coworker
(B) Redesign a product line
(C) Prepare some recipes
(D) Try out some devices

98. According to the speaker, where was a debit card used yesterday?

(A) At an international airport
(B) At an apparel retailer
(C) At a luxury resort
(D) At a fast food restaurant

99. Why must the listener place a call?

(A) To track some parcels
(B) To take advantage of a deal
(C) To confirm a purchase
(D) To make travel arrangements

100. Look at the graphic. Which office should the listener contact?

(A) Denver
(B) Seattle
(C) Tacoma
(D) Phoenix

정답 p.166 / 점수 환산표 p.167 / 스크립트 p.222 / 무료 해석 바로 보기(정답 및 정답 음성 포함)

▌정답 음성(QR)이나 정답(p.166)을 이용해 채점하시기 바랍니다. 정답 음성에서 Boy는 (B)를, David는 (D)를 나타냅니다.
▌다음 페이지에 있는 Self 체크 리스트를 통해 자신의 문제 풀이 방식과 태도를 점검해 보세요.

TEST 10 PART 4 **161**

Self 체크 리스트

TEST 10은 무사히 잘 마치셨죠?
이제 다음의 Self 체크 리스트를 통해 자신의 테스트 진행 내용을 점검해 볼까요?

1. 나는 테스트가 진행되는 동안 한 번도 중도에 멈추지 않았다.

   □ 예   □ 아니오

   아니오에 답한 경우, 이유는 무엇인가요?

2. 나는 답안지 표기까지 성실하게 모두 마무리하였다.

   □ 예   □ 아니오

   아니오에 답한 경우, 이유는 무엇인가요?

3. 나는 Part 2의 25문항을 푸는 동안 완전히 테스트에 집중하였다.

   □ 예   □ 아니오

   아니오에 답한 경우, 이유는 무엇인가요?

4. 나는 Part 3를 풀 때 음성이 들리기 전에 해당 질문과 보기를 모두 먼저 읽었다.

   □ 예   □ 아니오

   아니오에 답한 경우, 이유는 무엇인가요?

5. 나는 Part 4를 풀 때 음성이 들리기 전에 해당 질문과 보기를 모두 먼저 읽었다.

   □ 예   □ 아니오

   아니오에 답한 경우, 이유는 무엇인가요?

6. 개선해야 할 점 또는 나를 위한 충고를 적어보세요.

* 교재의 첫 장으로 돌아가서 자신이 적은 목표 점수를 확인하면서 목표에 대한 의지를 다지기 바랍니다. 개선해야 할 점은 반드시 다음 테스트에
  실천해야 합니다. 그것이 가장 중요하며, 그래야만 발전할 수 있습니다.

정답

점수 환산표

스크립트

Answer Sheet

《해커스 토익 실전 1000제 1 Listening》
무료 해석은 해커스토익(Hackers.co.kr)
에서 다운로드 받거나 QR 코드를 스캔하여
모바일로도 확인할 수 있습니다.

▪TEST 01

1 (D)	2 (B)	3 (A)	4 (C)	5 (A)
6 (B)	7 (A)	8 (B)	9 (C)	10 (C)
11 (A)	12 (C)	13 (B)	14 (B)	15 (A)
16 (B)	17 (A)	18 (C)	19 (A)	20 (B)
21 (B)	22 (A)	23 (C)	24 (A)	25 (B)
26 (A)	27 (C)	28 (A)	29 (C)	30 (B)
31 (C)	32 (B)	33 (C)	34 (C)	35 (B)
36 (A)	37 (D)	38 (B)	39 (D)	40 (B)
41 (B)	42 (D)	43 (A)	44 (D)	45 (B)
46 (A)	47 (D)	48 (C)	49 (A)	50 (D)
51 (A)	52 (B)	53 (C)	54 (D)	55 (A)
56 (C)	57 (B)	58 (D)	59 (C)	60 (D)
61 (B)	62 (D)	63 (C)	64 (A)	65 (D)
66 (C)	67 (C)	68 (A)	69 (D)	70 (C)
71 (C)	72 (A)	73 (D)	74 (B)	75 (A)
76 (D)	77 (B)	78 (C)	79 (C)	80 (A)
81 (D)	82 (B)	83 (D)	84 (D)	85 (C)
86 (A)	87 (B)	88 (C)	89 (A)	90 (C)
91 (D)	92 (A)	93 (B)	94 (D)	95 (A)
96 (B)	97 (C)	98 (A)	99 (B)	100 (D)

▪TEST 02

1 (D)	2 (C)	3 (B)	4 (C)	5 (A)
6 (D)	7 (C)	8 (B)	9 (B)	10 (A)
11 (B)	12 (C)	13 (A)	14 (C)	15 (C)
16 (B)	17 (A)	18 (A)	19 (B)	20 (A)
21 (A)	22 (C)	23 (A)	24 (B)	25 (B)
26 (B)	27 (A)	28 (C)	29 (B)	30 (C)
31 (A)	32 (A)	33 (C)	34 (A)	35 (D)
36 (B)	37 (B)	38 (C)	39 (D)	40 (D)
41 (C)	42 (A)	43 (D)	44 (D)	45 (C)
46 (B)	47 (B)	48 (B)	49 (B)	50 (B)
51 (C)	52 (B)	53 (C)	54 (B)	55 (D)
56 (D)	57 (B)	58 (D)	59 (B)	60 (A)
61 (B)	62 (D)	63 (A)	64 (D)	65 (D)
66 (B)	67 (B)	68 (D)	69 (B)	70 (D)
71 (B)	72 (C)	73 (A)	74 (C)	75 (B)
76 (B)	77 (D)	78 (D)	79 (A)	80 (C)
81 (C)	82 (B)	83 (B)	84 (C)	85 (A)
86 (D)	87 (A)	88 (C)	89 (C)	90 (D)
91 (D)	92 (B)	93 (C)	94 (C)	95 (C)
96 (B)	97 (B)	98 (B)	99 (C)	100 (D)

▪TEST 03

1 (A)	2 (B)	3 (D)	4 (B)	5 (D)
6 (C)	7 (A)	8 (B)	9 (C)	10 (B)
11 (A)	12 (C)	13 (C)	14 (B)	15 (A)
16 (C)	17 (C)	18 (A)	19 (B)	20 (B)
21 (A)	22 (C)	23 (C)	24 (B)	25 (A)
26 (B)	27 (C)	28 (A)	29 (C)	30 (A)
31 (B)	32 (B)	33 (D)	34 (A)	35 (D)
36 (B)	37 (B)	38 (A)	39 (D)	40 (D)
41 (C)	42 (C)	43 (A)	44 (C)	45 (D)
46 (A)	47 (C)	48 (D)	49 (D)	50 (D)
51 (B)	52 (C)	53 (D)	54 (B)	55 (C)
56 (B)	57 (A)	58 (A)	59 (C)	60 (C)
61 (B)	62 (D)	63 (C)	64 (C)	65 (A)
66 (C)	67 (D)	68 (B)	69 (D)	70 (B)
71 (D)	72 (A)	73 (D)	74 (A)	75 (D)
76 (B)	77 (C)	78 (D)	79 (B)	80 (C)
81 (B)	82 (A)	83 (D)	84 (A)	85 (B)
86 (D)	87 (A)	88 (B)	89 (D)	90 (A)
91 (D)	92 (A)	93 (C)	94 (B)	95 (C)
96 (B)	97 (B)	98 (C)	99 (D)	100 (C)

▪TEST 04

1 (D)	2 (B)	3 (C)	4 (A)	5 (A)
6 (D)	7 (C)	8 (A)	9 (B)	10 (C)
11 (B)	12 (C)	13 (B)	14 (C)	15 (A)
16 (C)	17 (B)	18 (C)	19 (C)	20 (B)
21 (C)	22 (C)	23 (C)	24 (A)	25 (B)
26 (B)	27 (C)	28 (C)	29 (B)	30 (C)
31 (C)	32 (C)	33 (C)	34 (C)	35 (B)
36 (D)	37 (A)	38 (C)	39 (A)	40 (D)
41 (B)	42 (D)	43 (C)	44 (B)	45 (B)
46 (C)	47 (A)	48 (C)	49 (B)	50 (C)
51 (B)	52 (A)	53 (B)	54 (A)	55 (B)
56 (B)	57 (C)	58 (A)	59 (B)	60 (D)
61 (A)	62 (A)	63 (C)	64 (B)	65 (C)
66 (C)	67 (B)	68 (B)	69 (B)	70 (D)
71 (A)	72 (A)	73 (B)	74 (C)	75 (D)
76 (D)	77 (D)	78 (A)	79 (B)	80 (D)
81 (A)	82 (A)	83 (D)	84 (A)	85 (C)
86 (D)	87 (B)	88 (B)	89 (D)	90 (B)
91 (A)	92 (B)	93 (B)	94 (C)	95 (C)
96 (B)	97 (B)	98 (A)	99 (B)	100 (D)

▌TEST 05

1 (A)	2 (D)	3 (C)	4 (C)	5 (C)
6 (B)	7 (B)	8 (A)	9 (C)	10 (B)
11 (B)	12 (A)	13 (C)	14 (A)	15 (C)
16 (B)	17 (C)	18 (B)	19 (A)	20 (A)
21 (C)	22 (C)	23 (A)	24 (A)	25 (B)
26 (C)	27 (A)	28 (A)	29 (B)	30 (C)
31 (A)	32 (C)	33 (A)	34 (C)	35 (B)
36 (D)	37 (C)	38 (D)	39 (B)	40 (C)
41 (D)	42 (C)	43 (A)	44 (C)	45 (C)
46 (B)	47 (D)	48 (A)	49 (D)	50 (A)
51 (D)	52 (A)	53 (A)	54 (C)	55 (B)
56 (D)	57 (B)	58 (A)	59 (D)	60 (B)
61 (C)	62 (B)	63 (B)	64 (D)	65 (B)
66 (C)	67 (B)	68 (A)	69 (D)	70 (B)
71 (C)	72 (B)	73 (A)	74 (D)	75 (C)
76 (A)	77 (C)	78 (D)	79 (A)	80 (C)
81 (B)	82 (A)	83 (B)	84 (A)	85 (D)
86 (B)	87 (A)	88 (A)	89 (B)	90 (D)
91 (D)	92 (B)	93 (A)	94 (D)	95 (C)
96 (D)	97 (A)	98 (C)	99 (D)	100 (B)

▌TEST 06

1 (C)	2 (B)	3 (D)	4 (D)	5 (A)
6 (B)	7 (C)	8 (C)	9 (B)	10 (A)
11 (C)	12 (C)	13 (A)	14 (B)	15 (A)
16 (C)	17 (B)	18 (B)	19 (A)	20 (C)
21 (A)	22 (B)	23 (A)	24 (C)	25 (B)
26 (A)	27 (C)	28 (A)	29 (B)	30 (C)
31 (C)	32 (D)	33 (C)	34 (B)	35 (C)
36 (D)	37 (A)	38 (D)	39 (A)	40 (B)
41 (C)	42 (D)	43 (A)	44 (B)	45 (B)
46 (D)	47 (C)	48 (D)	49 (A)	50 (B)
51 (C)	52 (A)	53 (C)	54 (B)	55 (A)
56 (D)	57 (B)	58 (D)	59 (C)	60 (D)
61 (A)	62 (B)	63 (C)	64 (A)	65 (D)
66 (B)	67 (B)	68 (A)	69 (B)	70 (C)
71 (B)	72 (C)	73 (A)	74 (B)	75 (B)
76 (A)	77 (C)	78 (D)	79 (A)	80 (D)
81 (D)	82 (C)	83 (A)	84 (C)	85 (D)
86 (C)	87 (A)	88 (B)	89 (C)	90 (C)
91 (D)	92 (B)	93 (D)	94 (A)	95 (B)
96 (B)	97 (D)	98 (C)	99 (D)	100 (A)

▌TEST 07

1 (A)	2 (C)	3 (B)	4 (B)	5 (B)
6 (D)	7 (A)	8 (C)	9 (A)	10 (A)
11 (C)	12 (A)	13 (B)	14 (C)	15 (A)
16 (C)	17 (C)	18 (B)	19 (B)	20 (B)
21 (C)	22 (A)	23 (B)	24 (A)	25 (B)
26 (A)	27 (A)	28 (C)	29 (B)	30 (A)
31 (B)	32 (C)	33 (D)	34 (B)	35 (A)
36 (B)	37 (C)	38 (A)	39 (A)	40 (D)
41 (B)	42 (D)	43 (C)	44 (D)	45 (A)
46 (B)	47 (B)	48 (A)	49 (C)	50 (A)
51 (B)	52 (B)	53 (C)	54 (B)	55 (B)
56 (D)	57 (C)	58 (C)	59 (D)	60 (B)
61 (D)	62 (A)	63 (B)	64 (D)	65 (A)
66 (B)	67 (C)	68 (B)	69 (C)	70 (A)
71 (B)	72 (A)	73 (D)	74 (D)	75 (C)
76 (D)	77 (D)	78 (A)	79 (B)	80 (C)
81 (D)	82 (A)	83 (C)	84 (A)	85 (D)
86 (D)	87 (B)	88 (D)	89 (A)	90 (D)
91 (A)	92 (B)	93 (D)	94 (B)	95 (C)
96 (B)	97 (D)	98 (B)	99 (D)	100 (C)

▌TEST 08

1 (D)	2 (A)	3 (A)	4 (B)	5 (A)
6 (C)	7 (C)	8 (B)	9 (A)	10 (B)
11 (C)	12 (A)	13 (C)	14 (B)	15 (B)
16 (A)	17 (C)	18 (C)	19 (B)	20 (C)
21 (C)	22 (A)	23 (C)	24 (B)	25 (C)
26 (C)	27 (B)	28 (A)	29 (A)	30 (A)
31 (C)	32 (B)	33 (D)	34 (B)	35 (C)
36 (A)	37 (B)	38 (C)	39 (C)	40 (A)
41 (D)	42 (B)	43 (C)	44 (D)	45 (A)
46 (A)	47 (C)	48 (A)	49 (D)	50 (C)
51 (A)	52 (D)	53 (B)	54 (D)	55 (A)
56 (C)	57 (D)	58 (C)	59 (A)	60 (B)
61 (D)	62 (D)	63 (C)	64 (B)	65 (A)
66 (C)	67 (C)	68 (D)	69 (C)	70 (B)
71 (B)	72 (A)	73 (C)	74 (C)	75 (A)
76 (B)	77 (C)	78 (A)	79 (D)	80 (B)
81 (D)	82 (C)	83 (C)	84 (D)	85 (D)
86 (B)	87 (D)	88 (C)	89 (D)	90 (D)
91 (C)	92 (A)	93 (C)	94 (B)	95 (B)
96 (C)	97 (B)	98 (D)	99 (C)	100 (C)

TEST 09

1 (C)	2 (D)	3 (B)	4 (D)	5 (D)
6 (C)	7 (A)	8 (C)	9 (C)	10 (A)
11 (C)	12 (A)	13 (B)	14 (A)	15 (A)
16 (B)	17 (C)	18 (B)	19 (A)	20 (B)
21 (B)	22 (A)	23 (C)	24 (C)	25 (B)
26 (A)	27 (A)	28 (B)	29 (B)	30 (A)
31 (C)	32 (B)	33 (B)	34 (A)	35 (A)
36 (D)	37 (B)	38 (B)	39 (C)	40 (D)
41 (C)	42 (D)	43 (A)	44 (C)	45 (D)
46 (C)	47 (C)	48 (B)	49 (D)	50 (D)
51 (C)	52 (A)	53 (C)	54 (B)	55 (A)
56 (B)	57 (D)	58 (B)	59 (C)	60 (B)
61 (C)	62 (D)	63 (C)	64 (A)	65 (A)
66 (C)	67 (C)	68 (B)	69 (A)	70 (C)
71 (B)	72 (C)	73 (C)	74 (D)	75 (B)
76 (B)	77 (C)	78 (B)	79 (B)	80 (A)
81 (B)	82 (C)	83 (D)	84 (C)	85 (A)
86 (B)	87 (B)	88 (A)	89 (D)	90 (C)
91 (D)	92 (D)	93 (B)	94 (A)	95 (C)
96 (B)	97 (D)	98 (D)	99 (B)	100 (A)

TEST 10

1 (D)	2 (B)	3 (A)	4 (A)	5 (C)
6 (C)	7 (C)	8 (B)	9 (A)	10 (B)
11 (A)	12 (C)	13 (C)	14 (B)	15 (A)
16 (B)	17 (A)	18 (C)	19 (A)	20 (B)
21 (C)	22 (B)	23 (C)	24 (C)	25 (B)
26 (B)	27 (C)	28 (C)	29 (B)	30 (B)
31 (C)	32 (B)	33 (A)	34 (B)	35 (C)
36 (A)	37 (B)	38 (C)	39 (D)	40 (D)
41 (A)	42 (C)	43 (A)	44 (A)	45 (D)
46 (B)	47 (D)	48 (C)	49 (C)	50 (D)
51 (A)	52 (B)	53 (A)	54 (C)	55 (D)
56 (C)	57 (A)	58 (B)	59 (A)	60 (B)
61 (C)	62 (D)	63 (A)	64 (B)	65 (C)
66 (B)	67 (B)	68 (D)	69 (A)	70 (C)
71 (A)	72 (D)	73 (A)	74 (B)	75 (A)
76 (B)	77 (C)	78 (D)	79 (D)	80 (A)
81 (B)	82 (B)	83 (B)	84 (B)	85 (D)
86 (D)	87 (C)	88 (A)	89 (A)	90 (D)
91 (B)	92 (B)	93 (A)	94 (A)	95 (C)
96 (B)	97 (D)	98 (B)	99 (C)	100 (D)

* 아래 점수 환산표로 자신의 토익 리스닝 점수를 예상해봅니다.

정답수	리스닝 점수	정답수	리스닝 점수	정답수	리스닝 점수
100	495	66	305	32	135
99	495	65	300	31	130
98	495	64	295	30	125
97	495	63	290	29	120
96	490	62	285	28	115
95	485	61	280	27	110
94	480	60	275	26	105
93	475	59	270	25	100
92	470	58	265	24	95
91	465	57	260	23	90
90	460	56	255	22	85
89	455	55	250	21	80
88	450	54	245	20	75
87	445	53	240	19	70
86	435	52	235	18	65
85	430	51	230	17	60
84	425	50	225	16	55
83	415	49	220	15	50
82	410	48	215	14	45
81	400	47	210	13	40
80	395	46	205	12	35
79	390	45	200	11	30
78	385	44	195	10	25
77	375	43	190	9	20
76	370	42	185	8	15
75	365	41	180	7	10
74	355	40	175	6	5
73	350	39	170	5	5
72	340	38	165	4	5
71	335	37	160	3	5
70	330	36	155	2	5
69	325	35	150	1	5
68	315	34	145	0	5
67	310	33	140		

※ 점수 환산표는 해커스토익 사이트 유저 데이터를 근거로 제작되었으며, 주기적으로 업데이트되고 있습니다. 해커스토익(Hackers.co.kr) 사이트에서 최신 경향을 반영하여 업데이트된 점수환산기를 이용하실 수 있습니다. (토익 > 토익게시판 > 토익점수환산기)

TEST 01 스크립트

* 무료 해석은 해커스토익(Hackers.co.kr)에서
다운로드 받을 수 있습니다.

* QR 코드로
바로가기

PART 1

1 [3e] 미국식 발음
(A) A woman is fixing a device.
(B) A woman is taking a wallet out of her handbag.
(C) A woman is arranging flowers in a vase.
(D) A woman is examining some clothing on a rack.

2 [3e] 호주식 발음
(A) Some tools are scattered on the ground.
(B) A tree is surrounded by some tents.
(C) They are looking in a box.
(D) They are assembling cameras.

3 [3e] 영국식 발음
(A) They are walking side by side.
(B) They are wearing ties.
(C) They are going into a building.
(D) They are standing under an umbrella.

4 [3e] 캐나다식 발음
(A) A painting is beside a lamp.
(B) There is a tablecloth over the table.
(C) A cushion is propped up on an armchair.
(D) A clock is mounted on the wall.

5 [3e] 영국식 발음
(A) The man is mopping the floor.
(B) The man is repositioning a bulletin board.
(C) The woman is carrying a bucket.
(D) The woman is plugging in a television.

6 [3e] 미국식 발음
(A) A bottle cap is being removed.
(B) A wall is covered in brick.
(C) Some plants are placed on a table.
(D) Some shelves have been emptied.

PART 2

7 [3e] 캐나다식 발음 → 미국식 발음
What play have you decided on going to see?
(A) The new one with Judd Kinsley.
(B) She is a famous movie producer.
(C) No, it's going really well.

8 [3e] 영국식 발음 → 캐나다식 발음
Who called you earlier this morning?
(A) Later in the afternoon.
(B) One of my clients.
(C) In my office.

9 [3e] 미국식 발음 → 호주식 발음
Would you like to switch to a corner room?
(A) Turn the lights off, please.
(B) Around the corner.
(C) That would be nice.

10 [3e] 호주식 발음 → 영국식 발음
Are we going to fix the broken copier soon?
(A) No, I can't go this time.
(B) I've got my copy right here.
(C) A new one would be cheaper.

11 [3e] 영국식 발음 → 호주식 발음
How can I check the balance in my account?
(A) You can log on to the bank's Web site.
(B) Just charge it and pay later.
(C) The deal is fair for both parties.

12 [3e] 미국식 발음 → 호주식 발음
We need to increase our social media efforts.
(A) An ancient society.
(B) The media will be there.
(C) I agree, but I am no expert.

13 [3e] 캐나다식 발음 → 영국식 발음
Where is your company's headquarters?
(A) He works at the local branch.
(B) In Madrid, Spain.
(C) We're a food manufacturing company.

14 [3e] 캐나다식 발음 → 미국식 발음
When is the technician supposed to come?
(A) It's technologically very advanced.
(B) I left a memo on your desk.
(C) She's highly qualified for the task.

15 [3e] 호주식 발음 → 영국식 발음
It feels like the brakes are not working properly.
(A) You came to the right place to fix them.
(B) The property is quite large.

(C) You can take your break now.

16 [3] 미국식 발음 → 호주식 발음

Could I get a bit more of the dressing for the salad?
(A) There is no dress code for the event.
(B) The bottle is over there.
(C) You don't have to prepare all the ingredients.

17 [3] 영국식 발음 → 캐나다식 발음

Would you prefer the first or second option for our new logo?
(A) The darker blue one.
(B) Yes, I love it.
(C) Because we hired a designer.

18 [3] 캐나다식 발음 → 미국식 발음

This is the restaurant where you're having your retirement party, isn't it?
(A) No, on the 25th of next month.
(B) That was a great party.
(C) I'm still trying to decide.

19 [3] 영국식 발음 → 호주식 발음

We could add one more salesperson to the team.
(A) We do need some extra help.
(B) Bonuses were given to all employees.
(C) At the team meeting.

20 [3] 캐나다식 발음 → 영국식 발음

Where can I find Cathy's office?
(A) With a large fine.
(B) Right down the hallway.
(C) We should get more office space.

21 [3] 호주식 발음 → 미국식 발음

Why hasn't Mr. Marx given us our work schedule for next week?
(A) I marked the date on my calendar.
(B) It's posted on the company intranet board.
(C) You should get it done quickly.

22 [3] 캐나다식 발음 → 영국식 발음

The room you reserved has just been cleaned.
(A) Great, I can't wait to put my bags down.
(B) Near the swimming pool.
(C) We will buy more cleaning supplies.

23 [3] 미국식 발음 → 영국식 발음

The exhibition only runs until next month, right?
(A) A monthly exercise.
(B) I'm sorry, I was running late.
(C) It ends this week.

24 [3] 호주식 발음 → 미국식 발음

Are you looking at our latest financial figures?
(A) Yes. They're incredible.
(B) That's what I figured.
(C) I'm still looking for freelance work.

25 [3] 캐나다식 발음 → 호주식 발음

Which phone application do you use the most?
(A) Use it with care.
(B) The file-sharing one.
(C) Ms. Nixon usually makes the call.

26 [3] 영국식 발음 → 캐나다식 발음

Where should I take the clients after the conference?
(A) Why don't you ask them directly?
(B) As soon as they arrive.
(C) Yes, I think that would be perfect.

27 [3] 캐나다식 발음 → 미국식 발음

Aren't you going to the design meeting that's about to start?
(A) Yes, I was there on Friday.
(B) The founder has resigned from the board.
(C) Finishing this file will only take a few minutes.

28 [3] 호주식 발음 → 미국식 발음

How much will the next order cost approximately?
(A) Should be the same as last time.
(B) We can go to the next store now.
(C) It'll take approximately a week.

29 [3] 캐나다식 발음 → 영국식 발음

Can we renovate the staff break room?
(A) It took three months to finish.
(B) How about ordering some coffee?
(C) We don't have enough funds in our budget.

30 [3] 미국식 발음 → 호주식 발음

The waiting area in the Clark Gallery looks bigger than it did before.
(A) Before you come in.
(B) They removed one wall.
(C) Please wait five minutes.

31 [3] 영국식 발음 → 호주식 발음

Can we have Veramo's spring collection in our stores within two months?
(A) Store the boxes downstairs.
(B) I'll collect information on the software.
(C) We're not going to order it.

PART 3

Questions 32-34 refer to the following conversation.

🔊 영국식 발음 → 캐나다식 발음

W: We have to prepare the rooftop so we have a place for the new solar panels.

M: But don't we already have enough empty space for them on the north side of the roof? I'm worried because there are air conditioning units and fans on the rooftop.

W: Yes. But the panels must be on the south side rather than the north side so they receive direct sunlight. Maybe we should consider moving the air conditioner units to the north side of the rooftop.

Questions 35-37 refer to the following conversation.

🔊 호주식 발음 → 영국식 발음

M: Ace Cable Television. How can I help you?

W: Hi. This is Jessica Pendleton. I'm moving out of my house next month, and I was wondering if I could transfer my cable account to my roommate. There's still another year on the contract, and I'd like to avoid the fee for early termination.

M: Yes, we do allow that. First, we'll need your address and account number. Then please tell us when you would like the transfer to take place.

W: OK, sounds good. I don't have my account number on hand, but I know it's included on the electronic bill I received. Let me check my e-mail.

Questions 38-40 refer to the following conversation with three speakers.

🔊 미국식 발음 → 캐나다식 발음 → 호주식 발음

W: Everyone, I'm coordinating with the caterer for our annual awards dinner on January 3, and I want to make sure that we get food everyone can eat. Have you returned the form with your team members' dietary restrictions, Harold?

M1: I'm sorry. It's not complete. I think a few may be vegetarians. What about on yours, Lamar?

M2: I'll have to ask if anyone has any special needs. If you can wait until this afternoon, I can get the form to you.

W: No problem. Since I have you both here now, can you quickly review this seating chart? I want to be sure everyone is in the best possible place.

M2: Yeah, of course.

Questions 41-43 refer to the following conversation.

🔊 캐나다식 발음 → 미국식 발음

M: Hey, Stacey. As you know, the marketing campaign that we're creating for Dawson Foods is due next Tuesday. I'm wondering if we can spend the next hour talking about how to best utilize our budget.

W: Right now, I'm going to fill out and submit my quarterly employee survey. It needs to be handed in today.

M: I understand. Do you have time tomorrow morning?

W: I do. I'll stop by your office at 9 A.M., and we can spend an hour or two on the task.

M: OK. I'll see you then. Good luck with the questionnaire.

Questions 44-46 refer to the following conversation.

🔊 영국식 발음 → 호주식 발음

W: Our fast food chain is going to open a new branch downtown. While we already have one location there, the market has enough demand for two branches.

M: That's a great idea. Customers at the current branch have been complaining about long lines. When do we hope to open?

W: The goal is sometime in late March.

M: If that's the case, we should start looking for a property to buy.

W: Yes, I agree. Plus, our CEO will be visiting us here at the regional headquarters next month. She'll probably want to discuss the costs of potential properties, so we should have some estimates by then.

M: That's true. I'll start researching properties today.

Questions 47-49 refer to the following conversation with three speakers.

🔊 캐나다식 발음 → 호주식 발음 → 미국식 발음

M1: Since we started allowing remote work, the office has been nearly empty. I think we should consider moving to a more appropriately sized place.

M2: I agree. It seems unnecessary to rent such a large office. We probably only need about one-fifth of the space we currently have.

M1: We could even look at a shared office space . . . Hey, Angie. What's that shared office place by the Denver Tower called?

W: It's called Our Room. I heard the rates there are pretty reasonable.

M1: It could be a good option then. I'll make a reservation to visit the facility after lunch.

M2: Great idea. I'm free this afternoon, so I'll join you.

Questions 50-52 refer to the following conversation.

🔊 캐나다식 발음 → 미국식 발음

M: Excuse me. When I was running earlier today, I dropped my key somewhere. Now I don't have any way to access my apartment. Do you have one I can make a copy of?

W: Of course. Follow me to the security office. We have copies of all the keys in the safe there. Do you know where you are going to make a copy?

M: I figured I'd go to a shop somewhere along 19th street. I've seen some key makers around there.

W: I like to use Nick's Hardware Store. They get it done in less than a minute. They provide the fastest service in town.

Questions 53–55 refer to the following conversation.

호주식 발음 → 영국식 발음

M: Did you hear that Joo-hee is sick, and James and Nekima are stuck in traffic? They texted me just before the store opened to customers.

W: Yes, I did. I read some posts on the employee management system from them all a few minutes ago. We usually require 12 people to run the store, but I think we'll be able to manage.

M: There are only nine here. Also, we're supposed to get a large shipment of shoes from our main distributor this morning.

W: OK, that could be a problem. I'll call some of our workers who are off today to see if anyone can come in on short notice.

Questions 56–58 refer to the following conversation.

미국식 발음 → 캐나다식 발음

W: Daniel, do you know how we're supposed to arrange the flowers for tonight's banquet? A courier just dropped off all 50 of our bouquets.

M: Honestly, I'm not sure. I don't usually handle the flower arrangements. However, I know that our manager distributed a handout with instructions. Why don't you refer to that?

W: Oh, right. I forgot about that. I'll look it over.

M: Great. I'll be back later to check on your progress, but I need to talk to Janet Nelson, the photographer we hired for the event. There were some last-minute changes made to the list of shots we need.

W: Yes, of course. That's more important.

Questions 59–61 refer to the following conversation.

영국식 발음 → 호주식 발음

W: Hayato, can we talk quickly? I'd like to pay a professional accountant to manage our gift shop's tax filing this year. How do you feel about that?

M: It would save us a lot of time and trouble, but it will probably cost a lot. I'm afraid it may not be worth the investment.

W: In my opinion, hiring a specialist would definitely be helpful. Doing it ourselves takes too much time and is inefficient. If you're worried about the cost, I've heard there are online accounting companies that cost much less than traditional ones.

M: Doing it online seems like a great option. Could you get some estimates?

W: Sure. I'll get some quotes now.

Questions 62–64 refer to the following conversation and product catalog.

캐나다식 발음 → 미국식 발음

M: Excuse me. I'm interested in buying a sofa for a dental office that I recently opened. But I can't make up my mind which model to get.

W: I'm happy to help you. Personally, I'm a fan of our Ridgeport and New Hampton models. Both are very stylish.

M: Yes, they're nice. Do you think they'd fit comfortably in a small waiting room?

W: If space is a concern, then the Wellington model is the best choice. It's also extremely comfortable and comes in six colors.

M: I think you're right. I'll go with that.

W: Great. And since the item costs over $500, you qualify to have it dropped off at no additional charge.

Questions 65–67 refer to the following conversation and flight ticket.

영국식 발음 → 호주식 발음

W: Good morning. Is there anything I can do for you today?

M: Hi. Yes. I'm traveling to Barcelona for a work conference, but I'd like to change something with my flight ticket.

W: Oh, what seems to be the matter?

M: Well, I'd like a different seat, if possible. I want to stay in an aisle seat, but I'd prefer one that is closer to the front of the plane. The online flight information suggests that there's an opening in Row 15.

W: Ah, yes. I can take care of that for you.

M: Thanks a lot. Also, I'd like to check this suitcase while I still have time.

W: Sure. I can handle that.

Questions 68–70 refer to the following conversation and bar graph.

캐나다식 발음 → 미국식 발음

M: Leslie, did you hear that Kenrick Jackson is stepping down as branch supervisor? He took a job at another electronics retailer.

W: Yes, I heard. You should apply for his position when it becomes available. His branch has the largest number of workers, so it'd be an excellent career opportunity.

M: Do you think so? I'd welcome the promotion, but I'm not sure my experience is adequate.

W: I disagree. You're more than qualified. If you're interested and decide to submit one, I'd be happy to help you prepare your application form.

M: Thanks for the offer. I'll think about it and let you know.

PART 4

Questions 71-73 refer to the following tour information.

[3ₙ] 호주식 발음

Welcome to the virtual tour of the Wilson Home, architect Neil Grady's last, unfinished project. Though most of the rooms on the first floor are completed, some areas, including the second floor and the basement, are only partially constructed. Thus, we'll be mainly viewing rooms on this floor. As we navigate through this house, you may notice question mark icons on some items. Feel free to click on these to get more information about the objects. I'll be telling you all about the history of the building's construction, and the people who have attempted to complete it over the years. Let's start.

Questions 74-76 refer to the following talk.

[3ₙ] 미국식 발음

Hello, everyone. I'm the leader of today's training session for new workers. We're running a little behind schedule, so let's begin. If you turn to the first page in your informational packet, you'll see the program for today's training. This morning, we'll discuss what to do in the event of a fire, earthquake, or other natural disaster. We'll break for lunch around noon. Then, at 1 P.M., we'll resume the training. We'll perform some activities designed to help you learn what to do if someone becomes seriously injured or ill in the workplace. At the end of the day, you'll each receive proof of completion of your workplace safety training for this year.

Questions 77-79 refer to the following talk.

[3ₙ] 캐나다식 발음

I'd like to thank our employees who volunteered at the job fair at the Anderson Community Center last week. For a small marketing company like ours, these events are essential for finding potential applicants. Thanks to your efforts, I have lined up several interviews in the coming week. My goal is to have at least two new copywriters on staff by November 27. That is when we will start working on the print advertisements for Green Gardens Florists, which is our biggest and most important client yet. With any luck, this project will lead to us having more clients on our list to work with next year.

Questions 80-82 refer to the following announcement.

[3ₙ] 영국식 발음

Attention, passengers. Due to severe weather conditions at our destination airport in Sydney, this flight has been delayed. We were scheduled to depart at 12:00 P.M., but we are now looking at an approximate takeoff time of 3:30 P.M. I apologize on behalf of the airline. I know you have taken your seats already. Now, everyone should return to the terminal. We will start boarding again at 2:30 P.M. To make the wait more comfortable, we will provide all passengers with a voucher for a free drink at any airport establishment. Please enjoy your drink and wait for further updates.

Questions 83-85 refer to the following introduction.

[3ₙ] 호주식 발음

Thank you everyone for attending today's product launch. I'd also like to welcome viewers from around the world as we are streaming this live on our Web site. Before you get a first glimpse at the new Moyo phone, CEO Margret Tucker will talk about her vision for the company's future. After taking this position last month, she now has the chance to talk to the world directly. After our presentation, I will guide all of the attendees to our lounge where they can actually use the phone. And here is the best part, one lucky raffle winner will walk away with one of the new phones. But now, let's welcome Margret Tucker.

Questions 86-88 refer to the following advertisement.

[3ₙ] 캐나다식 발음

Our mission at Fren Beauty Incorporated is to provide you with the most effective chemical-free products on the market. However, our commitment to making better products doesn't stop with our ingredients. Even our packaging has become eco-friendly. It's created from biodegradable and recycled materials. This applies to all the products we sell, from face wash and shampoo to foot scrubs. After years of direct sales, we are now happy to announce that you can find our product line at www.shopbeautysmart.com starting this April. If you would like to see our products on shelves, ask your local store to carry our brand today.

Questions 89-91 refer to the following report.

[3ₙ] 미국식 발음

This is Amanda Peters with the latest local news. Many residents do not know that the park is full of free activities. For example, The Friartown Park Association is hosting yoga classes on weekdays in Friartown Park from 7 A.M. to 8 A.M. On the weekends, you can enjoy aerobics classes at the same time. Both activities will last until the end of September. There are also monthly classical concerts on the first Friday of each month. Visit the association's Web site for daily updates and information about the artists playing at the concerts.

Questions 92-94 refer to the following telephone message.

[3ₙ] 영국식 발음

Hello, Jennifer. This is Celia Swanson calling from

Swanson Bakery. I received your message from Friday about the cake you are thinking of ordering for your party. As you requested, I've set up a cake tasting for you on Saturday, March 2, at 12:30 P.M. There is no obligation to purchase anything at that time. But if you do decide to place a cake order, please be informed that it generally takes us two days to fulfill an order for a basic sheet cake, but the cake you asked about has multiple layers. In addition, you mentioned wanting some lettering and special decorations. You can talk about those at Saturday's activity with our assistant, Genevieve. She'll be able to tell you if they're possible and how much extra they would cost.

Questions 95-97 refer to the following talk and table.

[호주식 발음]

Good morning, everyone. I hope you've enjoyed your first night at Carson Island Resort. Today, we have a number of complimentary activities for you to enjoy. If you refer to your welcome packet, you'll find a table with all of them listed. As you can see, most involve getting wet, so I recommend putting on a bathing suit and non-slip shoes. If you want to take the scuba diving course, please let me know. I'm the instructor and I'll have to get you some special equipment. Now, I'll let you enjoy your breakfast and decide what you want to do for the day.

Questions 98-100 refer to the following telephone message and map.

[미국식 발음]

Hello, this is Marcy Williams from Central Valley Electric. I have received your inquiry about your power being out. In fact, power is out all across Thomas County due to the severe weather we experienced last night. Central Valley Electric crews from the station there are working hard to restore service. At the moment, I advise you to stay calm and use emergency candles. However, if you still do not have electricity by 2 P.M. tomorrow, please call back to let me know. I can dispatch a technician to your property. You can reach me at 555-1920.

■TEST 02 스크립트

* 무료 해석은 해커스토익(Hackers.co.kr)에서
다운로드 받을 수 있습니다.

*QR 코드로
바로가기

PART 1

1 ③ 캐나다식 발음

   (A) The woman is carrying a shovel.
   (B) The woman is hiking in a field.
   (C) The woman is filling a watering can.
   (D) The woman is kneeling on the grass.

2 ③ 영국식 발음

   (A) Some people are walking along a road.
   (B) One of the men is brushing off his shirt.
   (C) Construction work is being done.
   (D) A hose has been set on the ground.

3 ③ 호주식 발음

   (A) A guitar is being played.
   (B) A room is unoccupied.
   (C) An instrument is being repaired.
   (D) A box is propping a door open.

4 ③ 영국식 발음

   (A) The woman is hanging up a blanket.
   (B) The woman is sorting some towels.
   (C) The woman is making a bed.
   (D) The woman is turning off a light.

5 ③ 캐나다식 발음

   (A) Some items are on display.
   (B) A woman is standing by a cash register.
   (C) Produce is being handed to a shopper.
   (D) Some people are pushing a shopping cart.

6 ③ 미국식 발음

   (A) Curtains separate the work areas.
   (B) A monitor has been turned on.
   (C) A remote control is lying on a chair.
   (D) A desk is illuminated by a lamp.

PART 2

7 ③ 영국식 발음 → 호주식 발음

   Who is in charge of the budget report?
   (A) It's standard procedure.
   (B) She is an excellent reporter.
   (C) I think Maria is.

8 ③ 캐나다식 발음 → 영국식 발음

   Where is the nearest post office located?
   (A) It's a nearby store.
   (B) About three blocks south.
   (C) I bought some stamps.

9 ③ 영국식 발음 → 호주식 발음

   Why wasn't the recycling taken out?
   (A) The garbage can.
   (B) Scott forgot to do it.
   (C) Oh, a collection agency.

10 ③ 미국식 발음 → 캐나다식 발음

   How much is this office's rental fee?
   (A) $3,000 monthly.
   (B) For government officials only.
   (C) Both items were free.

11 ③ 영국식 발음 → 미국식 발음

   Would you mind opening the window?
   (A) The account has been closed.
   (B) Isn't it too cold outside?
   (C) No, not until last spring.

12 ③ 캐나다식 발음 → 호주식 발음

   The projector in the conference room isn't working.
   (A) If there's enough room.
   (B) Yes, a presentation.
   (C) Holly also reported that problem.

13 ③ 미국식 발음 → 캐나다식 발음

   When will we update the dessert options on our menu?
   (A) Two types of cake were just added.
   (B) The screening is next Friday.
   (C) Those are very good suggestions.

14 ③ 호주식 발음 → 미국식 발음

   How are you going to finish your speech by the deadline?
   (A) A list of speakers.
   (B) I completely agree.
   (C) I'm concerned about that too.

15 [3ㅁ] 미국식 발음 → 캐나다식 발음

You're scheduled for the night shift, correct?
(A) The goods shifted during transit.
(B) Last night's videoconference.
(C) Not this evening.

16 [3ㅁ] 캐나다식 발음 → 미국식 발음

Were enough gift bags purchased for banquet attendees?
(A) I think you'll like your present.
(B) We were a few short.
(C) Programs for the event.

17 [3ㅁ] 영국식 발음 → 호주식 발음

Would you be interested in a beverage?
(A) Thanks, but I'll pass.
(B) No, neither of the plates.
(C) What an interesting outfit!

18 [3ㅁ] 미국식 발음 → 캐나다식 발음

Will it be a while until the train arrives?
(A) I haven't heard anything.
(B) I registered for a training session.
(C) Directly from Berlin.

19 [3ㅁ] 호주식 발음 → 영국식 발음

Can you please listen to your music with earphones?
(A) I can't use my phone.
(B) Yes. Sorry to disturb you.
(C) Where's the musical being held?

20 [3ㅁ] 캐나다식 발음 → 미국식 발음

What was the result of the promotional event this week?
(A) I've been away on a business trip.
(B) We're offering a trial period for new accounts.
(C) Turn in your sales report tomorrow.

21 [3ㅁ] 호주식 발음 → 영국식 발음

Where should these wooden boards be stacked?
(A) Beside the garage.
(B) It's high-quality wood.
(C) You should consider going as well.

22 [3ㅁ] 미국식 발음 → 캐나다식 발음

Who rearranged the layout of the lobby?
(A) Sure, I can arrange a taxi for you.
(B) Please lay the shirts on the shelves.
(C) The office manager.

23 [3ㅁ] 호주식 발음 → 영국식 발음

When will workers receive their annual bonuses?
(A) With their next paychecks.
(B) Yes, a generous amount.

(C) I have the receipt in my bag.

24 [3ㅁ] 미국식 발음 → 호주식 발음

The battery in this wristwatch needs to be replaced.
(A) I watched that movie yesterday.
(B) Oh, I didn't realize it was dead.
(C) Thanks for coming to my place.

25 [3ㅁ] 영국식 발음 → 캐나다식 발음

A shipment of notepads arrived at the school this morning.
(A) I'd recommend taking a cruise ship.
(B) But I just ordered pens and pencils.
(C) Middleton High School.

26 [3ㅁ] 호주식 발음 → 미국식 발음

Does Ms. Wallace have time to meet us this afternoon?
(A) I appreciate you getting together with me on short notice.
(B) I'll check her schedule.
(C) She reviewed the project timeline.

27 [3ㅁ] 캐나다식 발음 → 미국식 발음

Why are the display cases near our store's entrance empty?
(A) To make room for new inventory.
(B) Next to the exit.
(C) Please empty them out.

28 [3ㅁ] 영국식 발음 → 미국식 발음

Don't these hats have to be returned to the manufacturer?
(A) A popular line of winter apparel.
(B) A factory supervisor.
(C) Yes, they have defects.

29 [3ㅁ] 영국식 발음 → 호주식 발음

Are any of the seats on the flight to Rome still available?
(A) I've traveled to Rome twice.
(B) No, they are fully booked.
(C) I can help you find your seat in the theater.

30 [3ㅁ] 캐나다식 발음 → 영국식 발음

What did you want to talk to me about earlier today?
(A) That's correct. Today and tomorrow.
(B) As early as possible.
(C) My transfer to our overseas office.

31 [3ㅁ] 호주식 발음 → 캐나다식 발음

The winner of the fiction prize will be announced sometime this week.
(A) How will we be notified?

(B) I was surprised that he won.

(C) This year's fiction book fair was a huge success.

PART 3

Questions 32-34 refer to the following conversation.

🎧 영국식 발음 → 캐나다식 발음

W: Thank you for calling Index Shipping. My name is Valerie. How can I help you?

M: I want to report a mistaken delivery. When I came home from work today, I noticed a large box outside my door. It has my address on it but someone else's name.

W: Oh, I see. These things sometimes happen due to typos. Do you recognize the sender's information?

M: No, not at all.

W: Hmm . . . The sender probably wrote the wrong address on the parcel. I'll have a courier stop by your place and pick it up tomorrow morning.

Questions 35-37 refer to the following conversation with three speakers.

🎧 미국식 발음 → 캐나다식 발음 → 호주식 발음

W: Steve, this is our newly hired laboratory technician, Edward Germaine. Edward, this is Steve Meyers, our senior researcher.

M1: Welcome to Milton Research Firm. Will you be working on the upcoming allergy medicine study?

M2: I don't know yet. My orientation is today, so I haven't been assigned to a project yet.

W: Ms. Adams will tell him which team he'll be on tomorrow. By the way, Steve, would you be able to show Edward around the laboratory at some point today?

M1: Of course. When is a good time for you, Edward?

M2: I should be free at 1 P.M. Is that OK?

M1: Certainly. Let's meet in the break room.

Questions 38-40 refer to the following conversation.

🎧 호주식 발음 → 영국식 발음

M: Hi. I'm calling to see if your library has the book *Distant Stars* available to check out.

W: Just a minute . . . Yes, we have it, sir. But, well . . . that publication is part of our rare book collection. Books in that section cannot be taken out of our facility.

M: I see. In that case, I guess I'll have to look over the book there. Would it be possible to reserve a private reading room from 4 P.M. to 7 P.M. today?

W: For that, I'll have to transfer you to our facilities department. Please stay on the line while I connect you.

Questions 41-43 refer to the following conversation.

🎧 캐나다식 발음 → 미국식 발음

M: Hi. I'm repainting my house, and I was wondering if you sold paint and brushes.

W: Absolutely. The painting section is just between the aisles for plumbing and electrical supplies. Do you have any idea what color you want to use?

M: I have a picture of a house from a magazine that's a really nice color. Here, let me show you. Do you have this color?

W: Oh, yes. I think we do. And that paint is on sale for members of our loyalty club. If you're not a member, you can fill out some forms to join now.

M: I'm not a member. I will fill out the paperwork.

Questions 44-46 refer to the following conversation with three speakers.

🎧 영국식 발음 → 미국식 발음 → 호주식 발음

W1: I think customers would appreciate it if our company produced limited edition blends. With the holidays coming up, special holiday edition tea sets would make great gifts.

W2: I completely agree. That would really boost our sales.

M: We should bring it up to management. I could do it myself, but I'd need some guidance. I've never done anything like that before.

W1: The best option would be to make a proposal about it that we could present at our upcoming regional meeting.

W2: Yes. The company's regional director, Mr. Martin, will be there.

M: We could all work together on a presentation about it. What do you think, Olivia?

W1: Sure, let's start right now.

Questions 47-49 refer to the following conversation.

🎧 캐나다식 발음 → 영국식 발음

M: Young-mi, is anyone interested in the house you're trying to sell?

W: Actually, the real estate agent I hired called me about that an hour ago. He said that there's a woman who's interested. She contacted him this morning to set up a time to view my home. I guess she saw some pictures of it and was very impressed.

M: Well, I hope she decides to put an offer on the place.

W: I'm feeling optimistic. Apparently, the potential buyer was very happy when my agent told her that there is a grocery store and a fitness center nearby.

Questions 50-52 refer to the following conversation.

[3)] 미국식 발음 → 호주식 발음

W: Good morning. I'm here to pick up my clothes that I dropped off yesterday. I requested the express cleaning service.

M: I'm very sorry, ma'am, but your items are not quite ready yet. One of our machines unexpectedly broke down last night. It is currently being fixed.

W: I really needed everything this morning. That's why I chose to pay a premium.

M: I understand. We will refund you the extra amount, of course. And if you give us your address, we'll deliver the clothes to your residence at no extra charge this evening.

W: OK. Do you have a pen I can use?

Questions 53-55 refer to the following conversation.

[3)] 영국식 발음 → 캐나다식 발음

W: Hi. I'm wondering if you can assist me. There's an issue with the smartphone I bought here recently. It turns on fine, but I noticed a small crack on the display.

M: Yes, I see what you mean. When did you buy the device?

W: Just last Tuesday, when a special discount on the product was being offered.

M: Well, you're still within our 90-day store warranty period.

W: So, does that mean the display can be fixed for free?

M: Even better. We'll give you another unit at no cost.

W: Oh, wonderful! Thank you.

Questions 56-58 refer to the following conversation.

[3)] 호주식 발음 → 미국식 발음

M: Excuse me. I have an appointment with Gina Patel on the 18th floor. How can I access the elevators?

W: First, visitors must check in here. If you show me a piece of identification, I'll provide an electronic pass. Your ID will be kept here until you return.

M: Will my passport be suitable? I left my driver's license at my apartment.

W: That's fine. And now you just need to complete this form. It asks you for some personal details—your phone number, the purpose of your visit, and so on.

M: OK . . . I'll do that now.

Questions 59-61 refer to the following conversation.

[3)] 영국식 발음 → 캐나다식 발음

W: How does everyone on your team feel about the newly implemented filing system, Trent?

M: Well, they definitely like that sharing files online is much easier now. That's really helpful when we're considering designs to use for advertising campaigns.

However, it was running a bit slow yesterday, so that caused some delays.

W: OK. I'll call the IT department and ask them to check on that. By the way, Mr. Nolan just asked me about the status of the Glowfresh Cosmetics commercial.

M: Janice Miller just uploaded some storyboard files to the system. If you log in and click on Designs, you can see what she has done so far.

Questions 62-64 refer to the following conversation and floor plan.

[3)] 캐나다식 발음 → 영국식 발음

M: Marcy, I'm finalizing the floor plan for the office move that is scheduled for tomorrow afternoon. Do you have a room preference?

W: I would love an office with lots of light. Is there anything like that available?

M: Yes. The one next to the break room is available. It's a corner office with large windows on two sides. There will be a lot of traffic there, though.

W: That's fine. I don't mind a little noise as long as the office is bright.

M: OK, but I recommend you install shades to keep out some of the sunlight.

Questions 65-67 refer to the following conversation and concert poster.

[3)] 영국식 발음 → 캐나다식 발음

W: Carl, I want to let you know that I've confirmed the venue for the charity concert that we're organizing. I spoke with the park manager yesterday, and everything is set.

M: Oh, we got Helmsley Park. That's great. It already has a stage, so we won't have to build one. But wasn't there a conflict with the date that we selected?

W: No. The date we requested works after all.

M: Good. There's still one issue we must deal with, though.

W: Really? What's the problem? I hope it's not too serious.

M: The second band scheduled to play can't participate. They have another obligation. So, we'll have to find another option.

Questions 68-70 refer to the following conversation and shelving unit.

[3)] 호주식 발음 → 미국식 발음

M: Camilla, we will be selling our digital cameras and accessories at a discount next week. So, I'd like to reorganize that section of the store.

W: OK. What would you like me to do?

M: Please make sure that the cameras are prominently displayed. Um, why don't you move them to the shelf that currently holds the tripods?

W: Sure. It would be better to have the tripods on the bottom shelf anyway as they are much larger than the flashes and lenses.

M: Right. Uh, one more thing . . . We should also hand out some fliers to customers to publicize this event. I'll give you them to distribute once the shelves have been rearranged.

PART 4

Questions 71-73 refer to the following announcement.

〔3〕 미국식 발음

This announcement is for all passengers of Jet Winds Flight 391 from Brisbane, Australia to Busan, South Korea. Today's flight is fully booked. Therefore, all overhead compartments are expected to be filled. Please remember that suitcases should be placed in the bins with their top handles facing the aisle so as to allow for more items to fit. Also, if anyone is willing to check their bag prior to boarding, please see airline agents at the ticketing desk. All such volunteers will receive a voucher for one free in-flight snack or beverage. Passengers from economy class may now begin boarding. Thank you for listening.

Questions 74-76 refer to the following broadcast.

〔3〕 호주식 발음

Good afternoon, and welcome to *Getting Fit* on WQZP. Today I will be interviewing Mitchell Rothman. He is a nutritionist who is well-known for creating a popular one-month weight loss program, which focuses on eliminating junk food and introducing apple cider vinegar. Did you know that this type of vinegar can play a key role in helping to burn extra fat in our bodies? Mr. Rothman will explain how this works in a few minutes. But first, I'd like to play an audio recording of his opening address at the Pacific Health Conference. The ideas he presents are quite fascinating.

Questions 77-79 refer to the following telephone message.

〔3〕 영국식 발음

Hi, this is Melissa Walton from BRX Publishing for Liam Roberts. I'm calling because I reviewed the children's storybook you submitted with the other members of the editing committee. It was very well received! We hope to have a final manuscript prepared by the end of the month. Since we may need to make a few minor changes, I'd like you to come into our office next week to discuss details about the characters and plot with our team. Tuesday at 9 A.M. would be ideal, but we are flexible.

Questions 80-82 refer to the following excerpt from a meeting.

〔3〕 캐나다식 발음

As you know, this is the busiest time of the year for our hotel. We are fully booked until the end of August. In addition, the number of people joining our membership program is increasing. I'd like you all to continue concentrating on boosting those numbers. Also, I understand that many of you are confused about the overtime policy. Let me explain. You'll receive 150 percent of your hourly wage for any additional hours worked. And, if you work extra hours on holidays, then you'll receive double your normal rate. I hope this is clear.

Questions 83-85 refer to the following telephone message.

〔3〕 미국식 발음

Mr. Kunchai, this is Polly Jenkins calling. I'm sorry to bother you, but I've run into a small problem. It turns out that the paint I bought to use in your living room is the wrong color. Although the can says that it contains tan paint, the paint is actually a light green color. Anyway, I plan to head out after I get off the phone. I expect to lose at least an hour of work today by going to the store, which means I'll most likely need to return tomorrow to complete the project.

Questions 86-88 refer to the following excerpt from a meeting.

〔3〕 호주식 발음

I'd like to tell you about a new type of fabric that has lots of potential. Direct exposure to light breaks down any organic matter on it. It's the closest thing available right now to a textile that can clean itself. Making clothing from this would be very beneficial for the environment. For instance, consumers would be able to cut down on the energy they use for their washing machines and dryers. Now, take a look at this shirt. It's obviously dirt stained, but check out what happens when I put it under this special lamp.

Questions 89-91 refer to the following telephone message.

〔3〕 미국식 발음

This is Wendy Barr calling for Curtis Dunlap. I work for Benton Athletics, a sustainable sportswear manufacturer. I was wondering if you would be interested in endorsing our company. You won a gold medal at the Olympics last month. I think people would be really excited to see you representing our company, and it would help increase their awareness of our brand. I am attending a trade show next week, so I'll have some samples with me. If you are interested, I could stop by your gym and show you our merchandise.

Questions 92–94 refer to the following news report.

[음성] 영국식 발음

In local news, the renowned Derby Botanical Society plans to invite expert gardener Lorenzo Granada to its biannual meeting at 7 P.M. on Wednesday. Ms. Granada, who will be traveling all the way from Barcelona, is scheduled to give a lecture on growing orchids. Usually, the association gathers at Lakeside Community Center for such events, but this time the meeting will take place at Selby Auditorium. The change is due to the fact that a large turnout is anticipated. You can pay $10 to enter or present a Derby Botanical Society member card for complimentary admission.

Questions 95–97 refer to the following talk and ratings site.

[음성] 호주식 발음

Our next speaker here at the Cape Town Finance Forum is Lisa Duval, an economist who works for the Department of Budget and Planning. Dr. Duval has also written a number of best-selling books, including one about the growth of technology companies—the first one she ever published. In fact, her most recent book, which was released a week ago, quickly topped sales charts and has been awarded four stars by PageFlipper.com. Anyway, today she'll be discussing the current direction of the solar panel industry here in South Africa. Please welcome her with a big round of applause.

Questions 98–100 refer to the following telephone message and schedule.

[음성] 캐나다식 발음

I'm not sure if you remember me, but my name is Hector Fuentes. We met last Thursday at the AIDQUEST Conference. After your talk on how to use social media to promote organizations, we chatted a bit regarding my own foundation, Education Now. I was very impressed with what you had to say, and I'd like to hire you as a consultant. If you're interested, we should meet to discuss the position. Next week would be ideal. Monday won't work for me because I've got to attend an event at a local university, but I'll be free on Tuesday.

PART 1

1 🔊 캐나다식 발음

    (A) A man is pouring a beverage.
    (B) A man is grasping a spoon.
    (C) A man is placing an order at a café.
    (D) A man is stacking some cups.

2 🔊 영국식 발음

    (A) The man is removing headphones.
    (B) The man is using a piece of equipment.
    (C) A path is lined with large stones.
    (D) A tree is being chopped down.

3 🔊 미국식 발음

    (A) People are fishing in a stream.
    (B) Some boots have been taken off.
    (C) A dam has been built in a river.
    (D) Some hikers are crossing a stream.

4 🔊 호주식 발음

    (A) They are collecting some rocks.
    (B) They are walking down a path.
    (C) They are strolling across a bridge.
    (D) They are going in opposite directions.

5 🔊 캐나다식 발음

    (A) Passengers are reviewing a digital board.
    (B) A book has been stored in a pocket.
    (C) The woman is taking a nap.
    (D) A bag has been placed next to the woman.

6 🔊 미국식 발음

    (A) A bike rack is mounted on the side of a wall.
    (B) A flag is flying from a pole.
    (C) A sign is posted near the road.
    (D) A road passes between some houses.

PART 2

7 🔊 호주식 발음 → 미국식 발음

    When were these windows installed?
    (A) About five years ago.
    (B) I just installed a new operating system.
    (C) At the back of the workroom.

8 🔊 영국식 발음 → 캐나다식 발음

    Where should we set up our fruit stand?
    (A) Any time before 9 A.M.
    (B) Right by the market entrance.
    (C) Feel free to have a seat.

9 🔊 호주식 발음 → 영국식 발음

    Has the elevator been fixed yet?
    (A) On the second floor.
    (B) Next to the stairs.
    (C) I used it this morning.

10 🔊 미국식 발음 → 캐나다식 발음

    Is the board meeting scheduled for Wednesday?
    (A) Some financial concerns.
    (B) No, Tuesday.
    (C) We'll meet with him too.

11 🔊 영국식 발음 → 호주식 발음

    What time should I make the reservation for?
    (A) Whenever we can get a table.
    (B) With the restaurant manager.
    (C) Through an online booking site.

12 🔊 영국식 발음 → 캐나다식 발음

    Has the architectural firm hired by Mayor Li started the project?
    (A) My company is based in Florida.
    (B) Yes, some upcoming elections.
    (C) Work got underway on May 1.

13 🔊 호주식 발음 → 미국식 발음

    Who still needs to submit a reimbursement form?
    (A) All the documents.
    (B) Patrick will drop you off.
    (C) No one that I know of.

14 🔊 캐나다식 발음 → 영국식 발음

    Which article will be printed on the front page?
    (A) I printed a new pattern.
    (B) One of the longer ones.
    (C) In Friday's issue.

15 　[3w] 미국식 발음 → 캐나다식 발음

Are many customers making use of our video streaming services?
(A) Far more than we expected.
(B) Personalized customer profiles.
(C) A link on the Web site.

16 　[3w] 호주식 발음 → 영국식 발음

The sleeves of this coat are a bit too long for me.
(A) Probably for an hour.
(B) A popular fabric.
(C) Our tailor can fix that.

17 　[3w] 호주식 발음 → 미국식 발음

When is the most convenient afternoon for you to lead the software demonstrations?
(A) On our latest computer applications.
(B) It's important for us to talk to them.
(C) My schedule is actually fairly flexible.

18 　[3w] 캐나다식 발음 → 미국식 발음

Who's going to present the flowers to Ms. Ellis at the retirement party?
(A) When is the gathering being held?
(B) A dozen, please.
(C) The first part of the movie.

19 　[3w] 영국식 발음 → 호주식 발음

Shouldn't the instructions for logging in to the system be written out?
(A) One of our system engineers.
(B) That won't be necessary.
(C) Yes, guidelines for the gym.

20 　[3w] 미국식 발음 → 캐나다식 발음

Should we hire a band for the banquet or use recorded music?
(A) We're enjoying the buffet.
(B) A live show would be more entertaining.
(C) I used to play the piano.

21 　[3w] 미국식 발음 → 호주식 발음

Betsy Glenn has been asked to return to our headquarters for a follow-up interview.
(A) She seems like the most qualified applicant.
(B) Oh, come back whenever you'd like!
(C) I can't answer that question now.

22 　[3w] 캐나다식 발음 → 미국식 발음

Where are the stage props for tonight's play?
(A) From a theater in Lima.
(B) Have you met the lead actress?
(C) Check behind the curtain.

23 　[3w] 영국식 발음 → 호주식 발음

What floor is Robby Bluth's office located on?
(A) He works overtime most days.
(B) The floors were carpeted in June.
(C) There's a building directory on that wall.

24 　[3w] 캐나다식 발음 → 영국식 발음

A freelance illustrator drew the pictures for your children's book, right?
(A) No, I'm not a talented artist.
(B) Yes, for my most recent publication.
(C) Let me recommend a photographer.

25 　[3w] 미국식 발음 → 캐나다식 발음

Would you like a ticket for the 9 o'clock screening?
(A) That would be great.
(B) Passes to the local zoo.
(C) OK, I can show it to you.

26 　[3w] 미국식 발음 → 호주식 발음

How many people will attend the presentation today?
(A) Sign the attendance sheet.
(B) Six in total.
(C) Tomorrow will be better.

27 　[3w] 호주식 발음 → 영국식 발음

Will the product developers require another deadline extension?
(A) Most of the merchandise.
(B) The other side is in good condition.
(C) I hope they won't.

28 　[3w] 영국식 발음 → 캐나다식 발음

When is tomorrow's train to Bern supposed to depart?
(A) Emma has the itinerary.
(B) Yesterday at 2 o'clock.
(C) In the overhead compartment.

29 　[3w] 미국식 발음 → 호주식 발음

Are staff expected to take part in the session on workplace communication?
(A) No, the machines weren't taken apart.
(B) Thanks again for leading the discussion on wages.
(C) Yes, the event is mandatory for all personnel.

30 　[3w] 캐나다식 발음 → 미국식 발음

Why do you want to avoid crossing Lower Town Bridge?
(A) A radio broadcaster said it's congested.
(B) Because she wants to bring a suitcase.
(C) I agree. We'll do that.

31 ③ 영국식 발음 → 호주식 발음

Ben Graber can mount this television to the wall,
can't he?
(A) Any amount you donate would be appreciated.
(B) You'll have to ask him directly.
(C) Isn't this the remote control for the device?

PART 3

Questions 32-34 refer to the following conversation.

③ 캐나다식 발음 → 미국식 발음

M: Louisa, I heard you're taking a vacation in Mexico
this summer.
W: I'm really looking forward to it, but I could use your
advice about something related to my trip.
M: Sure. How can I help?
W: Well, the mobile company I use charges high fees
for data usage outside of Canada. You mentioned a
while back that your phone bill was reasonable after
you traveled to France. Who is your service
provider?
M: Pacific Mobile. They have several packages with
very reasonable rates if you sign a one-year
contract.
W: Great. I'll stop by a Pacific Mobile branch this
evening and look into that.

Questions 35-37 refer to the following conversation.

③ 호주식 발음 → 영국식 발음

M: I need to request an employee parking permit. My
new apartment isn't near a subway station, so I will
have to drive to work from now on.
W: You should contact the human resources manager,
Mr. Hong. Just note that when I asked him about
getting one last month, I was told that there is a
waiting list.
M: Really? The lot in front of our building is never full,
though.
W: I guess the company needs to ensure that our
clients can find a place to park. So, staff aren't
allowed to park in the front two rows.
M: Hmm . . . Do you know Mr. Hong's extension? I'll
speak to him about this situation now.

Questions 38-40 refer to the following conversation.

③ 호주식 발음 → 미국식 발음

M: Lindsay, how are the contract negotiations with
Sutton Technical Consulting going?
W: Shannon is in charge of that, actually. She
mentioned that it hasn't been a smooth process.
M: That's unfortunate. Maybe we should check if she
needs our assistance. I heard that our manager
wants to review the contract on June 2. That's just

four days away.
W: No need to worry. Three other employees were just
added to her team.
M: She'll have plenty of time to finalize the contract,
then.
W: Also, you'll be glad to know the deadline has been
pushed back to June 8.
M: That's a relief.

Questions 41-43 refer to the following conversation with three speakers.

③ 캐나다식 발음 → 영국식 발음 → 미국식 발음

M: Excuse me. I'm interested in the property on State
Road that's featured on your agency's Web site.
W1: I should let you know that, by law, the land can
only be used for agriculture. You cannot open
another business there.
M: I'm planning to grow apples, actually. But I'd like to
check the condition of the soil.
W1: Melinda, can you take a customer on a tour of the
Hillwood Farm?
W2: Sure. I just need to make a quick phone call to a
client. It'll only take 15 minutes.
W1: I can show you a site map in the meantime.
M: That'll be great.

Questions 44-46 refer to the following conversation.

③ 호주식 발음 → 영국식 발음

M: I was just in the break room, and there's a sign on
the refrigerator saying that it still isn't working.
W: I know. Several staff members have complained
about it already.
M: I thought a technician was supposed to repair it last
night after the office closed.
W: That technician was here to inspect our fire
sprinkler system. We still need to schedule the
refrigerator repair.
M: We need to have it fixed as soon as possible. Why
don't you call the repairperson now? See if you can
arrange for him to visit our office this afternoon.

Questions 47-49 refer to the following conversation.

③ 미국식 발음 → 캐나다식 발음

W: Hello. Thank you for visiting Westford Post Office.
How can I help you?
M: About a week ago, my friend mailed me a package
with some books. But I just realized that I gave him
my old address. Now I'm worried I won't receive the
package.
W: Well, do you have the item's tracking number? I can
use it to look the package up in our system and see
whether it's been delivered yet. If not, I can halt the
shipment.
M: No, I don't have that.
W: In that case, you'll have to wait for the package to

be returned to the sender. Your friend will have to mail it out again to the proper address. Sorry.

Questions 50-52 refer to the following conversation with three speakers.

호주식 발음 → 미국식 발음 → 영국식 발음

M: Welcome to Home Land Retail. How can I help you?

W1: We need shelves to store some extra equipment at our gym.

M: I'd recommend the EZ Keep storage system. It's a rack that can be lowered to the floor, loaded, and then raised up to seven feet high. It's operated with a remote control.

W2: Sounds perfect. What's the price?

M: $800. Plus, we can ship it directly to your address.

W1: Could the item be delivered within the next two weeks?

W2: Yeah, we want to organize the equipment before a promotional event we're running.

M: All of our products are shipped in less than a week. Why don't we head over to the aisle with the storage racks now so that you can look at the EZ Keep?

Questions 53-55 refer to the following conversation.

호주식 발음 → 미국식 발음

M: I'm taking an afternoon flight to San Jose on Tuesday to attend the seminar on facility safety that we signed up for. When will you be traveling?

W: I'm scheduled to complete an inspection at our Tucson factory that day, so I'll be leaving later in the evening. I plan on staying at the Surfside Inn near the downtown area.

M: Oh, that's my hotel too! Let's have an early breakfast on Wednesday morning and drive to the workshop together . . . umm . . . if that's OK with you.

W: I was just going to say that. Let's meet in the lobby at 6:15 A.M.

Questions 56-58 refer to the following conversation.

미국식 발음 → 캐나다식 발음

W: Rick, I got a request from the human resources department to set up computers for two new accountants that will be joining the firm on Friday. They'll be sharing the empty office on the second floor. I'd like you and Donna to take care of this today, please.

M: Sure. Should I use the spare computers that are currently in the storage area?

W: No. We just received a shipment of new devices this morning. The boxes are in the main hallway.

M: OK. I'll stop by Donna's workspace first to tell her about this task. Then, we'll take care of everything.

Questions 59-61 refer to the following conversation.

캐나다식 발음 → 영국식 발음

M: Excuse me. Can you see if I still have any books checked out? I don't think I do, but I'm not certain. My account is under the name David Harris.

W: Just a minute . . . Well, it looks like you still have a novel by Brad Thompson called, uh, *Forgotten Time*. It was released just last month.

M: Oh, right. I forgot about that one. I'll be visiting my family in Tacoma for a few days, so I'll drop it off next week.

W: OK, but it's due tomorrow, which means you'll have to pay a late fee if you bring it back then. I can renew it now, if you'd like.

M: I'd appreciate that.

Questions 62-64 refer to the following conversation and list.

캐나다식 발음 → 영국식 발음

M: Ms. Williams, you wanted to talk to me?

W: Yes, Ryan. Have you been sharing copies of the inventory lists with all the stock room staff like I asked?

M: No, I thought you wanted me to give the lists to the store manager only. Sorry if I misunderstood your instructions.

W: That's all right. But, please do that for future deliveries.

M: Certainly. Is there anything else?

W: Yeah. I need you to order more inventory for our shop. Anything with fewer than 10 items in stock, aside from extra small sizes. They don't sell as quickly, so we only need to keep five of those products on hand at a time.

M: Right away, Ms. Williams.

Questions 65-67 refer to the following conversation and map.

캐나다식 발음 → 미국식 발음

M: Sabrina, our hotel will be hosting a VIP guest for the next week. His name is Mr. Graystone, and he's going to arrive at the airport at 3 P.M. today. I'd like you to go pick him up, since you're a veteran driver.

W: Not a problem. Do you know the terminal he's coming into?

M: Terminal 2. By the way, Lily Street will be shut down this afternoon, so you won't be able to go that way.

W: Yeah, I heard. But that's fine. There's another route that will also take less than 30 minutes. I'll take that one.

🎧 영국식 발음 → 호주식 발음

W: I just spoke with the CEO of Delver Group. She wants to hold a meeting with some representatives from our consultancy on Monday. She says it's urgent.

M: Is something wrong?

W: Sort of. Her company is trying to boost sales in Europe since the firm's profits hit a low for the year during the month when the company expanded overseas.

M: I see. Well, I'm free that afternoon. So, let's try to get together with her then.

W: All right. Beforehand, however, we need to brainstorm business ideas to present to her. I'll send you an e-mail today with what I come up with, and you can respond with your input.

PART 4

Questions 71-73 refer to the following talk.

🎧 영국식 발음

My name is Gloria Bloom, and I'm a financial consultant. I'll be leading this seminar, which is being hosted by my firm, Stanley Financial. Our plan for this morning is to discuss ways to improve your personal wealth portfolios. To start, I'm going to give a short talk about the potential risks of putting money into stocks, government bonds, and real estate. Following that, I'll show you a series of charts and graphs that explain which financial products are best suited for short-term gains and why establishing a retirement plan is crucial. All right, let's begin.

Questions 74-76 refer to the following telephone message.

🎧 호주식 발음

My name is Ernesto Agusta. A flat-screen television I ordered was sent to my home by your delivery firm. However, the item's box seems to have been torn during transit, leaving a long scratch across the screen. I plan to give the item away as a prize during a company event, and it is being held this Saturday. Please call me back to let me know your plan for dealing with the matter.

Questions 77-79 refer to the following talk.

🎧 미국식 발음

Working at a restaurant isn't easy. There are plenty of challenges that you'll face as newly hired staff, from dissatisfied customers to delayed orders to missing ingredients. Such difficulties will be the focus of today's orientation. I would like to start by having everyone write down a challenging situation that you've confronted at a previous job as well as how you managed it. In about 15 minutes, we'll all talk about the experiences as a group and then consider alternative ways that the situations could have been dealt with. OK, let's get started.

Questions 80-82 refer to the following telephone message.

🎧 캐나다식 발음

Jamie, it's Phillip. I have a favor to ask of you. I'm wondering whether I can borrow your car for a trip to Portland next weekend. I'm gonna visit my old college friend, and I'd prefer not to spend money on a rental. If I remember correctly, you'll be in San Diego meeting with a client anyway, so I figure it won't be a major inconvenience for you. I'd need the car from Saturday morning until Sunday afternoon and could return it early that evening. Either way, let me know sometime today in case I need to make other arrangements. I look forward to hearing from you.

Questions 83-85 refer to the following announcement.

🎧 영국식 발음

Attention all Alison Apparel customers. In preparation for our soon-to-be-released winter line, we have decided to mark down everything in the store beginning tomorrow. This includes all remaining shoes, shirts, pants, and dresses from our summer and fall collections. Plus, become a member of our store's rewards program today to receive a complimentary piece of jewelry. These specials will also be offered on our Web site. But you must act quickly! Product availability is limited to what we have in stock.

Questions 86-88 refer to the following talk.

🎧 미국식 발음

Welcome, everyone, to today's tour of our private school for young, talented artists. There are a lot of things for us to see and discuss, but prior to exploring the facility, we'll first listen to a special lecture from our director, Ronald Marks. Mr. Marks spent nearly 25 years as a director at the nearby Laurel Museum. Over the course of the museum's history, that stands as a record. Now, please follow me down the main hallway to the auditorium, where Mr. Marks is waiting for us. It's a short walk.

Questions 89-91 refer to the following talk.

🎧 호주식 발음

In about half an hour, the Rockton Hospital Charity Day is going to start. If you haven't done so already, you should visit the registration booth, where you can sign up for different races and events. Remember, for every person who takes part in each competition, our sponsors will be donating $75. Seeing as how the turnout this afternoon is much higher than it was last year, I'm hopeful that we'll raise a lot of money. Oh, one more thing. Race participants will be given one of these Rockton Hospital Charity Day sweatshirts at no cost.

Questions 92-94 refer to the following talk.

[3ⁿ] 호주식 발음

Our public library plans to modernize its catalog. Specifically, we'll be using some government funding we received in May to expand our online database of audiobooks. More members are interested than ever before in listening to audiobooks during their work commutes. Many people report using them two or three times weekly. In addition, beginning in June, we will place less of an emphasis on acquiring printed books and spend more money on digital versions. What I need you all to do is carry out some research to determine which books are most popular among members, so we can make sure to get copies of them.

Questions 95-97 refer to the following podcast and subscription options.

[3ⁿ] 영국식 발음

Welcome to another episode of Flix Games, a weekly podcast where we talk about the latest online games and strategies for playing them. I'm proud to announce that this episode is sponsored by Increda. If you haven't heard of them, they offer a meal kit delivery service featuring tons of delicious, easy-to-follow recipes. Also, they generously offer discounts to new users of their service all the time. In fact, I signed up for a three-month subscription last week and was pleasantly surprised. All right, let's get into the episode. Today we'll be talking with Harrison Rivers, who's here to discuss the upcoming release of the highly anticipated sequel to the racing game *Fireflies*.

Questions 98-100 refer to the following advertisement and coupon.

[3ⁿ] 캐나다식 발음

Do you have a headache that just won't go away? Then try Quick Refresh, a pain relief medication manufactured by SilverEdge Pharmaceuticals. Quick Refresh is scientifically proven to act faster on stubborn headaches than any other medicine on the market. Moreover, Quick Refresh is sold in various bottle sizes, including a recently launched economy-sized bottle for consumers looking to buy in bulk. Our product can be found in CityMart stores across the nation. So, why rely on less effective options? Use fast-acting Quick Refresh!

* 무료 해석은 해커스토익(Hackers.co.kr)에서 다운로드 받을 수 있습니다.

* QR 코드로 바로가기

PART 1

1 영국식 발음
   (A) The woman is touching a monitor.
   (B) The woman is counting some money.
   (C) The woman is zipping up a jacket.
   (D) The woman is wearing a backpack.

2 캐나다식 발음
   (A) They are installing some glass partitions.
   (B) Some helmets have been put on.
   (C) Some plans are posted on a pillar.
   (D) They are shoveling some dirt.

3 미국식 발음
   (A) A man is mixing salad in a bowl.
   (B) An umbrella is covering a grill.
   (C) A man is cooking near a metal fence.
   (D) A napkin has dropped from a table.

4 호주식 발음
   (A) Tripods have been set up near the water.
   (B) A man is taking photographs in a gallery.
   (C) A man is stepping over a small log.
   (D) Some boats are floating on a lake.

5 미국식 발음
   (A) Some people are sitting at tables.
   (B) Some people are carrying meals across a room.
   (C) Some people are placing chairs at the bar.
   (D) Some people are waving at each other.

6 영국식 발음
   (A) Treadmills are being used in a gym.
   (B) Wood floor panels have been removed.
   (C) Marks are being wiped off a mirror.
   (D) Fitness equipment has been lined up.

PART 2

7 영국식 발음 → 캐나다식 발음
   Who did you end up going to a movie with on Saturday night?
   (A) Yes, but on Sunday evening.
   (B) I think you'd really appreciate the film.
   (C) A group of friends from college.

8 호주식 발음 → 미국식 발음
   When will you finish fixing my printer?
   (A) By tomorrow afternoon.
   (B) At a print shop.
   (C) I asked for a receipt.

9 캐나다식 발음 → 미국식 발음
   Faulty merchandise can be returned for a refund, can't it?
   (A) The price tag says $20.
   (B) Yes, but a receipt is required.
   (C) Check the fall collection.

10 캐나다식 발음 → 미국식 발음
   How did the invitations to the company picnic turn out?
   (A) It'll be at Mooreland Park.
   (B) I prefer e-mail.
   (C) Let me show you.

11 캐나다식 발음 → 호주식 발음
   We'd like you to write the next quarterly report.
   (A) It may have been erased.
   (B) Sorry. I won't be able to do it.
   (C) Yes, a contract with Blake Jewelry.

12 캐나다식 발음 → 미국식 발음
   Why don't we visit the amusement park?
   (A) The parking lot across the street.
   (B) Let's wait until the new rides open in May.
   (C) Everyone thought the concert was entertaining.

13 호주식 발음 → 영국식 발음
   I'll mail this agreement to our lawyer if you'd like me to.
   (A) With a legal representative.
   (B) Sure, if you don't mind.
   (C) Underneath those forms.

14 미국식 발음 → 호주식 발음
   How can I help you apply for the position?
   (A) I'll apply that approach.
   (B) No, it's a factory job.
   (C) By proofreading my résumé.

15 [♪] 캐나다식 발음 → 영국식 발음

What project is Oakley Construction planning at the moment?
(A) A commercial building near the river.
(B) Yes, just a moment ago.
(C) Either of the projectors.

16 [♪] 미국식 발음 → 캐나다식 발음

Has Mr. Donovan mentioned anything about the training session?
(A) Because it's still raining.
(B) Yesterday afternoon.
(C) There have been no messages.

17 [♪] 호주식 발음 → 미국식 발음

Where did Ms. Sato transfer from?
(A) Almost two years ago.
(B) She was in our Tokyo office.
(C) I applied for a transfer.

18 [♪] 영국식 발음 → 호주식 발음

Will the office stay like this or will you redecorate it?
(A) Yes, I'll stay for the performance.
(B) At a graphic design agency.
(C) Barbara is handling it.

19 [♪] 미국식 발음 → 영국식 발음

What do you think of the new advertising campaign?
(A) In newspapers and magazines.
(B) We finished it last week.
(C) It's going to be effective.

20 [♪] 미국식 발음 → 캐나다식 발음

When will the representative from Ferdinand Appliance Center be here?
(A) Around 20 percent.
(B) It's hard to say.
(C) Yes, she could be.

21 [♪] 영국식 발음 → 미국식 발음

Did Robert explain why the guest departed early?
(A) Or I could submit it in advance.
(B) Who guessed it correctly?
(C) I thought he told you.

22 [♪] 호주식 발음 → 영국식 발음

Why do we have to rearrange the order of the convention talks?
(A) It was on a very interesting topic.
(B) One of the speakers is running late.
(C) A full range of models.

23 [♪] 캐나다식 발음 → 미국식 발음

Our supervisor scheduled an inspection for Thursday.
(A) Check at the reception desk.
(B) I won't be here.
(C) No, I didn't expect it.

24 [♪] 캐나다식 발음 → 호주식 발음

Everyone will be receiving a small raise this year, right?
(A) Yes, the entire team.
(B) An annual company picnic.
(C) Every one of those signs.

25 [♪] 호주식 발음 → 미국식 발음

Guests get a complimentary breakfast in the hotel's dining area.
(A) The lunch was delicious.
(B) Yes, I read that online.
(C) Thanks for the compliment.

26 [♪] 미국식 발음 → 호주식 발음

Didn't you write for the *Dallas Times* when you started out?
(A) At any newsstand.
(B) That was my first job.
(C) I enjoy being a writer.

27 [♪] 영국식 발음 → 캐나다식 발음

How often is the trash collected in this neighborhood?
(A) At least another three hours.
(B) Cardboard and glass bottles.
(C) Crews come through twice a week.

28 [♪] 캐나다식 발음 → 영국식 발음

Do the interns require an orientation, or is that unnecessary?
(A) Let's ask Ms. Smith.
(B) A three-month internship.
(C) While watching the instructional video.

29 [♪] 미국식 발음 → 호주식 발음

Did you see the new mural painted in the library?
(A) I need to renew my card.
(B) Impressive, isn't it?
(C) Some art supplies.

30 [♪] 영국식 발음 → 호주식 발음

Aren't we supposed to get an invoice from the landscaper?
(A) A large section of the lawn.
(B) My voicemail is working again.
(C) It arrived yesterday.

⒊⁾ 영국식 발음 → 캐나다식 발음

Is there any way we could finish the market analysis a day ahead of schedule?
(A) No, that ceremony already ended.
(B) A few days each week.
(C) If we work really hard.

PART 3

Questions 32-34 refer to the following conversation.

⒊⁾ 호주식 발음 → 영국식 발음

M: We need to discuss start-up funding for our healthcare device company. I just got off the phone with a bank representative. Although we qualify for a loan, the amount will only cover about half of our estimated costs.

W: Hmm. That's definitely an issue. I guess we'll have to try to attract some initial investors, then.

M: Right. I think we should reach out to my former colleague, Rebecca Holt. She works at an investment firm, and she may be able to introduce us to people interested in supporting us.

W: Good idea. Please contact with Ms. Holt and set up a time to have lunch with her at her earliest convenience.

Questions 35-37 refer to the following conversation with three speakers.

⒊⁾ 미국식 발음 → 캐나다식 발음 → 호주식 발음

W: Is everything ready for today's software training seminar for human resources staff?

M1: Um . . . There's a problem, actually. Several computers in the training room won't turn on.

W: We only have 30 minutes left until the training starts. Can the technical support team help repair the machines?

M2: I already texted them. Unfortunately, they're all busy addressing some e-mail system issues now. So, they won't be able to start fixing our problem until 2 P.M.

W: Hmm . . . Let's conduct the training somewhere else, then. I think there are laptops already set up in Conference Room C. I'll go there now and see if the space is available.

Questions 38-40 refer to the following conversation.

⒊⁾ 캐나다식 발음 → 영국식 발음

M: Ms. Ono, I really appreciate you coming to our station and talking with me. As I mentioned over the phone yesterday, we'd love for you to be featured as a celebrity guest on our culinary show *Good Eats*. A cooking demonstration from a chef like you would surely attract a lot of viewers.

W: It'd be my pleasure. Actually, I've already decided which dishes to prepare. Just keep in mind that they include a few unusual ingredients. I'll send you the complete list later this afternoon.

M: OK. And don't worry about the ingredients. We'll be able to provide whatever you need.

Questions 41-43 refer to the following conversation.

⒊⁾ 호주식 발음 → 미국식 발음

M: Hi, Joanna. This morning, I finished writing the press release explaining our company's merger with Grey Stone Partners. Do you have time to look at it?

W: Sorry, I'm leaving for a meeting now. However, Clarissa is a great writer. She'll review your work very thoroughly.

M: Thanks for letting me know. I plan to e-mail the release to several popular news bloggers. So, I'd appreciate any tips she has for improvement.

W: Well, you can ask for her help now. Clarissa went into her office a few minutes ago.

Questions 44-46 refer to the following conversation with three speakers.

⒊⁾ 캐나다식 발음 → 호주식 발음 → 영국식 발음

M1: Ms. Sawyer, thank you for your interest in our architectural assistant position. I'm Irving Wright, the company's human resources manager. My colleague here has joined us today as well. Bradley, why don't you start things off?

M2: Certainly. First, why do you want to leave your current company?

W: Well, Harding Development is a small firm with only eight employees. There aren't many opportunities for promotion.

M2: That certainly seems reasonable for a young professional like yourself.

M1: Now, just to confirm . . . You got a degree in architecture from Western University before beginning at Harding, right?

W: Yes. I finished my studies two years ago. And I received a full academic scholarship through the school.

Questions 47-49 refer to the following conversation.

⒊⁾ 미국식 발음 → 캐나다식 발음

W: Hello, Mr. Gordon. This is Stacy from Fullerton Electronics. I received your voice mail complaint yesterday. We're very sorry for shipping you a faulty air conditioner.

M: Thanks for the apology. If possible, I'd like to have the air conditioner replaced with a brand-new one.

W: Certainly. We'll send you a new one and cover all the delivery costs. I'll also e-mail you a coupon for $30 off your next purchase with us.

M: Thanks. I'm actually thinking of getting a small refrigerator for my office.

W: I'll include a product catalog with the shipment.

Questions 50-52 refer to the following conversation.

[오디오] 호주식 발음 → 영국식 발음

M: Hey, Lisa. Welcome back. Did you learn any useful techniques at the marketing conference?

W: Some. But, for me, the main point of the conference was to network with other people in our industry. And, actually, I met Michelle Morey, the host of *The Impact*.

M: Oh, wow! I was just listening to that podcast during my lunch break!

W: Yeah, I spoke with her about our company for a long time. She wants our CEO to appear on the show.

M: When you mention it to him, make sure to point out the size of its audience. It gets 500,000 downloads a month.

Questions 53-55 refer to the following conversation.

[오디오] 영국식 발음 → 캐나다식 발음

W: Fredrickson Electronics. This is Audrey from technical support. How can I help you?

M: Yesterday, my Robbins D70 printer ran out of black ink, so I went to an office supply store and bought another cartridge. However, the device still won't print.

W: And did you take off the plastic strip before inserting the cartridge? That's necessary.

M: I followed the instructions on the box.

W: OK. The Robbins D70 also has three other cartridges. Can you check whether any of those are running low?

M: Hold on . . . I guess the yellow one is empty. But I'm not printing in that color.

W: Yes, however, the D70 won't work if any of the four cartridges are empty.

Questions 56-58 refer to the following conversation.

[오디오] 미국식 발음 → 캐나다식 발음

W: Hey, Vince, did you hear that Greg Ewing, the famous basketball player, will be at Greyville Mall this weekend? He's signing autographs during a meet-and-greet event there on Saturday at 4 P.M. I'm planning to go, and I thought you might like to join.

M: Really? He's my favorite sports player! But . . . ah . . . my motorcycle is currently being repaired. Could you possibly drive me there?

W: Sorry, but I don't own a car. I plan on using a ridesharing service to get to the mall. There's a great mobile application called Rapid Ride. You should give it a try.

M: Oh, thanks. Yeah, I'll definitely do that.

Questions 59-61 refer to the following conversation.

[오디오] 미국식 발음 → 호주식 발음

W: Excuse me. Is your shop able to dryclean silk?

M: Yes. However, because silk is so delicate, we have to use a special cleaning process. So, there will be an extra charge.

W: Oh, that's not a problem as long as you can get this brown stain out. Also . . . it'd be great if this dress could be ironed by tomorrow afternoon. I have a banquet to attend that evening, and I'm considering wearing it.

M: Normally, we could perform a rush service for you, but we don't have enough staff working right now. The best we can do for you is a two-day service.

W: I see. I think I'll try another dry cleaner.

Questions 62-64 refer to the following conversation and chart.

[오디오] 미국식 발음 → 호주식 발음

W: Tyler, could you e-mail me the budget summary for our company's mobile application development project? You know—the one you modified yesterday afternoon.

M: Of course. Would you also like me to forward you the résumés I received this morning?

W: Yes, I need to review those . . . ah . . . since we'll be selecting candidates to join our team at tomorrow morning's meeting.

M: OK. By the way, all applicants meet our educational requirements. So, we should analyze and prioritize their past experience in the technology sector when making a selection.

Questions 65-67 refer to the following conversation and building directory.

[오디오] 미국식 발음 → 캐나다식 발음

W: Hello. My name is Cynthia Holmes. I have a 10:30 A.M. appointment for an interview with Mr. Rogers.

M: Welcome, Ms. Holmes. You're a few minutes early, but you can go up to the human resources department now. There's a waiting room you can use on their floor.

W: OK. Should I take the elevator to get there?

M: Yes, but an access card is required to use it. Here's a visitor's pass that is valid for one day. Just tap it on the sensor by the keypad and then click the floor you need.

W: Great. I'll do that. Thanks a lot for your help.

Questions 68-70 refer to the following conversation and map.

[오디오] 호주식 발음 → 영국식 발음

M: Hi, Mandy. I hear you're planning to participate in a race this Sunday afternoon that our company has organized.

W: That's right. It's a fund-raiser for an association that provides free tutoring to underprivileged students.

M: What a great cause! And, where is the event being held?

W: In Lansdowne State Park. Runners were originally supposed to follow the trail from the entrance to the waterfall, but some people complained it was too steep. So, we will be racing to the picnic area instead.

M: It sounds fun. Maybe I'll sign up as well.

W: You'd better contact Ms. Harris soon. Today is the final day that staff members can sign up.

M: Oh, really? I'll call now, then.

PART 4

Questions 71-73 refer to the following announcement.

[3%] 캐나다식 발음

Employees, it's your last chance this year to order staff uniforms. If you need a new company shirt, sweater, or other clothing item, please stop by our main conference room before 5:30 P.M. Branson Uniform representatives will be there to take your order. If you are uncertain about the size you require, they will help you figure it out. Remember, the company will pay for three new shirts along with one sweater or vest each year. However, you can purchase additional items if you choose to.

Questions 74-76 refer to the following speech.

[3%] 미국식 발음

My name is Melanie Chen. I am the longtime editor of renowned author Allen Short, and I have come here tonight to accept this award on his behalf. Unfortunately, Mr. Short is unable to attend this evening as he now lives in Italy and was unable to return to Canada on short notice. However, I can say with confidence that he is truly honored to be the 25th recipient of the Redmark Medal in honor of the exceptional literature for kids he has written. Although we met nearly 15 years ago, I continue to be amazed every day by his dedication to his work. I can think of no better person to receive this honor than Mr. Short.

Questions 77-79 refer to the following report.

[3%] 호주식 발음

And now for the weather . . . The city will continue to experience a serious thunderstorm tonight through tomorrow. Heavy rain will fall until Wednesday morning, and clouds will move out of the area later Wednesday afternoon. Due to the risk of flooding, public schools will remain closed on Tuesday. A Department of Education official plans to make an announcement in the afternoon

about whether the institutions will reopen on Wednesday. It's doubtful at this point, but be sure to refer to the school's Web site tomorrow to find out the latest information on the issue.

Questions 80-82 refer to the following instructions.

[3%] 영국식 발음

For those of you who are unfamiliar with how to operate the factory's new conveyor belt, let me explain it quickly. First, the machinery is controlled by this dial and switch. The switch is to turn the device on and off, whereas the dial adjusts how quickly the belt moves. Be sure to set the dial on the second setting unless instructed otherwise. And if the conveyor belt ever experiences any mechanical issues, please let Jane Fowl, the floor manager, know. That way she can inform our technician . . . Oh, one more thing. Always make sure the belt is turned off at the end of our shift. It's a necessary safety measure.

Questions 83-85 refer to the following talk.

[3%] 미국식 발음

I want to stress the importance of tonight's banquet for our catering company. Celebrities, state legislators, and business owners will be among the guests. So, please be attentive to the diners' requests and double-check all the orders. This will not only ensure that our guests get everything they need but will also give them a positive first impression of our business. That is essential for a new company such as ours. OK, let's begin setting up for the evening.

Questions 86-88 refer to the following excerpt from a meeting.

[3%] 호주식 발음

Welcome, everyone, to Pomerta Incorporated's annual regional managers meeting. This is the first time this event has been conducted virtually. There's a time restriction on this platform. We only have an hour. You have, therefore, all received the agenda and other relevant documents, and, hopefully, you read the materials in advance. As you can see, we'll be voting on some proposals regarding the company's plans to open new stores in the coming year. But first, our corporate secretary Lewis Thompson will start the meeting by taking us through this year's sales and profits. Now, let's begin.

Questions 89-91 refer to the following announcement.

[3%] 영국식 발음

Welcome to the Outdoor Living Expo. We hope you enjoy the many vendor booths, where you'll find the finest products available for swimming pools, patios, yards, and gardens. And if you stop by the Bingham Fencing booth, you can enter a drawing for a free fence installation package worth up to $4,500. All you have to do is watch a 60-second video. This year, over 1,000 people are expected to take part. Finally, make sure to get a coupon for 20 percent off a patio set from Truman's Outdoor Furniture. For a full description of the event's highlights, just grab a program from the information desk.

Questions 92–94 refer to the following excerpt from a meeting.

[3] 호주식 발음

Before we end this meeting, there's one more issue I'd like to discuss, which . . . um . . . Martin Keillor brought to my attention yesterday in an e-mail. Namely, at least a dozen boxes of old documents have been set in front of our floor's emergency exit, making it almost completely inaccessible. Since this poses a safety violation, we need to deal with the situation as soon as possible. So, let's all go move the files now. We'll take them down to the main floor for recycling.

Questions 95–97 refer to the following talk and map.

[3] 캐나다식 발음

Good afternoon. My name is Jerry Horace, and I'll be leading you around the office of our newspaper, *The Nashville Gazette*, today. I'll . . . ah . . . start by showing you the wall in the lobby where our various awards are displayed. One was even given to our publication by the mayor of Nashville shortly after our founding two decades ago. The second part of the tour will focus on our printing machine area, where you can see the equipment necessary to produce 50,000 copies of the newspaper daily. That area is immediately next to our manager's office. OK. Please follow me through these doors.

Questions 98–100 refer to the following excerpt from a meeting and line graph.

[3] 영국식 발음

Let's discuss our performance over the past few months. I was pleased to see that the number of readers jumped in the month after our TV commercial aired. However, following that success, numbers have dropped steadily. Although our firm intends to release new commercials in the near future, a deal will be offered to further encourage sales of issues to new readers. All new subscribers throughout January will have their fee for the first year reduced by 10 percent. Now, I want to move on to the new magazine we'll be launching shortly.

* 무료 해석은 해커스토익(Hackers.co.kr)에서
다운로드 받으실 수 있습니다.

• QR 코드로
바로가기

PART 1

1 캐나다식 발음
(A) A man is cutting a vegetable.
(B) A man is rinsing a knife in the sink.
(C) A man is taking a utensil from a drawer.
(D) A man is folding an apron.

2 영국식 발음
(A) A woman is wiping some glasses.
(B) A woman is preparing a beverage.
(C) Some cabinet doors have been left open.
(D) A ladder is leaning against a wall.

3 미국식 발음
(A) One of the women is adjusting a microscope.
(B) The man is pouring liquid into a dish.
(C) They are wearing lab coats.
(D) They are seated across from each other.

4 호주식 발음
(A) Some papers are being printed.
(B) The man is pushing up his sleeves.
(C) The shelf is behind the man.
(D) An apple is being cut.

5 캐나다식 발음
(A) Some cabin roofs are being repaired.
(B) Camping gear has been loaded into a truck.
(C) Tents have been set up on a lawn.
(D) Some leaves have been raked into a pile.

6 영국식 발음
(A) The woman is filling up a gas tank.
(B) The woman has tied back her hair.
(C) The car tire is being removed.
(D) The hood of a car is being lifted.

PART 2

7 캐나다식 발음 → 미국식 발음
When did you arrive at the airport?
(A) Yes, I sent it yesterday.
(B) An hour before my departure.
(C) At the international terminal.

8 호주식 발음 → 영국식 발음
Why don't you sign up for a tour of the stadium?
(A) I already did.
(B) A concert at the stadium.
(C) He works as a tour guide.

9 영국식 발음 → 캐나다식 발음
Who do you think deserves a bonus?
(A) I think so.
(B) There are incentives for participation.
(C) Every salesperson has done well so far.

10 미국식 발음 → 영국식 발음
How long has Kendrick been able to speak French?
(A) Is it a language test?
(B) For nearly a decade.
(C) We depart for France on June 3.

11 호주식 발음 → 미국식 발음
Why didn't someone come to fix the sewing machine?
(A) Right, a warranty.
(B) I've already taken care of that.
(C) I don't know anyone either.

12 미국식 발음 → 영국식 발음
Do guests who visit the hotel pool have to pay an entrance fee?
(A) I'm not sure.
(B) Yes, they came through the front entrance.
(C) Swimming classes are held on Sundays.

13 캐나다식 발음 → 영국식 발음
Which of our factories in Asia do you plan to visit?
(A) I'm delighted to see so many visitors.
(B) From Tuesday to Friday.
(C) Only the plants in Taiwan.

14 미국식 발음 → 호주식 발음
Do you want to catch a taxi or a bus to the expo center?
(A) I'd rather just walk.
(B) Yes, it's in the city center.
(C) I'll try renting a booth.

15 영국식 발음 → 호주식 발음

Where did you purchase the armchairs in the waiting room?
(A) No, it was inexpensive.
(B) For a few minutes.
(C) At the Furniture Finds outlet.

16 영국식 발음 → 호주식 발음

We are planning to hire more clerks for the holiday season.
(A) She has worked here since Christmas.
(B) How many do you need?
(C) I applied for a higher position.

17 호주식 발음 → 영국식 발음

A membership at the public library is free, right?
(A) No, I don't remember her.
(B) At a book signing event.
(C) If you live in town.

18 호주식 발음 → 캐나다식 발음

When did you become an accountant?
(A) By using a calculator.
(B) A little over two years ago.
(C) They're coming to our headquarters.

19 영국식 발음 → 미국식 발음

Where can I find a gas station?
(A) There are several on Clay Street.
(B) About $35.
(C) They were charged a parking fine.

20 호주식 발음 → 미국식 발음

How are you going to spend your time in Jamaica?
(A) I want to relax on the beach.
(B) For over a week.
(C) Enjoy your vacation.

21 캐나다식 발음 → 영국식 발음

Which bicycle store do you want to call?
(A) Whichever museum they want to go to.
(B) I know of a great trail.
(C) The one by my house.

22 호주식 발음 → 미국식 발음

Have you adjusted the shop's design plans to include a storage closet?
(A) Here's the item you asked for.
(B) Mr. Finch designed our Web site.
(C) I'm working on them.

23 호주식 발음 → 영국식 발음

Would you like me to order dinner if we have to work late?
(A) Yes, thank you.
(B) I like the roses as well.
(C) Is this table reserved?

24 미국식 발음 → 캐나다식 발음

Why hasn't Nicholas completed his review for the paper?
(A) He has more urgent tasks to take care of.
(B) Our branch sells paper products.
(C) Your piece is good.

25 영국식 발음 → 호주식 발음

Do you want to shop for more souvenirs, or can we go now?
(A) Gifts for some of my colleagues.
(B) I'm ready to go.
(C) The shop opened in August.

26 캐나다식 발음 → 미국식 발음

The blueprint was checked by the architect, wasn't it?
(A) It looks more red to me.
(B) Check the rules first.
(C) He'll go over it this afternoon.

27 미국식 발음 → 호주식 발음

Delivery of your food will take more than an hour.
(A) I'll just pick it up.
(B) An update is available online.
(C) Put them in order.

28 영국식 발음 → 캐나다식 발음

Who wrote the initial presentation for the microwave marketing campaign?
(A) I can find out for you.
(B) For our target market.
(C) Alan did most of the hiring.

29 영국식 발음 → 캐나다식 발음

Isn't it time to head to the book signing?
(A) You're ahead in the competition.
(B) Actually, it starts after lunch.
(C) Yes, I attended it.

30 미국식 발음 → 호주식 발음

Would you mind stopping by my desk in a bit?
(A) I've stopped buying those.
(B) Because none are mine.
(C) I think I'll be able to do that.

31 〔캐나다식 발음 → 호주식 발음〕

The container in the refrigerator belongs to me.
(A) Did you mark it with your name?
(B) While I was cleaning it out.
(C) Ms. Valero owns the land.

PART 3

Questions 32-34 refer to the following conversation.

〔캐나다식 발음 → 미국식 발음〕

M: Pardon me . . . Could you help me, please? I was trying to use one of your bank's cash machines, but the touch screen isn't responding.
W: I'm sorry. That error has been coming up repeatedly this morning. A repairperson should be on the way. Meanwhile, I recommend using the machine near the exit instead.
M: Ah . . . I also tried that one, and it's not working either. I'm in a rush, so I'll consult one of the tellers.
W: Of course. And to apologize for the inconvenience, here's a free desk calendar.

Questions 35-37 refer to the following conversation.

〔영국식 발음 → 호주식 발음〕

W: Hello. I oversee an apartment complex, and I'm interested in installing the home security cameras you sell. Do you carry the brand . . . ah . . . PointAlert?
M: Unfortunately, those products all sold out last week. We sell similar items, though, if you'd like to come by and check them out.
W: OK. Your chain has an outlet on Marigold Street, right?
M: Actually, that branch moved to a different area last month. If you download our free smartphone application, you can see the locations of all our current retail shops.
W: Thanks. I'll do that now.

Questions 38-40 refer to the following conversation with three speakers.

〔캐나다식 발음 → 호주식 발음 → 미국식 발음〕

M1: Excuse me. My friend and I are wondering why tonight's concert has yet to begin.
M2: According to our tickets, the show was scheduled to start at 7:00 P.M., but it's already 7:15.
W: Yes, I'm sorry. Unfortunately, a member of the band wasn't able to arrive on time. She just got here, so we expect everything to get underway no later than 7:30 P.M. An announcement is about to be made now.
M1: I see. Well, I guess we'll head back to our seats and wait for it to start, then.

Questions 41-43 refer to the following conversation with three speakers.

〔미국식 발음 → 캐나다식 발음 → 영국식 발음〕

W1: Marty and Jen, are you ready to leave the guesthouse and do some sightseeing?
M: Sure! I'm excited to see the amazing mountain views at the state park nearby.
W2: We're going there today? I thought we'd shop at the outlet mall.
M: Well, maybe we can split up. Renee and I want to spend the morning at the park. So, why don't we meet you at the outlet mall for lunch, Jen?
W2: OK, but I'm not sure where the mall is. Maybe I'll ask the front desk clerk.
M: Good idea. I'm sure she can tell you how to get there.

Questions 44-46 refer to the following conversation.

〔호주식 발음 → 미국식 발음〕

M: Hi, Claire. How are the preparations for Maya's birthday party going?
W: Pretty well. I sent out the invitations yesterday. And how about booking a table at the Korean restaurant she likes?
M: Sure. I have that place's phone number saved. I'll call right now and see if there are any private rooms available.
W: Great. And don't forget to make the reservation for 8 P.M. We're attending a budget meeting that day.

Questions 47-49 refer to the following conversation.

〔캐나다식 발음 → 영국식 발음〕

M: Hi. I'd like to place an order for 50 printed T-shirts for a race my company will sponsor.
W: OK. Have you ordered with us before?
M: Oh, yes. Our corporate account number is 48827.
W: Great. And when do you need the items delivered by?
M: May 10, if possible. The event is being held on May 15.
W: Hmm . . . To meet that date, we can provide an expedited service. But there will be an additional charge of $20, which brings the total amount to $170. Is that all right?
M: Yes, that's fine. I'll e-mail you the design now.

Questions 50-52 refer to the following conversation.

〔호주식 발음 → 영국식 발음〕

M: Before we start the interview, I want to point out that the personal trainer position needs to be filled for one month only.
W: Yes, I saw that in the job advertisement. I'm going to move overseas in six weeks, so I need a short-term job.

M: Good. Our gym will be very busy in January. And the new employee will assist our director, Antoine Hart, during that time.

W: Are you expecting more customers because it's the new year?

M: Partly, but also because we're running a big promotion since we replaced some of our workout machines last month . . . Anyway, now I'll ask you some questions about your past work experience.

Questions 53-55 refer to the following conversation.

3) 미국식 발음 → 캐나다식 발음

W: Guess what, Andrei? Our pizza shop ordered some self-service kiosks.

M: Ah . . . Are they able to send text message notifications about orders to customers' phones?

W: That's right. I expect they'll help us boost sales as many people find them very convenient.

M: Hmm . . . I'm not so sure. I know many customers who prefer dealing directly with staff here.

W: Well, let's see how patrons respond on the first day the machines are available. An hour ago, I called the technician who will install them, and he said they'll be ready this Friday.

Questions 56-58 refer to the following conversation.

3) 영국식 발음 → 호주식 발음

W: The lease for our salon is almost over, Francis. And, according to our landlord, Brenda Frost, our monthly rent will be increased by $300 per month next year.

M: Wow! That's a big change. But I don't think it would be wise to try to relocate.

W: Not at all. We've established a large client base in the neighborhood. But I'm not sure if we can afford the new rental rate.

M: I think we can manage it. Our budget looks OK for this year.

W: You're right. I'll call Ms. Frost this afternoon to tell her about our decision to stay here.

Questions 59-61 refer to the following conversation.

3) 영국식 발음 → 호주식 발음

W: This is Candace Keller on *WGN Top Radio* in Austin. As advertised, I will now interview Jason Carter, a successful financial consultant and host of the new TV show *Deal Me In*. So, Jason, can you tell us about this new show?

M: Certainly. The program is filmed like a talk show and focuses on people's financial concerns, like their investments.

W: Sounds interesting. And what tips can you give our listeners now about managing their money?

M: The most important thing is to keep track of one's spending.

W: I see. Well, let's listen to some phone calls now from the people out there who've tuned in to this radio show.

Questions 62-64 refer to the following conversation and sign.

3) 미국식 발음 → 캐나다식 발음

W: Excuse me. I've just recently moved to this city, and I don't know my way around well. Could you tell me which bus travels to Windsor Station?

M: Hmm . . . You have a few options. But the quickest is the express bus.

W: Thanks, I'll take that one! And, um . . . Do you think I'll be able to get to where I'm going by noon? I'm running late for a dental appointment.

M: Oh, certainly. The bus arrives every five minutes, and you'll only be traveling 10 blocks or so.

Questions 65-67 refer to the following conversation and manual.

3) 미국식 발음 → 호주식 발음

W: Thanks for attending the second session of our training workshop for Styx Photo Editing software. Before I start, does anyone have questions about yesterday's session?

M: Yeah, I do. Can you show us how to switch color ranges again, please?

W: Sure, I'll show you in a few minutes. And in the future, you can find that information in the user manual.

M: Yes, I glanced through it. But I couldn't find anything in the Tools section about color ranges.

W: Oh, it's not in that section. It's actually on page 7. So you should check there. At any rate, you should review all the content to get ready for our exam tomorrow.

Questions 68-70 refer to the following conversation and survey.

3) 영국식 발음 → 캐나다식 발음

W: How's the analysis of our customer survey going, Casey?

M: I just need to type up the report . . . I'll submit it by the end of this week. But would you like to look at what I've got so far?

W: Sure. Hmm . . . I can understand why most customers rated our choice of calling plans as very poor. However, I'm surprised to see another category is poorly rated.

M: I wasn't expecting that either. What do you think we should do to address this issue?

W: I propose hiring an expert in this area to consult with us. Warren Jordan at Handler Consulting Agency might be a good choice since he helped us improve our call center.

PART 4

Questions 71-73 refer to the following telephone message.

[3번] 캐나다식 발음

Hello, Ms. Vincent. This is Howard Rogan from Division Center Supplies. I'm calling about the white printer paper you ordered for your office. Well, there's a problem. The manufacturer of the product you selected—Wellington Paper Products—just went out of business. You paid for 50 boxes, but we only have 20 in our warehouse. However, we do carry other paper products of a similar quality, which we can send instead. But first, I'd like to review your choices with you. Call me back at your earliest convenience, and I'll be happy to go over the options.

Questions 74-76 refer to the following talk.

[3번] 영국식 발음

Good morning, and I apologize for rescheduling this tour at the last minute. As you know, it was originally planned for yesterday, but electricity in the building had to be temporarily cut off. So it wasn't safe to walk around. Now, the first part of the new community center I want to show you all is the indoor pool. It'll be used for youth swimming classes. We'll be posting fee information and schedules for those courses on our Web site next week. And . . . um . . . we're hoping to offer other types of classes, too. Please share your suggestions now or after this tour.

Questions 77-79 refer to the following advertisement.

[3번] 호주식 발음

There's nothing more frustrating than needing to charge your smartphone when you don't have access to an outlet. Well, try the Renew charger! Our device is different from those of our competitors because it includes a standard cord for charging as well as a built-in solar panel. What's more, we're certain you'll appreciate the Renew's high-quality components and charging efficiency. But don't take our word for it! Visit www.renewcharger.com to read feedback from hundreds of satisfied customers.

Questions 80-82 refer to the following excerpt from a meeting.

[3번] 캐나다식 발음

I'd like us to turn our attention to next month's schedule. In June, half of our customer service representatives will be attending a weeklong workshop. If no preparations are made, customers will be inconvenienced. It's okay if customers have to wait up to 10 minutes to speak to a representative, but anything longer than this is not acceptable. To help us avoid long service delays, our recruitment agency will provide us with a few temporary workers. Regarding that, I'm going to need one of you to conduct training for several hours on May 20. I'll decide who will get this assignment later today.

Questions 83-85 refer to the following announcement.

[3번] 호주식 발음

Attention all tournament attendees. A list of this afternoon's matches is posted at the information desk near the entrance of Lilly Park. Please note, however, that there is one change to today's program. Famed tennis star Mary O'Reilly, who was supposed to play an exhibition match during the tournament, is unable to join us. She's apparently sick and not able to travel. It's quite unfortunate, as I know many of you were looking forward to meeting Ms. O'Reilly. And as a last reminder, coverage of today's activities and matches will be aired on WXTC Radio, our media partner for the event. You can listen in on 99.7 FM.

Questions 86-88 refer to the following radio broadcast.

[3번] 미국식 발음

Coming up next on *Book Talk*, we'll be continuing yesterday's discussion on e-books and why some genres are better suited for this digital format than others. For example, mystery and science fiction releases tend to sell well as e-books. But when it comes to photo books and travel guidebooks, readers prefer printed copies. Why is this so? Publishing industry expert Gail Boyd is on our show again and will go over all of this and more. Now, Ms. Boyd, let's begin by having you give us a quick overview of your professional background in publishing.

Questions 89-91 refer to the following telephone message.

[3번] 영국식 발음

Mr. Richards, this is Chloe Friedman from Breckendale Catering. I want to thank you for considering our company as you make arrangements for your upcoming music awards dinner. Regarding the message you left me, we're happy to accommodate people with dairy allergies. In fact, I talked to our head chef about the matter this morning, and we came up with a number of great dishes. Finally, you mentioned that you were uncertain about whether a company as small as ours could handle 250 guests. There were 300 people at an event we catered yesterday. If you'd like a specific estimate, I'm available to talk at your convenience.

Questions 92-94 refer to the following talk.

[3번] 호주식 발음

Welcome to the Preston Coffee roasting factory. My name is Arnold, and I'll be leading you on our tour today. Our first stop will be our storeroom, where I'll explain how we source our beans as well as what countries they come from. After that, we'll head to the main floor to watch the actual roasting process. Finally, we'll return to the administrative office, at which point you'll get a chance to taste our world-famous coffee before going home today. All right, let's get started.

Questions 95–97 refer to the following excerpt from a meeting and floor plan.

[3M] 미국식 발음

Amanda, thanks for giving us a summary of what's been done so far to get ready for the Buckley Pharmaceutical Conference. However, one detail still needs to be discussed. Our company is sponsoring the conference once again, which means we're entitled to distribute our magazine to all participants. Last year's event was also at the Astor Conference Center, and we . . . ah . . . set the magazine rack in Seminar Room 1—the room directly across from the stage. However, only 70 copies were taken. That's why we'll be placing the rack in the space beside the stage this year.

Questions 98–100 refer to the following telephone message and bar graph.

[3W] 캐나다식 발음

Good afternoon, Ms. Flores. I looked into live chat programs as you asked and have sent you the user ratings for four programs that I think could help improve our customer engagement. They are all rated above 4.5 out of 5, so they're probably all good. However, I think the most highly rated one is too expensive. The one with the third-highest rating is a bit cheaper, and it offers a 30-day free trial. I think we should go for it. I've already downloaded it on the computer in my office. If you have a few minutes, I can show you how it works.

PART 1

1 ⓒ 캐나다식 발음

(A) He is rolling up a carpet.
(B) He is removing his hat.
(C) He is measuring an item on the floor.
(D) He is kneeling to put on his shoes.

2 ⓒ 영국식 발음

(A) One of the men is putting some groceries into a basket.
(B) One of the men is standing in front of the counter.
(C) The woman is selecting some merchandise.
(D) The woman is making a payment.

3 ⓒ 미국식 발음

(A) A man is watering a plant.
(B) A man is using a photocopier.
(C) There is a bulletin board on the wall.
(D) A drawer has been pulled open.

4 ⓒ 호주식 발음

(A) A man is pointing out a window.
(B) A man is taking notes on a computer.
(C) Some people are setting up a table.
(D) Some people are listening to a presentation.

5 ⓒ 영국식 발음

(A) Some outdoor furniture is covered in snow.
(B) A lamp post has fallen down.
(C) A car is parked on the street.
(D) Some houses are under construction.

6 ⓒ 미국식 발음

(A) The men are painting a house.
(B) A part of the house is unfinished.
(C) A chimney is being repaired.
(D) The men are facing each other.

PART 2

7 ⓒ 호주식 발음 → 미국식 발음

When is the flight scheduled to take off?
(A) I need to take this sweater off.
(B) At Terminal B.
(C) In about 10 minutes.

8 ⓒ 영국식 발음 → 캐나다식 발음

Why don't we apply for a loan to open a second store?
(A) Apply the payment to the account.
(B) The bank on Second Avenue.
(C) I've never thought about it.

9 ⓒ 미국식 발음 → 캐나다식 발음

Who did you meet with after the conference yesterday?
(A) She should be there a bit after 11 A.M.
(B) One of the organizers.
(C) At a café close by.

10 ⓒ 캐나다식 발음 → 미국식 발음

All positions have already been filled, haven't they?
(A) No. Some are open.
(B) Fill it up to the top, please.
(C) A job applicant.

11 ⓒ 영국식 발음 → 호주식 발음

Where did you put the other form?
(A) Before April 2.
(B) Yes, I just read over it.
(C) In the file cabinet.

12 ⓒ 캐나다식 발음 → 미국식 발음

How much does a ferry ticket to Liverpool cost?
(A) The final cost analysis.
(B) There is a half-hour delay.
(C) It's $43 each way.

13 ⓒ 영국식 발음 → 호주식 발음

You can stop by my house later this evening if you want to.
(A) I won't have any time.
(B) A real estate agent.
(C) Oh, I'm late this morning.

14 ⓒ 미국식 발음 → 영국식 발음

Which documents do I have to sign?
(A) Mr. Lee let me use his pen.
(B) Some of the employment contracts.
(C) That's a beautiful design.

15 [호주식 발음 → 영국식 발음]

What kind of artwork would you like to purchase?
(A) I don't want anything that's too big.
(B) Over the fireplace in the living room.
(C) I bought it at the Foxworth Gallery.

16 [미국식 발음 → 호주식 발음]

Have you been to the new restaurant at the lakefront?
(A) I am not sure which font to use.
(B) He's a classically trained chef.
(C) Yes. The food is amazing.

17 [캐나다식 발음 → 영국식 발음]

When can I expect my bicycle repairs to be completed?
(A) The bike lane ends on the corner.
(B) We're having trouble finding parts for it.
(C) Actually, I haven't used it.

18 [영국식 발음 → 호주식 발음]

Would you rather contact the client yourself or have me do it?
(A) Sure, my phone number is 555-1212.
(B) I can take care of it.
(C) Canastar is our biggest client.

19 [캐나다식 발음 → 미국식 발음]

The Array Master software is really fast, isn't it?
(A) Because it's the latest version.
(B) I've already reported the problem.
(C) Our new smartphones will arrive soon.

20 [호주식 발음 → 영국식 발음]

Where will the electric car advertisement air tomorrow?
(A) The air filter has been fully tested.
(B) Most cars are now more fuel-efficient.
(C) On radio and TV stations nationally.

21 [영국식 발음 → 캐나다식 발음]

Can I share a ride with you to the airport?
(A) My business trip was canceled.
(B) Approximately two hours.
(C) What do you want to have for lunch?

22 [호주식 발음 → 미국식 발음]

Orders must be received by noon to qualify for free shipping.
(A) You cannot change the order amount.
(B) I had better submit it now then.
(C) I think the shipment arrived yesterday.

23 [캐나다식 발음 → 영국식 발음]

What product should I use to clean the desk?
(A) The liquid in the blue bottle.

(B) Some new desktops.
(C) Before your shift ends.

24 [영국식 발음 → 캐나다식 발음]

How long did it take you to become an attorney?
(A) The law office is just across the street.
(B) Hiring a good attorney can be expensive.
(C) I'm still working on it.

25 [영국식 발음 → 호주식 발음]

All first-class passengers can enter the train station's lounge for free.
(A) I prefer to book online.
(B) Oh, I will take advantage of that.
(C) No. I missed my flight.

26 [캐나다식 발음 → 영국식 발음]

Isn't it too late to get tickets for the concert?
(A) There are some balcony seats left.
(B) Please be on time.
(C) At the box office.

27 [미국식 발음 → 캐나다식 발음]

Why hasn't your daily work schedule been updated?
(A) Sure, it won't take very long.
(B) Install the updates before you leave.
(C) I'm going to do it this afternoon.

28 [캐나다식 발음 → 호주식 발음]

Are all the snack samples ready to be distributed, or shall I wait?
(A) Can you come back in five minutes?
(B) I like the design of the sample page.
(C) Its distribution network is vast.

29 [미국식 발음 → 캐나다식 발음]

Is there a chance to go backstage before the event starts?
(A) The lights are ready.
(B) Yes. The director approved it.
(C) It was a great show.

30 [호주식 발음 → 미국식 발음]

Didn't the books you ordered arrive last week?
(A) Please put them in order.
(B) His last novel is really famous.
(C) They're still in transit.

31 [미국식 발음 → 호주식 발음]

Have you visited the Hotel Venoby rooftop at sunset?
(A) Yes, my room was very spacious.
(B) Let's set the table now.
(C) The view is the best.

PART 3

Questions 32-34 refer to the following conversation.

호주식 발음 → 영국식 발음

M: Hi, Andrea. It's Kevin. I just submitted the financial report you helped me with. If you don't have plans, I'd like to treat you to lunch today. I was thinking of heading to India Palace. Is that OK with you?

W: That would be great. I can call them to reserve a table. They're always crowded at lunch.

M: I already did. They said they had a table for two available.

W: Perfect. Why don't we meet in the lobby in 15 minutes? I'd like to respond to one more e-mail quickly.

Questions 35-37 refer to the following conversation.

미국식 발음 → 캐나다식 발음

W: Good morning, I'm wondering if you ever got around to unpacking the shipment of produce that our grocery store received from the farm. It includes cucumbers, bell peppers, and onions.

M: I meant to do that this morning, but I've just been too busy. I'm sorry. I can start now if you'd like me to.

W: Yes, please do. I'll ask Stephen to help you take everything out of the boxes. If you two work together, you should be able to finish pretty quickly.

Questions 38-40 refer to the following conversation with three speakers.

호주식 발음 → 미국식 발음 → 영국식 발음

M: Excuse me. Do you still have this coat in green? If so, I'd like a medium.

W1: Actually, I don't think it comes in that color. I believe it's only available in blue and red.

M: A friend of mine bought it in green last week from this very store.

W1: Oh, really? My mistake. Well, let me find out for you . . . Amy? Do we have this garment in green?

W2: A new shipment of merchandise was just delivered. I can look for some green coats now if the customer has some time.

W1: Great. Can you wait a few minutes, sir?

M: Sure. That's no problem.

Questions 41-43 refer to the following conversation.

미국식 발음 → 캐나다식 발음

W: Overall, last month's research effort was a success. The customers who participated in the survey had some very valuable insights that we can use as we develop our next smartwatch model.

M: What in particular did you learn?

W: Customers really enjoy the clarity and durability of the display in our latest model, the X31. They made it very clear that the same one should be used in the next model.

M: That's very encouraging.

W: Yes, definitely. However, one issue that came up multiple times is how many people find the X31 too large for their wrist.

M: The X32 is going to be smaller than the X31.

Questions 44-46 refer to the following conversation.

영국식 발음 → 호주식 발음

W: I'm wondering how much longer you and your crew will be working in our staff break room. Are you almost done fixing the leaky pipes and installing the new sink?

M: It's nearly complete, but, unfortunately, we're almost out of the pipe we need for the job. That's going to slow down the process for us.

W: Oh, I see. Does that mean you're going to have to return tomorrow?

M: No. I'm going to have one of my employees drive to a store to get the necessary items. We should still be able to complete the job this afternoon.

Questions 47-49 refer to the following conversation.

영국식 발음 → 캐나다식 발음

W: I'm done examining your coffee shop, Mr. Miller. Overall, the space is clean and meets most of our state's health and safety guidelines. However, I did notice one issue.

M: Really? What seems to be the problem?

W: I didn't see any fire extinguishers in the shop. Commercial spaces are required by law to have two separate extinguishers accessible at all times.

M: Oh! I have them, but I forgot to put them out. They're actually in the box just behind you.

W: In that case, I can certify that your business is ready to open. Next week, you should get an operating license. Best of luck with your venture.

Questions 50-52 refer to the following conversation.

호주식 발음 → 미국식 발음

M: Hey, Carla. I've been meaning to talk to you about this weekend's exhibition. I'm pleased with the art pieces that we're going to display, but I feel like they could be better promoted.

W: I actually agree with you. How about setting up a selfie spot inside the exhibition hall? People could take pictures in front of the statue of Victory.

M: That's a great idea. We should also run a promotion on our social media accounts. We could ask people to share posts about the exhibition and select some users to get free passes to our next event.

Questions 53–55 refer to the following conversation with three speakers.

🔊 호주식 발음 → 미국식 발음 → 캐나다식 발음

M1: We need to get ready to present details about our new tablet model at the upcoming shareholders meeting. How are things coming along?

W: I'm almost done with the layout of the report. I just need to add pictures of the products.

M1: Thanks, Sylvia. Let me know if you need help.

M2: I'm concerned about the time limit. We may have to edit the speech a bit. We only have 10 minutes in total to give our presentation.

W: Do you think it's much longer than that?

M2: Yes. When I practiced, it took more than 15 minutes.

M1: That does seem too long. Our CEO will be there, so I want everything to go smoothly.

Questions 56–58 refer to the following conversation.

🔊 영국식 발음 → 캐나다식 발음

W: Hello, Shan-Woo. We are going to have to postpone the marathon. Hanford Grocery Store has pulled their sponsorship.

M: That's unexpected. Did they give a reason?

W: They merged with a national grocery store chain that is not interested in sponsoring the event. We are looking for another solution, but, in the meantime, I need you to inform the runners about the delay.

M: Should I e-mail all the runners?

W: I don't think that will work. Our registration form didn't require e-mail addresses, so we don't have them for everyone.

M: Hmm . . . In that case, how about sending them text messages, instead? Surely, we have their phone numbers.

W: Great. That's probably a better idea.

Questions 59–61 refer to the following conversation.

🔊 캐나다식 발음 → 미국식 발음

M: Gabriella, this morning, I read through the quality-control report you wrote and really liked your suggestions. I'd like you to join me when I share them with the production team manager later this week after we return from our trip to Boston.

W: Sure, I don't mind. The entire production team seems to be in the office today. Maybe we could go talk to him now? It shouldn't take that long.

M: A taxi will be here in 15 minutes. It's taking us to the airport for our 1 P.M. flight.

W: Oh, right. I suppose we'll have to wait, then. Actually, I should go to my office quickly. I left my suitcase there.

Questions 62–64 refer to the following conversation and order form.

🔊 영국식 발음 → 호주식 발음

W: Excuse me, Mr. Landry. I'm wondering if you've already bought the office supplies for this month. I need to make a correction to my order.

M: No, I haven't done it yet. I'm planning to this afternoon. You asked for more folders, right? What do you want to change about your order?

W: Actually, I requested black ink cartridges for my department's printer. I need one more than I originally indicated.

M: OK. I just need to talk to the accounting manager first to get approval for the budget. I'm on my way to do that now.

Questions 65–67 refer to the following conversation and map.

🔊 캐나다식 발음 → 미국식 발음

M: Yumi, it's Patrick calling. Sorry I'm running late. I know I'm supposed to be there already, but printing out our brochures took longer than expected.

W: That's OK. We have plenty of time to set the booth up . . . Since you're still at the office, can you do me a favor? I forgot our banners on my desk. Can you bring them when you come?

M: Sure. But I've never been there before. What's the best way to get there by bus?

W: Take the 115 bus from our office to the stop in front of Elmwood Park. Then, walk to Raymond Lane, and turn right. You'll see the conference center.

Questions 68–70 refer to the following conversation and calendar.

🔊 미국식 발음 → 호주식 발음

W: Hello, this is Fernlake Auto. I'm Cheryl. How can I help you?

M: Hi, I'm shopping for a new car. My current one is only a couple of years old, but I'm worried about its effect on the environment. I was interested in getting an electric car instead of something that burns gas.

W: A lot of our customers feel the same way. That's why the Sparrow electric car is our top-selling model at the moment. Actually, we got the new model in today. Would you like to come in and test drive it?

M: Sure. That would work for me.

W: OK. I'll get the car ready as soon as we hang up.

M: Perfect. I'll see you soon.

PART 4

Questions 71-73 refer to the following advertisement.

[3ω] 영국식 발음

Stop by Willis Tires this Saturday and Sunday to take advantage of our two-day sale. Everything in our stores will be marked down. Those who buy a set of Waterline tires will also receive a $100 voucher good for any future purchase. Don't miss your chance to save hundreds on your next set of car or truck tires! Visit our Web site at www.willistires.com for a list of Willis Tires locations in your neighborhood.

Questions 74-76 refer to the following talk.

[3ω] 호주식 발음

Good afternoon, and welcome to the Turner Expo. It is sponsored by Gatwick City. I'm Richard Atkins, and I've been a professional gardener for over 20 years. I started my career as an assistant gardener. I was then hired as the general manager of Hawthorne Gardening. Our company manages the gardens and lawns of many local hotels, athletic fields, and college campuses. Today, I'd like to discuss some of the steps that amateur gardeners like you can take to keep your plants safe and healthy. We'll review some methods of natural pest control and discuss which gardening chemicals are safe to use around children. Let's get started.

Questions 77-79 refer to the following excerpt from a meeting.

[3ω] 미국식 발음

I have some good news. The limited edition Cosmic Drink Mix has already sold out. I asked Kathy to create a wait list for the beverage mix yesterday, and there are already 1,000 individual customers on it. The question now is whether to produce another limited edition or include this mix in our permanent product line. In my opinion, wait lists and special editions are effective marketing tools. What do you all think? I am open to suggestions. No matter the decision, I'll have to tell the marketing manager about it as soon as we end the meeting.

Questions 80-82 refer to the following announcement.

[3ω] 캐나다식 발음

Good morning, everyone. I want to discuss our remote work policy. Its implementation has been smooth in many ways, but there is room for improvement. For one, some employees have not been actively using the messenger program while working from home. Since they do not reply to messages, I've had to make phone calls about urgent issues. Occasionally, I've had to wait 30 minutes for an answer. I want to make sure that our work-from-home system is successful, so everyone must use the program effectively. I've e-mailed everyone the work-from-home communication guidelines regarding the messenger program. Please take some time to review them, and follow them closely.

Questions 83-85 refer to the following recorded message.

[3ω] 영국식 발음

Hello, you've reached the administrative office of the Charles P. Harrison Museum of Fine Arts. Unfortunately, we are closed at the moment. Our office is open during the museum's regular hours. These are from 10 A.M. to 7 P.M. on weekdays and from 10 A.M. to 5 P.M. on weekends. Throughout the month of August, the museum will be hosting an exhibition of Impressionist paintings in the Redwood Wing. This will include French paintings from the 19th century. Entrance will be free to our members and $15 for all other visitors. If you are interested in purchasing a membership or reserving a ticket to the event, visit www.HarrisonMFA.org.

Questions 86-88 refer to the following talk.

[3ω] 캐나다식 발음

Thank you for joining us today. As we all know, self-employment rates have risen recently. Many people are starting their own businesses or taking on freelance work, but managing your own bookkeeping isn't easy. That's why I'm proud to debut the latest version of the FastTrack bookkeeping program. This software allows you to easily create and send invoices. It also allows you to set a budget for your business and easily track your expenses. Best of all, FastTrack keeps track of your income and provides automated reports you can use to file your annual taxes. Most users can complete their forms in a few hours. Let me demonstrate how easy this software is to use.

Questions 89-91 refer to the following news report.

[3ω] 호주식 발음

Welcome to Local Nine News. Heavy rainfall last winter has contributed to a spectacular display of wildflowers throughout Sonoma Hills. Hikers, photographers, and other nature lovers have visited the area in large numbers this month. Several of our viewers were thrilled to share their images of the hills covered in colorful flowers. But experts anticipate that the wildflower season will only last for two more weeks, so viewers who want to see the blooms in person are encouraged to take a trip to Sonoma Hills Nature Preserve right away. Those who want to visit the park for a day trip may do so freely, but a camping permit must be purchased for overnight trips.

Questions 92–94 refer to the following telephone message.

[발음] 미국식 발음

Hi, Ms. Ellison. This is Samantha from Palm Beach Floral Designs. I received your message and wanted to let you know that we can provide floral arrangements for your August 17 wedding. I understand that you're planning to hold the ceremony and reception at Amethyst Springs Resort & Spa. We've worked extensively with that hotel in the past, so we are familiar with the location. In addition, we've arranged exceptional wedding packages with them. They are only available for the next two months. I'd be happy to set up an appointment to go over those packages in more detail. We also provide custom-made floral arrangements for an additional fee.

Questions 95–97 refer to the following talk and presentation slide.

[발음] 호주식 발음

While I have all our employees in the room, I'd like to briefly review our updated dress code. We sent out an e-mail last week covering this topic in detail. But I'd like to remind everyone that closed-toe shoes are mandatory while you're on the premises. As we work with a lot of heavy machinery, this is an important safety precaution. Employees who are entering the processing rooms or shipping facilities must also remember to remove all jewelry, ties, and other accessories that can get pulled into the machinery. Again, I want to make sure you follow these regulations as they were created to prevent serious injuries.

Questions 98–100 refer to the following news report and agenda.

[발음] 영국식 발음

This is KLWA 6 News. I'm Emily Garcia. Water conservation was the topic at yesterday's town hall meeting. Several residents made speeches supporting Mayor Cooper's new regulations. However, other residents suggested that these regulations may be too drastic and could negatively affect their day-to-day lives. Under the new rules, local homeowners would be prohibited from washing their cars or hosing down their driveways at their homes. City Councilman Tom Loughlin acknowledged that these regulations place a significant burden on local residents. But he insisted that strict water conservation is needed to cope with the drought that has gripped the Green Meadows area for the past six months.

PART 1

1 [3n] 캐나다식 발음
   (A) Products are stacked on shelves.
   (B) A keyboard is being moved.
   (C) A man is tightening a tie.
   (D) The people are exchanging clipboards.

2 [3n] 미국식 발음
   (A) She is looking out of a window.
   (B) She is fastening a seat belt.
   (C) She is reading a magazine.
   (D) She is lowering a tray table.

3 [3n] 호주식 발음
   (A) A man is opening a toolbox.
   (B) A computer has been taken apart.
   (C) A man is arranging items on a desk.
   (D) A potted plant has been left on a table.

4 [3n] 영국식 발음
   (A) Baked goods are being purchased.
   (B) Food has been laid out on a counter.
   (C) Some bread has been put into an oven.
   (D) Light fixtures are being hung up.

5 [3n] 미국식 발음
   (A) Someone is holding a lamp.
   (B) One of the men is pointing at a file.
   (C) One of the women is using a laptop.
   (D) Some people are installing a fan.

6 [3n] 호주식 발음
   (A) Some curtains are being replaced.
   (B) A flower arrangement is on a windowsill.
   (C) A rug has been set under the furniture.
   (D) Some cushions are on a sofa.

PART 2

7 [3n] 호주식 발음 → 영국식 발음
   Which musician will be performing at the award ceremony?
   (A) The same guitar player as last year.
   (B) A prize valued at $500.
   (C) Ms. Thomas discovered the defect.

8 [3n] 캐나다식 발음 → 미국식 발음
   Where can we hang our poster for the event?
   (A) The event organizer.
   (B) OK. I'll print more of them.
   (C) On the bulletin board.

9 [3n] 미국식 발음 → 캐나다식 발음
   Would you like to go to a new Chinese restaurant with us?
   (A) No, thanks. I've already eaten.
   (B) A plant opening in China.
   (C) Yes, I did.

10 [3n] 영국식 발음 → 호주식 발음
   When am I supposed to shut down the store?
   (A) At 8 P.M.
   (B) Just down the street.
   (C) We bought this candle there.

11 [3n] 호주식 발음 → 영국식 발음
   How many desktop computers were ordered for the library?
   (A) Up to five books can be checked out.
   (B) Set up on the desk.
   (C) Mr. Collins can provide that information.

12 [3n] 캐나다식 발음 → 미국식 발음
   This luggage is heavier than I thought it would be.
   (A) Would you like me to carry it?
   (B) At the baggage claim area.
   (C) We thought it was a nice hotel.

13 [3n] 영국식 발음 → 캐나다식 발음
   Can my phone plan be upgraded to include unlimited texting?
   (A) Your own work number.
   (B) I can take care of that.
   (C) No, seat upgrades are excluded.

14 [3n] 호주식 발음 → 미국식 발음
   I thought we could have shortened the presentation.
   (A) Actually, it's a pretty long hallway.
   (B) It was a present from a friend.
   (C) Yes, I completely agree.

15 [캐나다식 발음 → 영국식 발음]

Why wasn't the photocopier we ordered installed this afternoon?
(A) It was.
(B) From an electronics store.
(C) The installation instructions.

16 [캐나다식 발음 → 미국식 발음]

Should we organize the workshops for May or June?
(A) No, we didn't attend.
(B) Because the shop was empty.
(C) I'd prefer to have them earlier.

17 [호주식 발음 → 영국식 발음]

What type of fabric did you order for the scarves?
(A) At a trade fair.
(B) Because it's affordable.
(C) I want to get more samples first.

18 [캐나다식 발음 → 미국식 발음]

The company is investing in wind power generators, isn't it?
(A) It's really windy today.
(B) Right. Since last quarter.
(C) Let's install new appliances.

19 [미국식 발음 → 영국식 발음]

We should e-mail Mr. Murray about the contract changes.
(A) Various legal requirements.
(B) Yes, he'll want to know.
(C) I don't have exact change.

20 [캐나다식 발음 → 호주식 발음]

Where is the conference on biotechnology being hosted?
(A) Both medical products and services.
(B) A venue in downtown Boston.
(C) Mindy organized the retirement party.

21 [미국식 발음 → 캐나다식 발음]

Why don't you take the highway?
(A) I don't believe there are.
(B) That's the next rest stop.
(C) One of the lanes is closed until Friday.

22 [영국식 발음 → 미국식 발음]

Didn't Mr. Taylor buy some more envelopes?
(A) This is all we have left.
(B) No, I have his e-mail address.
(C) I passed a stationery store this morning.

23 [호주식 발음 → 영국식 발음]

We're offering a discount on cleaning supplies this month, right?
(A) I'll have to count them.
(B) That's a good question.
(C) It was returned on June 4.

24 [미국식 발음 → 호주식 발음]

Have we published more articles this year than last year?
(A) I haven't worked here long enough to say.
(B) The article is much too long.
(C) I thought you had edited it already.

25 [영국식 발음 → 호주식 발음]

Could you tell Leslie to park in the lot next door?
(A) A bus is stuck in traffic.
(B) She doesn't have a car.
(C) The house next door is for sale.

26 [호주식 발음 → 영국식 발음]

When is the budget proposal due?
(A) I sent out a memo about it.
(B) Yes, we need to cut costs.
(C) It's over budget.

27 [미국식 발음 → 호주식 발음]

Should we pick up the cake or have it delivered?
(A) Whichever is easier.
(B) Let's get chocolate.
(C) Usually within 30 minutes.

28 [캐나다식 발음 → 영국식 발음]

Who has agreed to travel to San Francisco for the medical convention?
(A) Well, only after the convention ended.
(B) The trip took almost five days.
(C) Isn't Dr. Kumar planning to go?

29 [호주식 발음 → 캐나다식 발음]

How will the marketing director choose which intern to hire?
(A) Would you rather have a direct flight?
(B) She already gave the job to Steven Davies.
(C) The internship lasts three months.

30 [영국식 발음 → 캐나다식 발음]

A box was just dropped off for Rita Fritz.
(A) Can you bring it to her?
(B) Check rates from other shipping companies.
(C) She never had a chance to taste them.

31 [3»] 미국식 발음 → 영국식 발음

Can a photo of our shop be added to our Web site?
(A) I'll check the online version.
(B) Yes. That's simple to do.
(C) They rent cameras, too.

PART 3

Questions 32-34 refer to the following conversation.

[3»] 미국식 발음 → 호주식 발음

W: I read an article this morning that was published in *Business Quarterly* magazine. It highlighted the fact that more companies are manufacturing TV screens abroad because doing so is much cheaper.

M: Hmm . . . That might create a problem for us if our competitors end up lowering their prices. If they do, I suppose we'll have to think of ways to encourage customers to buy our domestically produced goods.

W: What if we emphasize how our goods lead to more high-paying jobs in the United Kingdom? We could launch a marketing campaign about it.

M: That's a great plan. I think consumers here would respond well to that message.

Questions 35-37 refer to the following conversation.

[3»] 캐나다식 발음 → 영국식 발음

M: Louise, I can't access any Web sites on my computer. Do you know what the problem might be?

W: All staff are having the same issue. Our supervisor is discussing the matter over the phone with the IT department head now.

M: This is very frustrating . . . It's the third time this month that we've had Internet issues.

W: I know. I suspect it's the Internet provider we're using. Maybe the IT staff should consider switching back to our previous provider.

M: I agree. We never had issues like this in the past. I think I'll send out an e-mail making the suggestion now.

Questions 38-40 refer to the following conversation.

[3»] 호주식 발음 → 미국식 발음

M: Our coffee shop has had good sales so far since opening last week.

W: True, but I think we can do more to promote our line of freshly made sandwiches.

M: Yeah, I've seen many customers just walk past the section where they're displayed. Do you have any suggestions for advertising them better?

W: We could give out samples at our storefront.

M: Who should that task be assigned to, though? Both of us have other work to do, and Sarah is operating the cash register.

W: Isn't Andy going to be starting his shift at 11 A.M.?

M: Oh, right. I forgot. I'll ask him to do it once he arrives.

Questions 41-43 refer to the following conversation with three speakers.

[3»] 캐나다식 발음 → 영국식 발음 → 호주식 발음

M1: Sharon, I know we're supposed to put the extra hoses for the fire trucks in a new place here, but I was never told where. Can you help me out?

W: I was actually wondering the same thing. Our chief announced the change yesterday, but I wasn't here when he did. I saw Justin moving a hose this morning, though.

M2: Did someone just mention my name?

M1: Justin, hey. Sharon and I aren't sure where to put hoses that aren't being used.

M2: There's a spot in our smaller garage where they're being kept. Why don't I show you two?

M1: That'd be great. Thanks.

Questions 44-46 refer to the following conversation.

[3»] 호주식 발음 → 미국식 발음

M: Hey, Matilda. In two weeks, a group of business students from Madrid University will visit here to tour this factory and study our clothing production process. I heard that most of them only speak Spanish. Do you know of any interpreters we can hire?

W: Hiring an interpreter will be very expensive. Instead, let's ask one of our staff members for assistance. Elena from the customer service team often handles phone calls from Spanish-speaking customers. So, she may be able to help.

M: Excellent idea. We'll be taking part in a meeting in half an hour. I'll bring it up with her then.

Questions 47-49 refer to the following conversation.

[3»] 캐나다식 발음 → 영국식 발음

M: Some of the protective clothing in our laboratory's storage closet is getting worn out, and a group of new hires starts next week. They'll need fresh garments.

W: Hmm . . . Well, we won't have time to order them through our supplier. That usually takes two to three weeks for delivery. But maybe there's a faster method.

M: Actually, I know of a uniform store located downtown. If we're only getting a few items, I'm sure we can find what we need there.

W: Great. Why don't you go to that store later today? Here, charge whatever you get to this company credit card. Thanks a lot.

Questions 50-52 refer to the following conversation.

호주식 발음 → 미국식 발음

M: Hi, Christi. Have you heard the news? Ms. Fleming is going to retire a year earlier than expected. She shared her decision with our CEO this morning.

W: Really? That will be a big loss for our department.

M: Yeah, I agree . . . But that's not all. I had a meeting with our CEO this morning, and he offered me Ms. Fleming's job. I got promoted to the position of department manager.

W: Congratulations! I'm sure you'll do an excellent job. And you'll have a great view of the city from Ms. Fleming's office.

M: I'm quite comfortable where I am . . . I figure creating another conference room would be more useful for the department.

Questions 53-55 refer to the following conversation.

미국식 발음 → 캐나다식 발음

W: Excuse me. I was here about an hour ago to open a new savings account. I think I accidentally left my cell phone here. Has anyone found it?

M: What does the device look like?

W: It's black and has a brown leather case.

M: Let me check our lost and found box . . . um . . . Sorry, I don't see anything like that here. Are you sure you didn't misplace it elsewhere?

W: Well, I went to the library earlier this morning. I plan to check there next.

M: OK. And I'll e-mail our staff and tell them to immediately report it if they find anything.

Questions 56-58 refer to the following conversation.

영국식 발음 → 캐나다식 발음

W: I'm currently looking for a programmer who can improve our restaurant reservation application, but I'm having trouble finding the right person. I might contact VHD Tech Staffing Services for help.

M: Don't you remember what happened the last time we used that service? They kept changing their price.

W: Do you have any other ideas then? Last week, half of the bookings in the system just disappeared.

M: If you've already placed a job posting and are not receiving many responses, maybe we should contact programmers on freelancer Web sites directly.

W: OK. If you think it will help, I'll start working on that now.

M: Great. I'll help you, too, since this is urgent.

Questions 59-61 refer to the following conversation with three speakers.

캐나다식 발음 → 미국식 발음 → 영국식 발음

M: Welcome to Paterson's Baked Goods! How can I help you?

W1: It's my supervisor's birthday tomorrow, and she wants a strawberry cake. But she doesn't eat dairy.

M: No problem. I can make one without any milk or butter. It won't be ready until tomorrow at 11 A.M., though. Is that OK?

W1: Let me call a coworker quickly to check . . . Hello, Beth. When will the party for Ms. Larson be held?

W2: Um, at 1 P.M. Once everyone returns from lunch.

W1: Thanks . . . Uh, 11 A.M. is fine.

M: Great. Would you like to pick it up? It can also be brought to your office for a $10 charge.

W1: I'll come get it myself.

Questions 62-64 refer to the following conversation and floor plan.

호주식 발음 → 영국식 발음

M: Pardon me. I'm supposed to participate in an orientation session organized by the human resources department. It should've started at 1:30 P.M., but it's 1:35 P.M. now, and no one has arrived yet. That's the main conference room over there, right?

W: Yes, it is. But, your meeting was moved to one of our other conference rooms.

M: Oh, thanks. I'm still settling in here since it's my first day of work. Can you tell me where I should go?

W: Sure. Head to the 14th floor. When you get off the elevator on that floor, go right. The meeting is taking place in the space directly across from the break room.

Questions 65-67 refer to the following conversation and seating chart.

캐나다식 발음 → 미국식 발음

M: Hi. I'm interested in seeing the musical *Coral Sea*. Are there any tickets available for the opening show on Saturday?

W: A few left, but they're going fast. The leading actor was nominated for several awards last year, so there is a lot of interest in the play.

M: Great, I'm glad some seats are still available. I'd like two that are next to each other and as close to the stage as possible.

W: OK. And will you be paying with cash or credit card?

M: You can run this card. And I need a receipt, please.

Questions 68-70 refer to the following conversation and schedule.

🎧 미국식 발음 → 캐나다식 발음

W: A friend from university told me she went to a figure drawing class here last week. I was wondering if I could join the next session.

M: Actually, that's our most popular class. Because the instructor is a very well-known artist, it fills up quickly. In order to get a spot, you'll need to sign up immediately.

W: Oh. I'll register for it now then. Do you take credit cards?

M: We accept credit cards and also bank transfers. But please keep in mind that there is a $25 fee for canceling after you've registered.

W: That's no problem. I don't plan on canceling.

PART 4

Questions 71-73 refer to the following excerpt from a meeting.

🎧 캐나다식 발음

Thank you all for coming in before we open the bistro for lunch. I want to give everyone an update on the latest menu changes. As you all know, the owners would like to offer a variety of traditional Italian foods in addition to our pizzas. And ever since Chef Michael Trager joined our team last week, our cooks have been working on some new recipes. This morning you'll get to sample the menu items and provide feedback about the dishes, which we'll begin serving on October 23.

Questions 74-76 refer to the following telephone message.

🎧 미국식 발음

This message is for Derek Hastings. My name is Judy, and I work at Blue Circle Pharmacy. I've had a chance to listen to the voice mail you left yesterday. Regarding your question, we're unable to mail regularly refilled prescriptions to your home. We don't offer this service for safety and liability reasons. So you'll have to pick them up at our store yourself. If you have any other questions about the matter, feel free to contact Vincent Mitchel, my manager.

Questions 77-79 refer to the following instructions.

🎧 캐나다식 발음

Welcome to today's lecture on modern sculpture here at the Claremont Creative Alliance. If you look at the information sheet you received earlier, you will see today's schedule of events. You will first hear a talk by Dr. Arthur Sorenson, an art history professor from Richfield University. Following that, we will screen a short documentary about abstract art. After that, there will be a 15-minute intermission. Finally, we will conclude with a question-and-answer session with the professor. Dr. Sorenson usually doesn't take part in these. I hope you appreciate it.

Questions 80-82 refer to the following excerpt from a meeting.

🎧 호주식 발음

Before we finish up, let's discuss the charity bike ride that some of you will be representing our firm in next week. Those going should've received special T-shirts for the race. They were distributed yesterday by . . . um . . . my assistant, Marcelle. If you weren't at your desk then, please get one from her later today. Multiple sizes are still available. But please note that there are only a few left in the small size. Also, some of you paid the entry fee in advance. The company will reimburse you for this in cash next week. All right, that's all for now.

Questions 83-85 refer to the following announcement.

🎧 영국식 발음

May I have your attention, everyone? I've got some exciting news to share with you. As of today, our soft drink company will be partnering with the Las Vegas Aces soccer team. In fact, I signed the agreement this morning, making it official. This is a big deal for us. Not only will our drinks be exclusively offered at the Aces' stadium, but we'll also be allowed to use the team logo in our marketing materials. Considering how popular the team is, there's a great chance that this will significantly boost the public's awareness of our brand.

Questions 86-88 refer to the following broadcast.

🎧 캐나다식 발음

Over the weekend, city officials announced plans to allocate $2 million for building a new public library. The decision came after weeks of debate, during which city council members considered how to use a recent federal grant. Some people were hoping that the funds would be spent on road repairs. However, a majority of residents support Mayor Sherry Keenam's decision to approve the library proposal. As of now, no fixed timeline regarding construction has been established, but work is expected to start as soon as this September. To find out the latest details about this development moving forward, residents are welcome to take part in Town Hall meetings every Tuesday evening.

Questions 89-91 refer to the following excerpt from a meeting.

🎧 호주식 발음

While we have achieved record sales numbers for many of our products this year, car batteries have been an exception. Until recently, our line of automotive batteries was popular among consumers. However, it is now underperforming as more competitors have entered the market. As a result, management has decided to drop the A34 car battery model to reduce production costs. The impact is expected to be considerable. As for models that will remain in production, we'll be sending out an updated product catalog to retail outlets at the end of next week.

Questions 92-94 refer to the following talk.

[3ᵢ] 미국식 발음

It's my pleasure to welcome you all to this workshop on how to improve interpersonal communication within office settings. Over the course of the morning, we'll be talking about a lot of very useful information. First, I'll explain how to encourage personnel to be more engaged and communicative by creating a welcoming working environment. Then, later this morning, we'll discuss a variety of group exercises that you can have employees do to build trust among team members— something essential to good communication. But before all of that, I'd like everyone to quickly tell the group your name and a few details about where you work. Let's start over here on the left.

Questions 95-97 refer to the following telephone message and calendar.

[3ᵢ] 영국식 발음

Mr. Hakeem, this is your assistant Peggy. I'm calling because the manager of Westwood Books wants to schedule a signing event to coincide with the release of your memoir. I know you're very busy next week, but I think it would be best to schedule the event on the same day as the awards ceremony. The hotel where the ceremony is being held is only a 10-minute drive from the bookstore, so you could easily do both. I can arrange for a taxi to pick you up, so you won't have to worry about driving yourself. If you agree with my suggestions, I'll take care of everything.

Questions 98-100 refer to the following telephone message and layout.

[3ᵢ] 미국식 발음

Hello, Ms. Coyle. This is Sandra Brink. I want to let you know that I've come to a decision regarding our lobby arrangement. I like the idea that you shared during our meeting last week about placing a table in the center of the room. Clients will appreciate having a place to set down their belongings as they wait to meet with staff. I also contacted my partner Marvin Griggs to get his input, and we agree that the design with a small chair and two long sofas facing each other is the most ideal one. You have my permission to order the appropriate furniture in the fabric styles we discussed before.

* 무료 해석은 해커스토익(Hackers.co.kr)에서
다운로드 받을 수 있습니다.

• QR 코드로
바로가기

PART 1

1 🎧 캐나다식 발음

(A) He is putting clothes into a washer.
(B) He is wiping a floor.
(C) He is cleaning a sink.
(D) He is taking apart a machine.

2 🎧 영국식 발음

(A) They're leaning on a railing.
(B) A backpack is resting on a bench.
(C) They're looking at each other.
(D) A boat is sailing down a river.

3 🎧 캐나다식 발음

(A) They are standing in front of easels.
(B) They are having a discussion.
(C) Some people are hanging up posters.
(D) Some people are viewing an exhibit.

4 🎧 호주식 발음

(A) Leaves are being gathered.
(B) Some sticks have been put into a pile.
(C) A man is warming his hands.
(D) A man is enjoying a beautiful view.

5 🎧 미국식 발음

(A) The doors of a barn have been shut.
(B) A tractor has been stored in a garage.
(C) Bushes are being trimmed.
(D) Tree branches are being piled up near a tower.

6 🎧 캐나다식 발음

(A) Suitcases are being loaded onto an aircraft.
(B) A man is leaning forward.
(C) A man is sitting in a waiting area.
(D) A plane is landing at an airport.

PART 2

7 🎧 호주식 발음 → 캐나다식 발음

How do you usually book your vacations?
(A) I'm open to all of those destinations.
(B) Here's a copy of the book.
(C) I use a travel agent.

8 🎧 영국식 발음 → 호주식 발음

I recommend purchasing the larger television for the studio.
(A) This is where the movie was filmed.
(B) OK, I'll consider it.
(C) That's my favorite show.

9 🎧 미국식 발음 → 캐나다식 발음

Does this dress shirt also come in white?
(A) I'll have to check.
(B) Fold down the collar, too.
(C) The black jeans look trendy.

10 🎧 영국식 발음 → 호주식 발음

Will my radio interview last for very long?
(A) Toward the end of the row.
(B) No more than 15 minutes.
(C) Oh, we talked about numerous issues.

11 🎧 캐나다식 발음 → 미국식 발음

Where did you find the extra training manuals?
(A) No, I didn't.
(B) Refer to page 34 to see it.
(C) In the supply closet.

12 🎧 미국식 발음 → 호주식 발음

Who typically manages Mr. Harper's schedule?
(A) His personal assistant, Ben.
(B) Sally usually shows up on time.
(C) Changes to the program schedule.

13 🎧 캐나다식 발음 → 영국식 발음

Who should I speak to about the proposal, Ms. Neilson or Mr. Shears?
(A) You shouldn't change the password.
(B) Have you written your acceptance speech?
(C) You should speak to both of them.

14 🎧 영국식 발음 → 호주식 발음

When can I expect the package to arrive?
(A) At the post office.
(B) Sometime next week.
(C) Because I sent it out yesterday.

15 캐나다식 발음 → 영국식 발음

The financial advisor hasn't dropped by yet, has he?
(A) No, the bank charges a monthly fee.
(B) He's visiting us next week.
(C) Thanks for your advice!

16 호주식 발음 → 미국식 발음

Could you give Ms. Delano directions to the train station?
(A) Sure, where is she now?
(B) The director's approval.
(C) It's a round-trip ticket.

17 미국식 발음 → 캐나다식 발음

One of the ovens in the café needs to be fixed.
(A) Apparently, the oven is available in silver.
(B) Both chefs are happy with the menu.
(C) Hopefully, a technician can come today.

18 영국식 발음 → 미국식 발음

You can work at the conference this weekend, can't you?
(A) I can't remember who was there.
(B) This is the right place.
(C) I'm available on Sunday.

19 호주식 발음 → 영국식 발음

Why is Mr. Liu sending a memo to staff members?
(A) Some of the original memos.
(B) I haven't been told the reason.
(C) Any worker can use it.

20 미국식 발음 → 캐나다식 발음

Our supervisor has offered to provide us with standing desks.
(A) Yes, the office needs better lighting.
(B) A drawer in my desk.
(C) I'm actually a fan of my current setup.

21 영국식 발음 → 호주식 발음

Would you like the order to be delivered to your front door?
(A) Yes, our hotel has vacancies.
(B) For the delivery person.
(C) That depends on when it arrives.

22 미국식 발음 → 캐나다식 발음

How many cars did our dealership sell this week?
(A) Records indicate a few dozen.
(B) Yes, it's on sale.
(C) My vehicle has excellent features.

23 캐나다식 발음 → 영국식 발음

Where should I place this box of cosmetics?
(A) A boxing match.
(B) I liked the makeup very much.
(C) There isn't any room here.

24 미국식 발음 → 호주식 발음

Which violin are you thinking about purchasing?
(A) And some other musical instruments.
(B) The one in the case, most likely.
(C) I bought them online.

25 호주식 발음 → 미국식 발음

Why don't we implement a summer internship program?
(A) Here are my spring travel plans.
(B) My internship starts next week.
(C) You should propose the idea to management.

26 캐나다식 발음 → 영국식 발음

Have Rebecca and James finished making graphs for the shareholders meeting?
(A) Only some of our stakeholders.
(B) To complete the entire lesson.
(C) I've got the graphs here.

27 호주식 발음 → 미국식 발음

Why can't Marcus work until 7 P.M. on Friday?
(A) Yes, he's very talented.
(B) Due to a medical appointment.
(C) It's currently 1 o'clock.

28 영국식 발음 → 호주식 발음

Is this project going to be discussed in person or via an online conference?
(A) The details haven't been announced.
(B) I assume you've visited the Web site before.
(C) What did they end up talking about?

29 캐나다식 발음 → 영국식 발음

Should I finish typing the staffing report for you?
(A) No, I'd rather do it myself.
(B) I like those types of dishes.
(C) Because of staffing problems.

30 호주식 발음 → 영국식 발음

Isn't the championship game tonight?
(A) It's going to be a great match.
(B) The delivery will arrive this evening.
(C) No, I prefer playing soccer.

31 미국식 발음 → 캐나다식 발음
When will the press statement be released to the local news media?
(A) I work at a regional newspaper.
(B) Not since the journalist called.
(C) Marcie said it will be a bit delayed.

PART 3

Questions 32-34 refer to the following conversation.
미국식 발음 → 캐나다식 발음

W: The sneakers our company released last month have been underperforming. I think we should put together a marketing campaign to raise awareness about them.
M: Yeah, that makes sense. However, I don't think we should use radio commercials like we did for our previous launch. They didn't effectively reach our target audience.
W: Actually, I think a social media campaign would be best. We can create banner advertisements and display them through online posts.
M: Good idea. But let's e-mail our director to get her input before making a final decision.

Questions 35-37 refer to the following conversation.
영국식 발음 → 호주식 발음

W: William, have you reviewed the invitation template I created for Richmond Library's reopening party?
M: Yes, but I noticed an issue. You wrote that the gathering will be held next Friday. However, the library's Web site says it's taking place next Thursday.
W: Well, when you were out sick yesterday, our team met with the head librarian. And she mentioned it will have to take place on Friday instead . . . uh . . . due to a scheduling conflict.
M: OK. In that case, the Web site will have to be updated. I'll call the head librarian now and tell her to do so.

Questions 38-40 refer to the following conversation.
영국식 발음 → 캐나다식 발음

W: Excuse me. Does your shop offer international shipping services? I'd like to get this teapot. But I'm worried it might break in my suitcase on my flight back to Spain.
M: We can't send items overseas, unfortunately. However, I can put the teapot in bubble wrap for you. That should protect it while you're traveling.
W: Wonderful . . . I love your store, by the way. I often travel to England and always stop in here.
M: Thank you. Would you like a card for our loyalty program then? You can earn points with everything you buy and use them to pay for future purchases.

Questions 41-43 refer to the following conversation with three speakers.
미국식 발음 → 영국식 발음 → 캐나다식 발음

W1: Ted and Megumi, the president of Norma Manufacturing just called. He's not pleased with the photos we recently took of his executive team.
W2: What's wrong with them?
W1: He said shadows are cast on people's faces, which makes it difficult to make out their features.
M: Don't worry. I can fix that issue with our digital editing software. I can brighten up the foreground a bit more.
W1: That's a relief! I thought we'd have to arrange another shoot. Um . . . I'm supposed to call the president's assistant this afternoon. So, Ted, how long will it take you to edit the photos?
M: A couple of hours. I'll upload the files to our server before 12 P.M.

Questions 44-46 refer to the following conversation.
호주식 발음 → 미국식 발음

M: Hello, Tina. It's me, Seth. I just got the package in the mail. Thank you for the sweater. It's so beautiful. You're a very talented knitter.
W: I'm glad you like it. I was actually thinking of selling my work.
M: Oh, do you know the flea market on Miller Street? There may be vacancies for vendors. It's just something I heard, though.
W: I doubt it. I spoke to a vendor the last time I went, and he said the market would be closing soon.
M: Maybe you should start your own e-commerce Web site. I have a friend who does very well selling jewelry online.

Questions 47-49 refer to the following conversation with three speakers.
호주식 발음 → 영국식 발음 → 미국식 발음

M: I want to replace the tiles on my kitchen floor since many of them have lost their color over time. Can either of you suggest a good flooring specialist?
W1: Tanya, didn't you have the same work done last year?
W2: I had carpeting installed in my living room. But the man I hired takes care of all types of flooring. His name is Frank, and his company is called HomeRefresh.
M: Actually, I already looked up HomeRefresh online, but I can't afford its high rates.
W1: Well, my neighbor recently remodeled his kitchen. Why don't I text him right now to see which

business he used? Maybe it will be a bit cheaper.

M: That would be very helpful. Thanks!

Questions 50-52 refer to the following conversation.

[3]] 캐나다식 발음 → 영국식 발음

M: Annabel, we need to plan a dinner for one of our biggest supporters, Henry Goodrich.

W: Oh, he's invested in our company for many years. When will he be in town?

M: He'll be here next Tuesday. I think it's important we take him out to dinner somewhere.

W: I agree. There's a new Thai place downtown that's getting great reviews for its creative dishes and excellent service. It's called the Chiang Rai Grill. Many of the reviewers say it's the best restaurant in town now.

M: Sounds like a good choice. Can you go ahead and make a reservation?

W: Sure. Before I do that, though, I want to confirm that Mr. Goodrich enjoys Thai food. I'll send him an e-mail.

Questions 53-55 refer to the following conversation.

[3]] 미국식 발음 → 캐나다식 발음

W: I recently discovered that we'll need some audiovisual devices for Jennifer Bailey's presentation at the Green Energy Conference. Apparently, she's decided to play video clips with her talk.

M: That's fine, but there will be an extra charge for the technical team at the event hall to set up everything.

W: I just got out of a meeting with our budgeting committee, and I'm sure we can handle that.

M: Great. I just have to edit our booking request on the hall's Web page to reflect this new requirement.

Questions 56-58 refer to the following conversation.

[3]] 영국식 발음 → 호주식 발음

W: Mr. Wesley, here's the completed inventory report you wanted. Ah . . . our shop is running low on stationery goods, like notebooks and pens.

M: OK. It seems that the free delivery service we offered in September helped us sell more of those items. Can you please order new stock by this weekend?

W: I was just about to do that. But I don't know what happened to the list of suppliers that used to be posted in the office.

M: Oh, sorry. It's locked in the top desk drawer because it contains confidential information. Let me grab a key for you to open that.

Questions 59-61 refer to the following conversation.

[3]] 미국식 발음 → 호주식 발음

W: Hello. This is Kelly McDermott from Sunshine Painters. We're scheduled to paint the outside of your realty office today. However, our truck just broke down, and we're unable to make it to your building this morning.

M: Oh, I'm sorry to hear that . . . When might you be able to do the work?

W: Well, the mechanic we spoke to said the vehicle will be fixed this evening. So, can we come by tomorrow?

M: That should be fine. I won't be at the office then, though, as I'm showing homes to prospective buyers all day. But my personal assistant Angela Dawson will be around. Once you arrive, she can answer any questions you may have.

Questions 62-64 refer to the following conversation and map.

[3]] 미국식 발음 → 캐나다식 발음

W: Charles, Jackson Street is gonna be closed this Thursday so new traffic lights can be installed. So, laboratory workers who use one of the lots on that road will need to park elsewhere. Could you send a memo informing staff?

M: Of course. Are there alternative arrangements for that day?

W: Yes. Our employees should park in the garage across from Bartow Manufacturing—you know, the one that's next to Pizza Palace.

M: But won't people be charged $15 to leave their cars there?

W: Our company will pay for employees to park there. They just have to submit an expense form along with the relevant receipts to be reimbursed.

Questions 65-67 refer to the following conversation and label.

[3]] 영국식 발음 → 호주식 발음

W: Thanks for rescheduling my personal training session, Devon. I can't come to the fitness center this afternoon today because I'm representing my company at a trade fair.

M: No problem. Should we get started with your workout?

W: Actually, I'd like to ask you about something first. My doctor recommends I take a supplement, and the PulseTrain Multivitamin offers 70 percent of the daily value for the vitamin I'm lacking. Have you heard of that brand before?

M: PulseTrain products are quite good. Um, I have some complimentary multivitamin packages that a PulseTrain representative left with me to hand out to my clients. Why don't you take one?

[캐나다식 발음 → 미국식 발음]

M: Sheryl, a word please? The talk on renewable energy is going to start 20 minutes behind schedule. The speaker texted to say cars are at a standstill on Highway 14.

W: OK. I'll notify the audience about the change.

M: Meanwhile, regarding the keynote lecture, over 200 people signed up to hear it.

W: I'm not surprised. Food waste is an important issue, and Andrea Parker has written a best-selling book on the topic.

M: Oh . . . I almost forgot. Sorry to say, but a valet parking driver called in sick. I know you're overseeing that team as well. Hopefully, you can make things work with one less person.

PART 4

Questions 71-73 refer to the following radio broadcast.

[캐나다식 발음]

Last week on *Around Town*, we talked about the new monument on Rockport Road. This time we'll focus on the renovations at Bloomington Medical Center. They've been in progress for six months and are now wrapping up. When the center opens its doors again next week, it will be considerably larger—with 25 percent more beds for patients and additional room for diagnostic equipment. I've got Director Roselyn Geddy on the phone right now. She's going to tell us about the ceremony that's been organized to mark the grand reopening.

Questions 74-76 refer to the following talk.

[호주식 발음]

I appreciate everyone coming today to make a laboratory training video for GenTech. I've spoken with Ms. Carver, GenTech's head researcher, about her hopes for the shoot. As chemicals are often used in GenTech's labs, she wants to focus on safety protocols. The video we're producing will demonstrate the correct procedures for dealing with any chemical spills or other laboratory accidents. There are some extra lab coats hanging on the wall. If all of you could please put one on, I'll begin preparing for the shoot.

Questions 77-79 refer to the following excerpt from a meeting.

[호주식 발음]

To start this meeting, I have some important news. Several government agencies have placed orders with us for laptops. As a result, 2,200 units of our latest computer models must be shipped out. They need the products next week, and today is Tuesday. My hope is that we'll be able to establish a long-term partnership with the government. So, let's all work hard to make sure this process goes as smoothly as possible.

Questions 80-82 refer to the following speech.

[영국식 발음]

Thank you all for joining me this evening to pay honor to legendary jazz musician Herb Jean. The statue of Mr. Jean being unveiled was made by sculptor Janice Longoria, who is herself a huge fan of the pianist. While many millions of people around the world have been moved by his music, very few know that he was raised right here in Brighton, England. That's why our city council decided to fund the creation of this incredible artwork. Even though Mr. Jean couldn't join us today due to tour obligations, he has informed us by letter just how grateful he is.

Questions 83-85 refer to the following advertisement.

[미국식 발음]

There's no better way to listen to music or your favorite podcasts than the Sable Portable Speaker from HomePerfect Electronics. The Sable has wireless connectivity, allowing users to stream content from the Internet without connecting any cables. Moreover, it is an entirely voice-controlled device, meaning you don't have to walk across the room every time you want to change songs or adjust the volume. Techtime Magazine gave it their highest rating. So what are you waiting for? Stop by your nearest major electronics retailer to try one out!

Questions 86-88 refer to the following talk.

[호주식 발음]

Thank you for attending today's lecture about global sports marketing. My name is Thomas Brast, and I'm going to present a slideshow about a marketing case study I did. The study, which involves the massive athletic apparel chain store Hashtag Goods, focuses on the impact social media advertising has on young adults worldwide. Following that, we'll watch a brief video regarding advertising methods used in various countries. I think you'll find it very informative as well as relevant as it compares practices common here in Canada to those in Egypt and Brazil. Now, let's get started.

Questions 89-91 refer to the following telephone message.

[미국식 발음]

Hi, Gavin. This is Carla from the product design team. I'm calling because I'm having trouble accessing my work e-mail through the company cell phone I received yesterday. Do you think you could come by my desk sometime today or tomorrow to help me resolve the matter? I'll have to get this done by Thursday morning at the latest since that's when I'll be leaving on a business trip for Madrid. I . . . ah . . . I'll be reporting back to headquarters during my trip about my client meetings, so this situation will have to be dealt with before then.

Questions 92-94 refer to the following speech.

[音] 캐나다식 발음

Once again, congratulations on being hired to lead tours for Auckland City Experience. We've come here to Auckland's main square because it's typically where we begin our city tour. Our customers are asked to arrive at least 10 minutes before their walking tour starts. You should be early as well to answer their questions. Remember! They are coming for the first time. This morning, the focus will be on our Heritage Tour. There are over a dozen attractions to visit around town. Pay close attention as we spend time at each location because this is our most popular route. Oh . . . but first let me hand out the relevant brochures.

Questions 95-97 refer to the following telephone message and list.

[音] 영국식 발음

Good afternoon. This is Iris calling from Hasberry Leather Goods. I'm sorry to tell you that our Web site was experiencing technical problems on the day you made your purchase. The handbag you bought is not actually in stock, even though the site indicated otherwise. This means that the delivery date will be postponed for one week—the package won't arrive at your address until September 15. And please note that the package will require a signature when it is dropped off at your residence. We're very sorry for the delay, and thank you for your business.

Questions 98-100 refer to the following telephone message and map.

[音] 미국식 발음

Good morning, Ms. Phelps. This is Debra calling from Ace Gardens. I just wanted to get in touch with you before my crew comes over this weekend. The orchids I originally included in the landscape plan aren't available right now, unfortunately. However, I was able to secure the magnolia trees from a local tree supplier. We will plant them in the area between the garden and the driveway. Also, you still want us to install decorative lights in your garden, right? Anyway, let me know what you'd like us to replace the orchids with. There are some options listed on our business Web site. Thank you!

PART 1

1 캐나다식 발음
(A) He is painting a fence.
(B) He is plugging in a device.
(C) He is talking on a phone.
(D) He is riding a bicycle.

2 미국식 발음
(A) They are unrolling a large rug.
(B) They are turning toward a bookcase.
(C) They are setting down some pillows.
(D) They are bending over to lift a sofa.

3 호주식 발음
(A) The man is writing on a clipboard.
(B) The man is looking into a container.
(C) The man is labeling a box.
(D) The man is emptying out a bin.

4 영국식 발음
(A) One of the women is removing her coat.
(B) One of the women is examining a document.
(C) The women are stepping onto an elevator.
(D) The women are descending a staircase.

5 캐나다식 발음
(A) Students are raising their hands.
(B) Papers are being distributed.
(C) Some furniture has been arranged in a circle.
(D) Whiteboards are on the classroom wall.

6 호주식 발음
(A) Chairs are being set up.
(B) The bottles are being filled with water.
(C) Some pictures have been hung.
(D) A laptop is being used at a meeting.

PART 2

7 영국식 발음 → 호주식 발음
Can you recommend a place to get my car washed?
(A) Yes, I'll text you the address.
(B) I drive to work every day.
(C) There's a dry cleaner on Main Street.

8 캐나다식 발음 → 영국식 발음
Where should I hang this team photograph?
(A) Anytime next week.
(B) A black and white photo.
(C) On the conference room wall.

9 영국식 발음 → 호주식 발음
Is the strategic business report due tomorrow?
(A) Behind the office printer.
(B) Vinnie Hansen works at that firm.
(C) There's extra time because our boss is away.

10 미국식 발음 → 캐나다식 발음
Why do you prefer this tablet?
(A) Its screen is a good size.
(B) OK, I'll switch it on.
(C) I don't know why it stopped.

11 영국식 발음 → 미국식 발음
Are these your bags, or do they belong to someone else?
(A) It was a memorable trip.
(B) This bag is pretty heavy.
(C) I believe they belong to that woman there.

12 캐나다식 발음 → 호주식 발음
Who is in charge of scheduling the roof repairs?
(A) Is there a problem?
(B) On Friday afternoon.
(C) I've got to hand it to you.

13 미국식 발음 → 영국식 발음
The dance studio is at the end of Maple Street, right?
(A) A dance competition.
(B) Yes, it is.
(C) At the beginning of the book.

14 호주식 발음 → 미국식 발음
When will you visit Andrew's house to drop off his coat?
(A) I stopped by there this morning.
(B) He has a black jacket.
(C) Visitors are waiting to be let in.

15 [3μ] 미국식 발음 → 캐나다식 발음

How did customers react to our latest TV commercial?
(A) Better than expected.
(B) I didn't hear how the match went.
(C) I'll be sure to let them know.

16 [3μ] 캐나다식 발음 → 미국식 발음

Could you double-check the sales figures in the annual report for me?
(A) That's our best-selling product.
(B) Sure. I'll look over it.
(C) My annual checkup is scheduled for next week.

17 [3μ] 영국식 발음 → 호주식 발음

Please don't forget to give these documents to the factory owner.
(A) A major manufacturing plant.
(B) I'll give the gloves to them.
(C) Thanks for the reminder.

18 [3μ] 미국식 발음 → 캐나다식 발음

Who should I select for the Employee of the Month award?
(A) I'm in complete agreement.
(B) The receptionist is quite deserving.
(C) During the selection process.

19 [3μ] 호주식 발음 → 영국식 발음

Our company newsletter is distributed once a month, isn't it?
(A) Every two weeks, actually.
(B) It contains useful information.
(C) On June 2.

20 [3μ] 캐나다식 발음 → 미국식 발음

Where should we have lunch today?
(A) Yes, we should.
(B) Oh, I can look for a place online.
(C) I've eaten there before.

21 [3μ] 호주식 발음 → 영국식 발음

Did any of the investors call you back?
(A) Here's my phone number.
(B) I've heard from Mr. Stevens.
(C) We invest in the stocks.

22 [3μ] 미국식 발음 → 캐나다식 발음

Why are we testing the new product at the end of July?
(A) That's when the prototype will be ready.
(B) I'm more productive in the morning.
(C) Oh, they're resting in the lobby.

23 [3μ] 호주식 발음 → 미국식 발음

When is Grand Avenue Books closing down?
(A) No, in three hours.
(B) They're closer than I thought.
(C) I'm pretty sure it already did.

24 [3μ] 미국식 발음 → 호주식 발음

Can't we move into this office space in August?
(A) We removed that device in advance.
(B) A new exhibit on outer space.
(C) An earlier date has been scheduled.

25 [3μ] 영국식 발음 → 캐나다식 발음

What was the best part of your vacation?
(A) Later tomorrow evening.
(B) Learning about the island's local history.
(C) For some vocational training.

26 [3μ] 호주식 발음 → 미국식 발음

Are the laptops set up for the newly recruited researchers?
(A) I just called technical support about that.
(B) No, the recruiter is.
(C) It's at the top of this legal form.

27 [3μ] 캐나다식 발음 → 미국식 발음

There's a minor leak in the hose beside the garage.
(A) OK, I'll go and take a look at it.
(B) No, it's a major award.
(C) I usually park my car inside.

28 [3μ] 영국식 발음 → 캐나다식 발음

Chris, would you book a taxi to pick up our clients from the airport?
(A) The delivery should arrive by then.
(B) I don't know how many people are coming.
(C) Parking is not allowed here.

29 [3μ] 영국식 발음 → 호주식 발음

Is the function hall going to be suitable, or is a larger venue required?
(A) That's right, a sales event.
(B) We need a bigger one.
(C) We're not going to be carpooling.

30 [3μ] 캐나다식 발음 → 호주식 발음

Can I make it to the immigration office within 45 minutes?
(A) Only if you drive down Highway 70.
(B) The officer left yesterday.
(C) It wasn't made very well.

호주식 발음 → 미국식 발음

How many publishers have shown interest in your novel?
(A) Five or six more novelists.
(B) The book has been praised by critics.
(C) I'm in contact with a couple at the moment.

PART 3

Questions 32-34 refer to the following conversation.

캐나다식 발음 → 미국식 발음

M: Welcome to City Hall. How can I assist you?
W: I'm looking for the recreation department. I'm running late for my meeting with Mr. Baxter this morning. He requested a presentation on the summer sports program my organization is planning.
M: You must be Dana Royce. We've been expecting you! The recreation department is on the third floor. I'll call Mr. Baxter now and tell him that you're here. The elevators are just to your right.
W: I'll go upstairs now. Thanks for your help!

Questions 35-37 refer to the following conversation.

호주식 발음 → 영국식 발음

M: Did you hear that Greg Colson will transfer to our Scottsdale branch?
W: Yes. Our department head wants me to recommend someone to take over the public relations team that Greg has been managing.
M: Is there anyone in particular you are considering for the position?
W: I was thinking of Brad Chan. He has worked here for several years and has been involved in some major projects. He wrote the press release when our firm purchased Polson Incorporated last year.
M: That's true. But what about Linda Ferris? She has a lot of experience as well.
W: Hmm . . . Good point. I've got to attend a training seminar now, but I'll go through her personnel record afterward.

Questions 38-40 refer to the following conversation.

미국식 발음 → 캐나다식 발음

W: This is the front desk of the Harborview Hotel. How may I help you?
M: Hello. I have a conference call at 3 P.M., but I can't connect to the wireless Internet in my suite.
W: I'm so sorry for the inconvenience, sir. Did you check your printed receipt? You have to enter the password for your specific room.
M: Yes, but it did not work.
W: Oh, I'm not sure exactly what the problem is then. While I'm looking into it, you can use the business lounge near our main entrance. There's complimentary wireless Internet.

Questions 41-43 refer to the following conversation.

호수식 발음 → 미국식 발음

M: Hello, and welcome to the Durban Fiction Seminar. May I have your name, please?
W: Sure. It's Janna Kruger.
M: Hmm . . . I don't seem to have a name tag here for you. Did you preregister online for the event?
W: I meant to, but I completely forgot about it until the registration period had ended. However, I was able to buy a ticket at the entrance.
M: In that case, you should go back to the admissions counter and ask the person working there to make you a name tag.

Questions 44-46 refer to the following conversation.

영국식 발음 → 캐나다식 발음

W: Thank you for calling the Cherry Tea Factory.
M: Hi. I signed up for a tour online this morning, but I haven't received a follow-up e-mail. I just wanted to make sure that my request has been processed.
W: Could I get your name, please?
M: Sure. It's Sam Redmond. Um, I selected the 2 P.M. tour on Saturday.
W: Just a moment . . . Um . . . It's odd that you weren't notified. Group of four, right?
M: Yes. Is there anything else I need to do?
W: Just pay the $15 fee when you arrive. Keep in mind that we only accept credit cards.

Questions 47-49 refer to the following conversation.

영국식 발음 → 캐나다식 발음

W: Mr. Sasaki, I recently received some new fabric from my supplier in India. It's a mixture of cotton and silk. Um . . . And it is mostly dark blue. Would you like to see it?
M: Thanks for letting me know, but that's not really what I'm looking for. The spring collection I'm designing for my clothing brand has to feature bright colors with some unique flower patterns.
W: Well, maybe I should ask my supplier to send several different fabric samples for you to look at. I could do that this week, if you'd like.
M: Good idea. That way I can choose the ones best suited for my collection before an order is placed.

Questions 50-52 refer to the following conversation with three speakers.

영국식 발음 → 호주식 발음 → 캐나다식 발음

W: I just had a meeting with Mr. Lewis. He complained that our advertising firm's logo is outdated. He wants us to start brainstorming ways to update it.
M1: That's a good idea. Luke and I were talking about

this a few weeks ago. We need a more modern logo design.

M2: Right. We should begin soon, I guess. Um, why don't I book the meeting room for this afternoon?

W: Not quite yet, Luke. Hold off until Maria Sutherland returns from her business trip to Paris. She recently joined our design team, and I want her to participate in the process as well.

Questions 53-55 refer to the following conversation.

호주식 발음 → 미국식 발음

M: Hello, Ms. Brandon. This is Mark Lawrence calling to let you know we've started working on the chairs specified in your order. Um . . . But we'll send them in two shipments because the trucks can only hold 50 units each.

W: No problem. We placed a larger order than usual this time. When will the shipments be delivered to our shop?

M: Well, I still have to confirm the exact date with the shipping company. I'll let you know by this Friday.

W: Excellent. Just make sure the items arrive before June 11—the first day of our summer sale.

Questions 56-58 refer to the following conversation with three speakers.

미국식 발음 → 영국식 발음 → 캐나다식 발음

W1: Hey, Lucy. Max and I are going to see *Northward* at Central Cinema. It starts at 7 P.M. Do you want to come with us?

W2: Actually, I need to stay at the office until 8 P.M. today. I'm getting everything ready for next week's board meeting.

M: Well, according to the schedule, there's another showing at 8:30 P.M.

W1: Would you be able to join us then?

W2: I think so. Um . . . I can't drive there, though. My car is currently being repaired.

M: We live in the same neighborhood, so why don't we share a taxi both ways?

W2: That would work.

Questions 59-61 refer to the following conversation.

호주식 발음 → 미국식 발음

M: Several employees have complained that the desks are uncomfortable at our office. Apparently, they're too high, and they can't be adjusted. What do you think?

W: Honestly, I agree with the staff. I know other companies use adjustable standing desks. They're very popular since workers have the option of either standing or sitting.

M: Hmm . . . Could you please look for some suitable options online and send me your findings by e-mail?

W: Sure. I'll get that information to you by 5 P.M. today.

M: Wonderful. In the meantime, I'll have Mr. Roland go around to each employee's workspace and ask about their preferences for new desks.

Questions 62-64 refer to the following conversation and receipt.

호주식 발음 → 영국식 발음

M: Welcome to Frasier Decorative Goods.

W: I bought this window blind here yesterday. But when I tried to hang it at home, I realized that it's too short. I want to return it, please.

M: Certainly. We stock blinds manufactured by Vincentio, Perfect Home, and others. Would you like to browse some of these?

W: I think I'll order some new curtains online. So, I'd rather just get a refund, actually.

M: All right. Do you have your receipt?

W: Yes. Here it is along with the credit card I used for my purchase.

M: OK. Give me a minute to make sure there is no damage, and then I'll process your refund.

Questions 65-67 refer to the following conversation and catalog.

미국식 발음 → 캐나다식 발음

W: We just got the new line of covers for laptop computers. There are several designs, and customers can even create their own using the manufacturer's online design tool.

M: Oh, customers are always asking about creating their own laptop covers.

W: We should create some sample designs using the customization tool so that customers know about the feature.

M: Good idea.

W: Since the face design is easy to modify, it will probably be very popular.

M: That should be our first sample, then.

W: Right, but we've got a lot of promotions going on. The tool might not draw as much attention as we expect.

M: Maybe we should post about it on social media.

W: I'll work on that.

Questions 68-70 refer to the following conversation and list.

호주식 발음 → 영국식 발음

M: Excuse me. I noticed a flyer the other day that said your store not only sells instruments but also offers music classes for beginners. Is that true?

W: That's right. We employ multiple instructors, all of whom are very experienced. Is there a particular instrument that you want to try?

M: I'm already familiar with the piano and violin. My current goal is to learn how to play guitar. Since

I have no experience, I'll need a very patient teacher.

W: We've got just the person to help you out. Now, let's head over to the counter. We can figure out a time that works for you and get you signed up for classes.

PART 4

Questions 71-73 refer to the following talk.

[3개] 미국식 발음

I'd like to thank everyone on the board of directors for coming to this year's strategy meeting. We're going to follow the same agenda that we had in previous years. This morning, we'll hear reports from the heads of the finance and product design departments. After lunch, we'll talk about revenue projections for the coming year. And at 3 P.M., we'll have an in-depth discussion about the mobile phone applications that we'll be releasing soon and how they can be used to capture a greater share of the market. Now, before we get started with those activities, I'd like to take the next few minutes to distribute some handouts.

Questions 74-76 refer to the following telephone message.

[3개] 캐나다식 발음

Hello, Ms. Brock. This is Matthew Zender from *Music Magazine*. I'm wondering if I could set up a photo shoot with you for next week. I'd like to take your picture in Pembroke Concert Hall, as you were recently named conductor of the regional orchestra. The images will be used in an upcoming article about . . . ah . . . the orchestra's new leadership. I realize that you have a busy schedule, but I'm guessing it'll just be half an hour or so. Could you please call our office and let me know whether you'd be interested?

Questions 77-79 refer to the following advertisement.

[3개] 호주식 발음

Are you looking for a unique hobby? Do you need more ways to express your creative side? If so, then come to the pottery class at the Midtown Artist Loft! We can accommodate people with a wide range of skill levels, from beginners to longtime enthusiasts. And from May to July, our visiting instructor will be Diego Bello, who has displayed his collection of vases at gallery events across Europe. Visit the Midtown Artist Loft online to see photos of our students' handmade pieces and to enroll today!

Questions 80-82 refer to the following excerpt from a meeting.

[3개] 영국식 발음

I know that you all are still new to our firm's accounting department and have yet to master our software for tracking travel reimbursements. However, entering and updating requests from staff is an important part of your job. And since some of you have mentioned that you find the software confusing, I've organized a training session on the matter. I've asked Mr. Nunes, a technology specialist, to explain the software. His talk shouldn't take more than 15 minutes. Before he begins, though, please pick up one of the software user guides from the stack on the table. He will be referring to this document throughout the workshop.

Questions 83-85 refer to the following announcement.

[3개] 미국식 발음

Thank you all for coming tonight to help raise money for our nonprofit dental organization, Clean Teeth. My name is Ashani Mia, and I'm the president of Clean Teeth. Now, before we begin, I'd like to make some brief announcements. First, I've prepared various brochures detailing past and current projects, such as our most recent initiative with low-income families in Detroit. They have been laid out on the table near the entrance. Second, the auction won't start until 7 P.M., but I suggest you check out the various donated goods up for auction. That way, you can familiarize yourself with the items, which will make the bidding process easier later.

Questions 86-88 refer to the following telephone message.

[3개] 영국식 발음

Good morning, Mr. Collins. My name is Alice Lee, and I'm calling to welcome you on behalf of our local neighborhood association. The organization was founded last year to help people who move into our area settle in. I have a welcome basket for you, which is filled with homemade treats from association members as well as coupons donated by local businesses. I'd like to bring it to your house within the week. The visit will only take a few minutes, although I'd be happy to stay longer to answer any questions you might have. Please call me back at the number I've used to reach you to set up a time.

Questions 89-91 refer to the following broadcast.

[3개] 캐나다식 발음

In other news, the Woodward County Fair will be held from October 2 to October 5 in Abbott City. The regional event will feature carnival rides, games, and amazing food. Also, a visual arts tent will be set up this year for the first time in order to promote artists from around the area. And as was done at past events, several bands will hold shows each afternoon. Finally, a special children's zone will include singers, clowns, and magicians. General admission tickets will be sold at the entrance gate of Hansen Park on each day of the event.

Questions 92–94 refer to the following talk.

3)) 미국식 발음

Starting next week, our orchestra hall is going to start accepting digital tickets in addition to traditional paper ones. In order to process a digital pass, you will have to scan the ticket barcode that is on the customer's smartphone. This can be done on the new machines that we had hooked up this morning. Although this will require staff to learn a new process, recent trends are clear. These days, smartphones are used in all sorts of ways. OK, I'd like you all to follow me to the front desk, so I can show everyone how to properly use the scanners.

Questions 95–97 refer to the following announcement and mall directory.

3)) 호주식 발음

Attention all Gibson Mall shoppers. This summer marks a number of changes to our shopping center. In addition to adding three new rides to our Wacky World amusement park, our food court has been expanded. Just this week, a brand new fast food restaurant—Burrito House—opened for business. To celebrate their opening, customers can get an order of chips and salsa at no additional cost with any entrée. But that's not all. Gibson Mall is also hosting many events these days! For instance, children's book author Jemma Harrison will be signing autographs to promote her newest publication. This event will take place at Readtopia from 1 to 3 P.M.

Questions 98–100 refer to the following excerpt from a meeting and survey.

3)) 영국식 발음

Since sales have been weak at our branch of Petra Motors for a while, the marketing department manager, Dan McGee, conducted an extensive customer survey about three months ago. After reviewing the feedback, we implemented some changes and then conducted a follow-up survey last week. Our lowest-scoring category last year is now our highest-rated one. That's certainly good news. However, customers are still not very impressed with our showroom's interior design and the speed of our services. I've put together a brief slide show that covers both of these issues, which I'll show you now. It offers multiple suggestions about how our mechanics can speed up their workflow.

* 무료 해석은 해커스토익(Hackers.co.kr)에서
다운로드 받을 수 있습니다.

• QR 코드로
바로가기

PART 1

1 캐나다식 발음
   (A) A kayak has been left on a beach.
   (B) The man is getting out of a boat.
   (C) A swimmer has jumped into a river.
   (D) The man is holding on to some paddles.

2 영국식 발음
   (A) Some people are checking information on a screen.
   (B) Some people are waiting in a line.
   (C) Some people are typing on keyboards.
   (D) Some people are filling out forms.

3 미국식 발음
   (A) Some water is spraying into the air.
   (B) A group is biking down the street.
   (C) A tourist is taking a photograph.
   (D) A man is looking at a map.

4 캐나다식 발음
   (A) He's holding up a machine's lid.
   (B) He's stacking some binders.
   (C) He's filing documents in an office.
   (D) He's getting up from a stool.

5 미국식 발음
   (A) Spectators are exiting a theater.
   (B) A staircase is positioned below a seating area.
   (C) Some people are performing on a stage.
   (D) Audience members are clapping their hands.

6 호주식 발음
   (A) Some lines are being painted on asphalt.
   (B) A ship is sailing under a bridge.
   (C) Some vehicles are parked in a row.
   (D) A road has been blocked off to pedestrians.

PART 2

7 캐나다식 발음 → 미국식 발음
   Who has the keys to the storage room?
   (A) That's a key position in the store.
   (B) We need to count our inventory.
   (C) Mr. Perez in the maintenance team.

8 호주식 발음 → 영국식 발음
   When should we meet at the bus station?
   (A) For the bus driver.
   (B) Anytime after 1:30 P.M.
   (C) Yes, I can meet then.

9 캐나다식 발음 → 호주식 발음
   How much more equipment do we need to order?
   (A) We have enough machines.
   (B) The order number.
   (C) It's equipped with a sensor.

10 영국식 발음 → 호주식 발음
   The sales meeting won't last all morning, will it?
   (A) Mostly online revenue.
   (B) No, just 30 minutes.
   (C) It's 10 feet long.

11 캐나다식 발음 → 미국식 발음
   Ms. Gordon left her purse on my desk.
   (A) I'll let her know.
   (B) The bag is discounted right now.
   (C) Head left at the intersection.

12 호주식 발음 → 영국식 발음
   Have you been to Benson Stadium since it was expanded?
   (A) I've known them since college.
   (B) Tickets for a game.
   (C) Yes, just last weekend.

13 호주식 발음 → 미국식 발음
   You should leave now for your appointment.
   (A) It was with a few clients.
   (B) The flight left on time.
   (C) Yes, there could be heavy traffic.

14 캐나다식 발음 → 영국식 발음
   Which photo should we use for the magazine's cover?
   (A) I can take photos of those.
   (B) The one on the left is the best.
   (C) The publication is quite popular.

15 ③ 호주식 발음 → 미국식 발음

How many of us are going to Sheldon's birthday party?
(A) Deloris can't come, so just 10.
(B) It's only partly painted.
(C) Most of the billing statements.

16 ③ 캐나다식 발음 → 영국식 발음

Where was the pack of printer paper set?
(A) For a copy machine.
(B) Cindy should know.
(C) Yes, I'll get it.

17 ③ 호주식 발음 → 미국식 발음

Has the finance team responded to your reimbursement request?
(A) No, nobody has contacted me yet.
(B) That's his department.
(C) To my checking account.

18 ③ 캐나다식 발음 → 영국식 발음

Do you know why the road is blocked?
(A) For a few days, I think.
(B) On Yale Street.
(C) There was a bad accident.

19 ③ 미국식 발음 → 캐나다식 발음

How did the medical convention go?
(A) Actually, I didn't participate in it.
(B) Conference Room 1 is available.
(C) I have a medical degree.

20 ③ 영국식 발음 → 호주식 발음

Please tell the shipping clerk that the package must arrive by noon on Wednesday.
(A) Overnight delivery rates.
(B) OK, I will.
(C) I got there on Friday.

21 ③ 호주식 발음 → 미국식 발음

When is the play *Lost in Time* running?
(A) A brief intermission.
(B) For another week.
(C) In about an hour.

22 ③ 캐나다식 발음 → 미국식 발음

I'd like to renew my monthly subscription to *Business Insight*.
(A) A seminar during October.
(B) I'm happy to help with that.
(C) No, we have few subscribers.

23 ③ 영국식 발음 → 호주식 발음

What messaging program should we use in the office?
(A) They should be arriving soon.
(B) I haven't seen him around today.
(C) Didn't you get Mr. Jackson's e-mail?

24 ③ 영국식 발음 → 캐나다식 발음

Did the sellers accept our final offer on the house, or did they reject it?
(A) We sold more properties last year.
(B) The open house was on Tuesday.
(C) Our agent said they agreed to it.

25 ③ 미국식 발음 → 호주식 발음

Why was I assigned to the Greenway Project?
(A) Because the door is locked.
(B) Mr. Dobson made that decision, not me.
(C) I'll consider your proposal.

26 ③ 캐나다식 발음 → 영국식 발음

Can't we stop for coffee on the way to work?
(A) Thanks for the tea.
(B) If there's enough time.
(C) I'm fine with my current job.

27 ③ 미국식 발음 → 영국식 발음

Which of the people who auditioned for the TV program do you like?
(A) It was an action film.
(B) I really like the dessert.
(C) They all did outstandingly well.

28 ③ 호주식 발음 → 미국식 발음

Are you still planning to go to the art show in the park this weekend?
(A) Park anywhere you like.
(B) They look good on your wall.
(C) It depends on the weather.

29 ③ 영국식 발음 → 캐나다식 발음

Could you send me a copy of the tax file?
(A) A copy of the updated schedule.
(B) The accountant will bring it tomorrow.
(C) We received a fine for paying it late.

30 ③ 미국식 발음 → 캐나다식 발음

We're still planning to go to the technology trade show, right?
(A) We don't need the parts any longer.
(B) Let me check with Bailey on that.
(C) Yes, we're planning on buying a few.

31 🔊 호주식 발음 → 영국식 발음

May I please talk to Mr. Himura from the marketing division?
(A) The talk was quite short.
(B) No, it was for a promotional campaign.
(C) Please hold while I transfer your call.

PART 3

Questions 32-34 refer to the following conversation.
🔊 호주식 발음 → 영국식 발음

M: Hey, Pauline. Have you registered for the engineering seminar in Beijing yet? I've just booked my flight there.
W: Not yet. I tried yesterday, but the event's Web site wasn't working.
M: Then you should probably just do it over the phone since registration ends today.
W: Good idea. I definitely don't want to miss out on the event.
M: Definitely not. I heard the famous engineer Eli Price will be a guest speaker. He actually developed the machines we use in our factory.
W: I know. I'm reading the book he published last month. He has some interesting ideas about robotics.

Questions 35-37 refer to the following conversation.
🔊 미국식 발음 → 호주식 발음

W: Sales of our dresses and pants have dropped by 5 percent since we started selling them through the Hadley Outlet.
M: Yes, Nancy told me about that after she finished analyzing last quarter's financial figures. That's a big problem, isn't it?
W: Absolutely. Accordingly, I've arranged an appointment with one of Hadley Outlet's representatives so we can brainstorm ways to boost revenues. We'll be getting together next Wednesday at 3 P.M., if you want to join us.
M: I wish I could, but I'm scheduled to train our interns on the accounting software that afternoon. Please e-mail me the notes from the meeting, though. I'd like to review what you discuss.

Questions 38-40 refer to the following conversation.
🔊 호주식 발음 → 영국식 발음

M: The weather forecast is not very favorable for the charity run on Saturday. It's supposed to be extremely hot with intense sunlight. What shall we do?
W: There isn't anything we can really do as postponing the event isn't an option. Let's prepare more

shades, water bottles, and ice boxes.
M: Good idea. Should we hire medical staff in case some of the runners can't handle the heat?
W: Some doctors are volunteering. I'd like them to be spread out along the route.
M: OK. I'll figure out the best places for them now.

Questions 41-43 refer to the following conversation.
🔊 호주식 발음 → 미국식 발음

M: Ms. Kearney, we're almost done bringing your belongings into your new home. Ah . . . but where should I place these boxes marked as decorations?
W: Oh, those are the ornaments for my living room. Please put them on the floor by the brown cabinet.
M: All right. That's everything, then. Would you like our company to e-mail you the invoice, or would it be better to mail you a paper copy?
W: An e-mail would be great, thanks. You should have my contact information on record. Do you happen to know how much my bill will be?
M: Yes. You'll be charged a flat rate of $350.

Questions 44-46 refer to the following conversation with three speakers.
🔊 미국식 발음 → 캐나다식 발음 → 영국식 발음

W1: Everyone, we're planning to open another branch of our public relations company in Tacoma.
M: Wow . . . That decision was made quickly! I thought the CEO wouldn't approve that until next year.
W2: Me too. It makes sense, though. Many companies are located there, so it's a promising market for us.
M: Right. Um . . . Kara, do you know who will manage the new branch?
W1: No, but the executive team will discuss that in next Thursday's meeting. I heard they are planning to consider both internal and external candidates.
M: Well, you should submit an application. You'd be a perfect fit.
W1: Thanks. I might give it a try.

Questions 47-49 refer to the following conversation.
🔊 캐나다식 발음 → 미국식 발음

M: My name is Tim Jones, and I'm calling to report a defective appliance. My order number is 44312.
W: Just a minute, Mr. Jones . . . OK, our records show that you ordered a Steelman 90B stove. Is that correct?
M: I purchased a Gateway 350. Again, the order number is 44312.
W: Oh, I misheard the last digit. My apologies. Yes, I see your purchase information now. What exactly is the problem?
M: I'm not sure. When I press the power button, nothing happens.

W: I see. Would you like me to arrange a time for a repairperson to visit your home?

M: Yes, please. Any time before noon on Friday would be convenient for me.

Questions 50-52 refer to the following conversation.

호주식 발음 → 영국식 발음

M: Hello, Ms. Beale. This is Dan Feingold from *BizLife Magazine*. Do you have any interest in being interviewed for our publication? We'd like to write a piece on your recently published book on management strategies.

W: Absolutely. I'm a big fan of your magazine!

M: That's wonderful to hear. Would you be able to come to our office in downtown Portland on Friday afternoon for the interview?

W: Actually, I'm having lunch with my company's CEO that day. Saturday is more convenient for me.

M: We can manage that. Oh, and are you willing to pose for some pictures? We want to print them next to the article.

W: Of course.

Questions 53-55 refer to the following conversation.

미국식 발음 → 캐나다식 발음

W: Good morning. My name is Maureen Price. I came to your office a week ago to discuss a Web site you said you could design for the new amateur baseball team that I manage.

M: Oh, right. Have you decided which features you'd like to include?

W: Yes. I'll need a page where people can reserve tickets. There should be a schedule of games, too.

M: Do you want any video content to be featured as well? We only charge an extra $100 to do so.

W: We intend to put up players' photos—but not any videos.

M: OK. Please take a seat, and I'll get a quote ready for you. It should only take a few minutes.

Questions 56-58 refer to the following conversation.

영국식 발음 → 캐나다식 발음

W: These crates are too heavy, Mike. We can't move them from this loading dock to the warehouse without using the truck.

M: But Kevin is using the truck right now. And we need to move this shipment before lunchtime.

W: Kevin told me earlier today that he'd be back by 11 A.M. So . . . uh . . . he should be here any minute now.

M: Oh, OK. In that case, I'll wait for him. In the meantime, could you please double-check that the crates are labeled properly? We've had issues with that in the past.

Questions 59-61 refer to the following conversation with three speakers.

캐나다식 발음 → 미국식 발음 → 영국식 발음

M: Unfortunately, our ski resort has had low occupancy numbers over the last few months. Could you two propose some ways to attract more visitors?

W1: How about building a new spa?

M: That's a nice thought, but we can't afford to build any new structures.

W2: Then why don't we create a sledding course? Guests could go up the mountain using our cable car and then sled down.

M: I like that. Our biggest competitor has something similar. Anything to add, Connie?

W1: Yes. I know several guests have mentioned that room rates are rather high. How about offering discounted prices as a promotion?

M: Excellent suggestions. I'll mention both ideas at the executive meeting this afternoon.

Questions 62-64 refer to the following conversation and e-mail inbox.

영국식 발음 → 캐나다식 발음

W: Tom, I want to let you know that I'm almost finished with the seating chart for Friday's banquet. I'm trying to seat all the winners near the front of the venue.

M: Yes, they should have easy access to the stage. And that reminds me. We got an e-mail from the caterer for the event about 30 minutes ago. Have you read it yet?

W: No. I've been focused on getting this chart finished. Beeman Corporation expanded its guest list this morning. Did the e-mail indicate that there will be some problems?

M: Everything's fine as we decided on the menu a month ago. The message just mentioned the number of vegetarian meals that will be provided.

Questions 65-67 refer to the following conversation and coupon.

호주식 발음 → 미국식 발음

M: Excuse me. I need a printer for my home office. Where are they stocked?

W: Oh, they're right over here. Do you have a specific brand in mind?

M: Well, I had a PaperPro device before, and I really liked it. So, something from that brand would be excellent.

W: I'd recommend the PaperPro 300, then. Um . . . Our store received them from the manufacturer just last Monday. They're even more user-friendly than previous models.

M: Perfect. I'll take one of those, please.

W: Certainly. Also, do you need any paper for the

printer? If so, here's a discount coupon for you to use. We're having a sale on those items today.

M: I'll take two packs.

Questions 68-70 refer to the following conversation and form.

[3w] 캐나다식 발음 → 영국식 발음

M: Good afternoon. I was biking this morning and noticed that my bicycle is making a lot of noise.

W: Let me take a look . . . Hmm . . . Quite a few parts need to be updated.

M: I see. Would you be able to take care of that today?

W: No, unfortunately. The parts have to be ordered. We could have it fixed by next week. As for the cost, let me check on everything . . . All right, the total will be $195.

M: That's pretty expensive! Is there any way to lower the price?

W: I suppose the chain you have will be OK for another few months.

M: Great. I'll get a new one later, then.

PART 4

Questions 71-73 refer to the following announcement.

[3w] 호주식 발음

May I have your attention, shoppers? A sweater was found in our bakery section. It was left beside a sale sign and is gray with a black stripe across the back. If this item belongs to you, come to the information desk, which is situated next to our milk and cheese aisle . . . Also, I'd like to remind everyone that Smiling Grocery recently introduced a new service. Buy as many goods as you like, and we'll bring them to your residence within an hour, as long as you live here in Allensville.

Questions 74-76 refer to the following telephone message.

[3w] 미국식 발음

Hi, Paul. This is Becky Landers. I looked over your proposal for redesigning my kitchen. I really like your choice of counter—the color matches the tiles on the wall. But regarding, um, the sink you picked out . . . I think it would be better to do things differently. I live by myself. So, it would be great if you could recommend a smaller model instead. Can we meet at 4 P.M. to discuss it? I think that would be more efficient than doing it on the phone.

Questions 77-79 refer to the following announcement.

[3w] 영국식 발음

I want you all to meet Ahmed Pearce, our new managing director. Mr. Pearce has overseen public

relations firms like ours for over a decade now, so he has plenty of experience. He's also received the Carter Prize from the National PR Society. I'm sure you'll all appreciate working under him. I've arranged for some bagels, muffins, and coffee to be delivered to our break room tomorrow morning for you to enjoy while introducing yourself to Mr. Pearce.

Questions 80-82 refer to the following excerpt from a meeting.

[3w] 캐나다식 발음

I'm sure you're all as eager as I am to see the new company logo that our graphic design team has been working on. It will be unveiled next week at the trade show, after which we'll give each of our clients small presents with the logo on them. For instance, we're planning to hand out pens as well as key chains. If you have ideas for other items we could distribute, I'm open to them. The more, the better.

Questions 83-85 refer to the following broadcast.

[3w] 영국식 발음

This is Haley Woodson, and you're listening to *Movies Today* on WMMZ 99.5 Radio. This morning, I'll be interviewing director Marcy Sawyer about her latest documentary film, *Wild Serengeti*, which was released just two weeks ago. It contains never-before-seen footage of endangered animals living in western Africa and advocates for the protection of wildlife in that region. In just a moment, Ms. Sawyer will tell us all about her joys and struggles living and working abroad for nearly four months. Critics have loved the film, and I've got no reason to doubt them. But first, let's take a few minutes to listen to the morning news highlights from our reporter Shirley Quinn.

Questions 86-88 refer to the following telephone message.

[3w] 캐나다식 발음

Hi, Clara. This is Shawn from BeBelle Hair Salon. I'm calling you regarding your cutting and styling appointment today with Steve. Unfortunately, he is running late today, and we're wondering whether you're open to coming an hour later than originally planned. I know this is an inconvenience, and we're very sorry. If you agree, we'd be happy to give you a complimentary bottle of shampoo. Oh . . . one more thing. Our building's elevator is currently out of service, so you'll have to take the stairs to the second floor whenever you arrive. I look forward to hearing from you.

Questions 89-91 refer to the following talk.

[3w] 미국식 발음

We will begin selling a new keyboard on Tuesday. As you will need to introduce this product to our customers, you should get to know its features as quickly as possible. It's called the Koring Pro, and it's made by Leino. What makes this item stand out is that it has no cord. It connects wirelessly to computers, tablets, and phones. And it's quite affordable. The price here at Gadget Warehouse will be $21. In time, I think it'll become one of our best sellers.

Questions 92-94 refer to the following news report.

미국식 발음

This is Catherine Long with BBS News. Our top business story today is about the launch of JarinSport's highly anticipated running shoe line. The shoes have been designed to include computer chips that record the wearer's distance traveled and calories burned and send the information to a smartphone application for review. Consumers who participated in the product testing carried out this spring showed promising levels of satisfaction. The line of shoes hits stores early this May. Unfortunately, JarinSport has stopped accepting advance orders due to an unexpectedly high volume of requests placed through its Web site.

Questions 95-97 refer to the following excerpt from a meeting and pie chart.

호주식 발음

I'd like to discuss one of our products. This morning, I heard that Westmore Home Goods has released a new product called the West2000 that will compete with our Master Baker. Although I believe our product is superior, I am worried as it is included in our second biggest product category. We can't risk such a popular product line being affected. I think we should brainstorm some ideas to ensure that the product line remains competitive. I've asked my assistant to go out and get a few West2000s. I'd like you all to test them out and compare them to ours. Then we can decide if we should increase our marketing to stay ahead.

Questions 98-100 refer to the following telephone message and table.

캐나다식 발음

Good afternoon. This is Jonathan Rivers calling from Partners Bank for Helen Wong. Ms. Wong, I'd like to let you know that your debit card may have been used by an unauthorized person. A purchase was made with your card yesterday at a luxury clothing store in Barcelona. However, our records indicate that you live in Seattle. In order to discuss the matter further, please call 555-3422. This number will connect you with the customer service center at our main branch, and a representative will assist you. Thank you.

무료 토익·토스·오픽·지텔프 자료 제공
Hackers.co.kr

Answer Sheet

TEST 02

LISTENING (Part I~IV)

TEST 02의 점수를 환산한 후 목표 달성기에 TEST 02의 점수를 표시합니다.
점수 환산표는 문제집 16페이지, 목표 달성기는 교재의 첫 장에 있습니다.

맞은 문제 개수: _____/100

자르는 선 ✂

Answer Sheet

TEST 01

LISTENING (Part I~IV)

TEST 01의 점수를 환산한 후 목표 달성기에 TEST 01의 점수를 표시합니다.
점수 환산표는 문제집 16페이지, 목표 달성기는 교재의 첫 장에 있습니다.

맞은 문제 개수: _____/100

무료 토익·토스·오픽·지텔프 자료 제공
Hackers.co.kr

Answer Sheet

TEST 04

LISTENING (Part I~IV)

1	Ⓐ Ⓑ Ⓒ	21	Ⓐ Ⓑ Ⓒ	41	Ⓐ Ⓑ Ⓒ Ⓓ	61	Ⓐ Ⓑ Ⓒ Ⓓ	81	Ⓐ Ⓑ Ⓒ Ⓓ
2	Ⓐ Ⓑ Ⓒ	22	Ⓐ Ⓑ Ⓒ	42	Ⓐ Ⓑ Ⓒ Ⓓ	62	Ⓐ Ⓑ Ⓒ Ⓓ	82	Ⓐ Ⓑ Ⓒ Ⓓ
3	Ⓐ Ⓑ Ⓒ	23	Ⓐ Ⓑ Ⓒ	43	Ⓐ Ⓑ Ⓒ Ⓓ	63	Ⓐ Ⓑ Ⓒ Ⓓ	83	Ⓐ Ⓑ Ⓒ Ⓓ
4	Ⓐ Ⓑ Ⓒ	24	Ⓐ Ⓑ Ⓒ	44	Ⓐ Ⓑ Ⓒ Ⓓ	64	Ⓐ Ⓑ Ⓒ Ⓓ	84	Ⓐ Ⓑ Ⓒ Ⓓ
5	Ⓐ Ⓑ Ⓒ	25	Ⓐ Ⓑ Ⓒ	45	Ⓐ Ⓑ Ⓒ Ⓓ	65	Ⓐ Ⓑ Ⓒ Ⓓ	85	Ⓐ Ⓑ Ⓒ Ⓓ
6	Ⓐ Ⓑ Ⓒ	26	Ⓐ Ⓑ Ⓒ	46	Ⓐ Ⓑ Ⓒ Ⓓ	66	Ⓐ Ⓑ Ⓒ Ⓓ	86	Ⓐ Ⓑ Ⓒ Ⓓ
7	Ⓐ Ⓑ Ⓒ	27	Ⓐ Ⓑ Ⓒ	47	Ⓐ Ⓑ Ⓒ Ⓓ	67	Ⓐ Ⓑ Ⓒ Ⓓ	87	Ⓐ Ⓑ Ⓒ Ⓓ
8	Ⓐ Ⓑ Ⓒ	28	Ⓐ Ⓑ Ⓒ	48	Ⓐ Ⓑ Ⓒ Ⓓ	68	Ⓐ Ⓑ Ⓒ Ⓓ	88	Ⓐ Ⓑ Ⓒ Ⓓ
9	Ⓐ Ⓑ Ⓒ	29	Ⓐ Ⓑ Ⓒ	49	Ⓐ Ⓑ Ⓒ Ⓓ	69	Ⓐ Ⓑ Ⓒ Ⓓ	89	Ⓐ Ⓑ Ⓒ Ⓓ
10	Ⓐ Ⓑ Ⓒ	30	Ⓐ Ⓑ Ⓒ Ⓓ	50	Ⓐ Ⓑ Ⓒ Ⓓ	70	Ⓐ Ⓑ Ⓒ Ⓓ	90	Ⓐ Ⓑ Ⓒ Ⓓ
11	Ⓐ Ⓑ Ⓒ	31	Ⓐ Ⓑ Ⓒ Ⓓ	51	Ⓐ Ⓑ Ⓒ Ⓓ	71	Ⓐ Ⓑ Ⓒ Ⓓ	91	Ⓐ Ⓑ Ⓒ Ⓓ
12	Ⓐ Ⓑ Ⓒ	32	Ⓐ Ⓑ Ⓒ Ⓓ	52	Ⓐ Ⓑ Ⓒ Ⓓ	72	Ⓐ Ⓑ Ⓒ Ⓓ	92	Ⓐ Ⓑ Ⓒ Ⓓ
13	Ⓐ Ⓑ Ⓒ	33	Ⓐ Ⓑ Ⓒ Ⓓ	53	Ⓐ Ⓑ Ⓒ Ⓓ	73	Ⓐ Ⓑ Ⓒ Ⓓ	93	Ⓐ Ⓑ Ⓒ Ⓓ
14	Ⓐ Ⓑ Ⓒ	34	Ⓐ Ⓑ Ⓒ Ⓓ	54	Ⓐ Ⓑ Ⓒ Ⓓ	74	Ⓐ Ⓑ Ⓒ Ⓓ	94	Ⓐ Ⓑ Ⓒ Ⓓ
15	Ⓐ Ⓑ Ⓒ	35	Ⓐ Ⓑ Ⓒ Ⓓ	55	Ⓐ Ⓑ Ⓒ Ⓓ	75	Ⓐ Ⓑ Ⓒ Ⓓ	95	Ⓐ Ⓑ Ⓒ Ⓓ
16	Ⓐ Ⓑ Ⓒ	36	Ⓐ Ⓑ Ⓒ Ⓓ	56	Ⓐ Ⓑ Ⓒ Ⓓ	76	Ⓐ Ⓑ Ⓒ Ⓓ	96	Ⓐ Ⓑ Ⓒ Ⓓ
17	Ⓐ Ⓑ Ⓒ	37	Ⓐ Ⓑ Ⓒ Ⓓ	57	Ⓐ Ⓑ Ⓒ Ⓓ	77	Ⓐ Ⓑ Ⓒ Ⓓ	97	Ⓐ Ⓑ Ⓒ Ⓓ
18	Ⓐ Ⓑ Ⓒ	38	Ⓐ Ⓑ Ⓒ Ⓓ	58	Ⓐ Ⓑ Ⓒ Ⓓ	78	Ⓐ Ⓑ Ⓒ Ⓓ	98	Ⓐ Ⓑ Ⓒ Ⓓ
19	Ⓐ Ⓑ Ⓒ	39	Ⓐ Ⓑ Ⓒ Ⓓ	59	Ⓐ Ⓑ Ⓒ Ⓓ	79	Ⓐ Ⓑ Ⓒ Ⓓ	99	Ⓐ Ⓑ Ⓒ Ⓓ
20	Ⓐ Ⓑ Ⓒ	40	Ⓐ Ⓑ Ⓒ Ⓓ	60	Ⓐ Ⓑ Ⓒ Ⓓ	80	Ⓐ Ⓑ Ⓒ Ⓓ	100	Ⓐ Ⓑ Ⓒ Ⓓ

맞은 문제 개수: ___ /100

TEST 04의 점수를 환산한 후 목표 달성기에 TEST 04의 점수를 표시합니다.
점수 환산표는 문제집 16페이지, 목표 달성기는 교재의 첫 장에 있습니다.

✂ 자르는 선

Answer Sheet

TEST 03

LISTENING (Part I~IV)

1	Ⓐ Ⓑ Ⓒ	21	Ⓐ Ⓑ Ⓒ	41	Ⓐ Ⓑ Ⓒ Ⓓ	61	Ⓐ Ⓑ Ⓒ Ⓓ	81	Ⓐ Ⓑ Ⓒ Ⓓ
2	Ⓐ Ⓑ Ⓒ	22	Ⓐ Ⓑ Ⓒ	42	Ⓐ Ⓑ Ⓒ Ⓓ	62	Ⓐ Ⓑ Ⓒ Ⓓ	82	Ⓐ Ⓑ Ⓒ Ⓓ
3	Ⓐ Ⓑ Ⓒ	23	Ⓐ Ⓑ Ⓒ	43	Ⓐ Ⓑ Ⓒ Ⓓ	63	Ⓐ Ⓑ Ⓒ Ⓓ	83	Ⓐ Ⓑ Ⓒ Ⓓ
4	Ⓐ Ⓑ Ⓒ	24	Ⓐ Ⓑ Ⓒ	44	Ⓐ Ⓑ Ⓒ Ⓓ	64	Ⓐ Ⓑ Ⓒ Ⓓ	84	Ⓐ Ⓑ Ⓒ Ⓓ
5	Ⓐ Ⓑ Ⓒ	25	Ⓐ Ⓑ Ⓒ	45	Ⓐ Ⓑ Ⓒ Ⓓ	65	Ⓐ Ⓑ Ⓒ Ⓓ	85	Ⓐ Ⓑ Ⓒ Ⓓ
6	Ⓐ Ⓑ Ⓒ	26	Ⓐ Ⓑ Ⓒ	46	Ⓐ Ⓑ Ⓒ Ⓓ	66	Ⓐ Ⓑ Ⓒ Ⓓ	86	Ⓐ Ⓑ Ⓒ Ⓓ
7	Ⓐ Ⓑ Ⓒ	27	Ⓐ Ⓑ Ⓒ	47	Ⓐ Ⓑ Ⓒ Ⓓ	67	Ⓐ Ⓑ Ⓒ Ⓓ	87	Ⓐ Ⓑ Ⓒ Ⓓ
8	Ⓐ Ⓑ Ⓒ	28	Ⓐ Ⓑ Ⓒ	48	Ⓐ Ⓑ Ⓒ Ⓓ	68	Ⓐ Ⓑ Ⓒ Ⓓ	88	Ⓐ Ⓑ Ⓒ Ⓓ
9	Ⓐ Ⓑ Ⓒ	29	Ⓐ Ⓑ Ⓒ	49	Ⓐ Ⓑ Ⓒ Ⓓ	69	Ⓐ Ⓑ Ⓒ Ⓓ	89	Ⓐ Ⓑ Ⓒ Ⓓ
10	Ⓐ Ⓑ Ⓒ	30	Ⓐ Ⓑ Ⓒ Ⓓ	50	Ⓐ Ⓑ Ⓒ Ⓓ	70	Ⓐ Ⓑ Ⓒ Ⓓ	90	Ⓐ Ⓑ Ⓒ Ⓓ
11	Ⓐ Ⓑ Ⓒ	31	Ⓐ Ⓑ Ⓒ Ⓓ	51	Ⓐ Ⓑ Ⓒ Ⓓ	71	Ⓐ Ⓑ Ⓒ Ⓓ	91	Ⓐ Ⓑ Ⓒ Ⓓ
12	Ⓐ Ⓑ Ⓒ	32	Ⓐ Ⓑ Ⓒ Ⓓ	52	Ⓐ Ⓑ Ⓒ Ⓓ	72	Ⓐ Ⓑ Ⓒ Ⓓ	92	Ⓐ Ⓑ Ⓒ Ⓓ
13	Ⓐ Ⓑ Ⓒ	33	Ⓐ Ⓑ Ⓒ Ⓓ	53	Ⓐ Ⓑ Ⓒ Ⓓ	73	Ⓐ Ⓑ Ⓒ Ⓓ	93	Ⓐ Ⓑ Ⓒ Ⓓ
14	Ⓐ Ⓑ Ⓒ	34	Ⓐ Ⓑ Ⓒ Ⓓ	54	Ⓐ Ⓑ Ⓒ Ⓓ	74	Ⓐ Ⓑ Ⓒ Ⓓ	94	Ⓐ Ⓑ Ⓒ Ⓓ
15	Ⓐ Ⓑ Ⓒ	35	Ⓐ Ⓑ Ⓒ Ⓓ	55	Ⓐ Ⓑ Ⓒ Ⓓ	75	Ⓐ Ⓑ Ⓒ Ⓓ	95	Ⓐ Ⓑ Ⓒ Ⓓ
16	Ⓐ Ⓑ Ⓒ	36	Ⓐ Ⓑ Ⓒ Ⓓ	56	Ⓐ Ⓑ Ⓒ Ⓓ	76	Ⓐ Ⓑ Ⓒ Ⓓ	96	Ⓐ Ⓑ Ⓒ Ⓓ
17	Ⓐ Ⓑ Ⓒ	37	Ⓐ Ⓑ Ⓒ Ⓓ	57	Ⓐ Ⓑ Ⓒ Ⓓ	77	Ⓐ Ⓑ Ⓒ Ⓓ	97	Ⓐ Ⓑ Ⓒ Ⓓ
18	Ⓐ Ⓑ Ⓒ	38	Ⓐ Ⓑ Ⓒ Ⓓ	58	Ⓐ Ⓑ Ⓒ Ⓓ	78	Ⓐ Ⓑ Ⓒ Ⓓ	98	Ⓐ Ⓑ Ⓒ Ⓓ
19	Ⓐ Ⓑ Ⓒ	39	Ⓐ Ⓑ Ⓒ Ⓓ	59	Ⓐ Ⓑ Ⓒ Ⓓ	79	Ⓐ Ⓑ Ⓒ Ⓓ	99	Ⓐ Ⓑ Ⓒ Ⓓ
20	Ⓐ Ⓑ Ⓒ	40	Ⓐ Ⓑ Ⓒ Ⓓ	60	Ⓐ Ⓑ Ⓒ Ⓓ	80	Ⓐ Ⓑ Ⓒ Ⓓ	100	Ⓐ Ⓑ Ⓒ Ⓓ

맞은 문제 개수: ___ /100

TEST 03의 점수를 환산한 후 목표 달성기에 TEST 03의 점수를 표시합니다.
점수 환산표는 문제집 16페이지, 목표 달성기는 교재의 첫 장에 있습니다.

자르는 선 ✂

무료 토익·토스·오픽·지텔프 자료 제공
Hackers.co.kr

Answer Sheet

TEST 06

LISTENING (Part I~IV)

#					#					#					#				
1	Ⓐ Ⓑ Ⓒ				21	Ⓐ Ⓑ Ⓒ				41	Ⓐ Ⓑ Ⓒ Ⓓ				81	Ⓐ Ⓑ Ⓒ Ⓓ			
2	Ⓐ Ⓑ Ⓒ				22	Ⓐ Ⓑ Ⓒ				42	Ⓐ Ⓑ Ⓒ Ⓓ				82	Ⓐ Ⓑ Ⓒ Ⓓ			
3	Ⓐ Ⓑ Ⓒ				23	Ⓐ Ⓑ Ⓒ				43	Ⓐ Ⓑ Ⓒ Ⓓ				83	Ⓐ Ⓑ Ⓒ Ⓓ			
4	Ⓐ Ⓑ Ⓒ				24	Ⓐ Ⓑ Ⓒ				44	Ⓐ Ⓑ Ⓒ Ⓓ				84	Ⓐ Ⓑ Ⓒ Ⓓ			
5	Ⓐ Ⓑ Ⓒ				25	Ⓐ Ⓑ Ⓒ				45	Ⓐ Ⓑ Ⓒ Ⓓ				85	Ⓐ Ⓑ Ⓒ Ⓓ			
6	Ⓐ Ⓑ Ⓒ				26	Ⓐ Ⓑ Ⓒ				46	Ⓐ Ⓑ Ⓒ Ⓓ				86	Ⓐ Ⓑ Ⓒ Ⓓ			
7	Ⓐ Ⓑ Ⓒ				27	Ⓐ Ⓑ Ⓒ				47	Ⓐ Ⓑ Ⓒ Ⓓ				87	Ⓐ Ⓑ Ⓒ Ⓓ			
8	Ⓐ Ⓑ Ⓒ				28	Ⓐ Ⓑ Ⓒ				48	Ⓐ Ⓑ Ⓒ Ⓓ				88	Ⓐ Ⓑ Ⓒ Ⓓ			
9	Ⓐ Ⓑ Ⓒ				29	Ⓐ Ⓑ Ⓒ				49	Ⓐ Ⓑ Ⓒ Ⓓ				89	Ⓐ Ⓑ Ⓒ Ⓓ			
10	Ⓐ Ⓑ Ⓒ				30	Ⓐ Ⓑ Ⓒ Ⓓ				50	Ⓐ Ⓑ Ⓒ Ⓓ				90	Ⓐ Ⓑ Ⓒ Ⓓ			
11	Ⓐ Ⓑ Ⓒ				31	Ⓐ Ⓑ Ⓒ Ⓓ				51	Ⓐ Ⓑ Ⓒ Ⓓ				91	Ⓐ Ⓑ Ⓒ Ⓓ			
12	Ⓐ Ⓑ Ⓒ				32	Ⓐ Ⓑ Ⓒ Ⓓ				52	Ⓐ Ⓑ Ⓒ Ⓓ				92	Ⓐ Ⓑ Ⓒ Ⓓ			
13	Ⓐ Ⓑ Ⓒ				33	Ⓐ Ⓑ Ⓒ Ⓓ				53	Ⓐ Ⓑ Ⓒ Ⓓ				93	Ⓐ Ⓑ Ⓒ Ⓓ			
14	Ⓐ Ⓑ Ⓒ				34	Ⓐ Ⓑ Ⓒ Ⓓ				54	Ⓐ Ⓑ Ⓒ Ⓓ				94	Ⓐ Ⓑ Ⓒ Ⓓ			
15	Ⓐ Ⓑ Ⓒ				35	Ⓐ Ⓑ Ⓒ Ⓓ				55	Ⓐ Ⓑ Ⓒ Ⓓ				95	Ⓐ Ⓑ Ⓒ Ⓓ			
16	Ⓐ Ⓑ Ⓒ				36	Ⓐ Ⓑ Ⓒ Ⓓ				56	Ⓐ Ⓑ Ⓒ Ⓓ				96	Ⓐ Ⓑ Ⓒ Ⓓ			
17	Ⓐ Ⓑ Ⓒ				37	Ⓐ Ⓑ Ⓒ Ⓓ				57	Ⓐ Ⓑ Ⓒ Ⓓ				97	Ⓐ Ⓑ Ⓒ Ⓓ			
18	Ⓐ Ⓑ Ⓒ				38	Ⓐ Ⓑ Ⓒ Ⓓ				58	Ⓐ Ⓑ Ⓒ Ⓓ				98	Ⓐ Ⓑ Ⓒ Ⓓ			
19	Ⓐ Ⓑ Ⓒ				39	Ⓐ Ⓑ Ⓒ Ⓓ				59	Ⓐ Ⓑ Ⓒ Ⓓ				99	Ⓐ Ⓑ Ⓒ Ⓓ			
20	Ⓐ Ⓑ Ⓒ				40	Ⓐ Ⓑ Ⓒ Ⓓ				60	Ⓐ Ⓑ Ⓒ Ⓓ				100	Ⓐ Ⓑ Ⓒ Ⓓ			

맞은 문제 개수: ___/100

TEST 06의 점수를 환산한 후 목표 달성기에 TEST 06의 점수를 표시합니다.
점수 환산표와 문제집 167페이지, 목표 달성기는 교재의 첫 장에 있습니다.

✂ 자르는 선

Answer Sheet

TEST 05

LISTENING (Part I~IV)

#					#					#					#				
1	Ⓐ Ⓑ Ⓒ				21	Ⓐ Ⓑ Ⓒ				41	Ⓐ Ⓑ Ⓒ Ⓓ				81	Ⓐ Ⓑ Ⓒ Ⓓ			
2	Ⓐ Ⓑ Ⓒ				22	Ⓐ Ⓑ Ⓒ				42	Ⓐ Ⓑ Ⓒ Ⓓ				82	Ⓐ Ⓑ Ⓒ Ⓓ			
3	Ⓐ Ⓑ Ⓒ				23	Ⓐ Ⓑ Ⓒ				43	Ⓐ Ⓑ Ⓒ Ⓓ				83	Ⓐ Ⓑ Ⓒ Ⓓ			
4	Ⓐ Ⓑ Ⓒ				24	Ⓐ Ⓑ Ⓒ				44	Ⓐ Ⓑ Ⓒ Ⓓ				84	Ⓐ Ⓑ Ⓒ Ⓓ			
5	Ⓐ Ⓑ Ⓒ				25	Ⓐ Ⓑ Ⓒ				45	Ⓐ Ⓑ Ⓒ Ⓓ				85	Ⓐ Ⓑ Ⓒ Ⓓ			
6	Ⓐ Ⓑ Ⓒ				26	Ⓐ Ⓑ Ⓒ				46	Ⓐ Ⓑ Ⓒ Ⓓ				86	Ⓐ Ⓑ Ⓒ Ⓓ			
7	Ⓐ Ⓑ Ⓒ				27	Ⓐ Ⓑ Ⓒ				47	Ⓐ Ⓑ Ⓒ Ⓓ				87	Ⓐ Ⓑ Ⓒ Ⓓ			
8	Ⓐ Ⓑ Ⓒ				28	Ⓐ Ⓑ Ⓒ				48	Ⓐ Ⓑ Ⓒ Ⓓ				88	Ⓐ Ⓑ Ⓒ Ⓓ			
9	Ⓐ Ⓑ Ⓒ				29	Ⓐ Ⓑ Ⓒ				49	Ⓐ Ⓑ Ⓒ Ⓓ				89	Ⓐ Ⓑ Ⓒ Ⓓ			
10	Ⓐ Ⓑ Ⓒ				30	Ⓐ Ⓑ Ⓒ Ⓓ				50	Ⓐ Ⓑ Ⓒ Ⓓ				90	Ⓐ Ⓑ Ⓒ Ⓓ			
11	Ⓐ Ⓑ Ⓒ				31	Ⓐ Ⓑ Ⓒ Ⓓ				51	Ⓐ Ⓑ Ⓒ Ⓓ				91	Ⓐ Ⓑ Ⓒ Ⓓ			
12	Ⓐ Ⓑ Ⓒ				32	Ⓐ Ⓑ Ⓒ Ⓓ				52	Ⓐ Ⓑ Ⓒ Ⓓ				92	Ⓐ Ⓑ Ⓒ Ⓓ			
13	Ⓐ Ⓑ Ⓒ				33	Ⓐ Ⓑ Ⓒ Ⓓ				53	Ⓐ Ⓑ Ⓒ Ⓓ				93	Ⓐ Ⓑ Ⓒ Ⓓ			
14	Ⓐ Ⓑ Ⓒ				34	Ⓐ Ⓑ Ⓒ Ⓓ				54	Ⓐ Ⓑ Ⓒ Ⓓ				94	Ⓐ Ⓑ Ⓒ Ⓓ			
15	Ⓐ Ⓑ Ⓒ				35	Ⓐ Ⓑ Ⓒ Ⓓ				55	Ⓐ Ⓑ Ⓒ Ⓓ				95	Ⓐ Ⓑ Ⓒ Ⓓ			
16	Ⓐ Ⓑ Ⓒ				36	Ⓐ Ⓑ Ⓒ Ⓓ				56	Ⓐ Ⓑ Ⓒ Ⓓ				96	Ⓐ Ⓑ Ⓒ Ⓓ			
17	Ⓐ Ⓑ Ⓒ				37	Ⓐ Ⓑ Ⓒ Ⓓ				57	Ⓐ Ⓑ Ⓒ Ⓓ				97	Ⓐ Ⓑ Ⓒ Ⓓ			
18	Ⓐ Ⓑ Ⓒ				38	Ⓐ Ⓑ Ⓒ Ⓓ				58	Ⓐ Ⓑ Ⓒ Ⓓ				98	Ⓐ Ⓑ Ⓒ Ⓓ			
19	Ⓐ Ⓑ Ⓒ				39	Ⓐ Ⓑ Ⓒ Ⓓ				59	Ⓐ Ⓑ Ⓒ Ⓓ				99	Ⓐ Ⓑ Ⓒ Ⓓ			
20	Ⓐ Ⓑ Ⓒ				40	Ⓐ Ⓑ Ⓒ Ⓓ				60	Ⓐ Ⓑ Ⓒ Ⓓ				100	Ⓐ Ⓑ Ⓒ Ⓓ			

맞은 문제 개수: ___/100

TEST 05의 점수를 환산한 후 목표 달성기에 TEST 05의 점수를 표시합니다.
점수 환산표와 문제집 167페이지, 목표 달성기는 교재의 첫 장에 있습니다.

무료 토익·토스·오픽·지텔프 자료 제공
Hackers.co.kr

Answer Sheet

TEST 08

LISTENING (Part I~IV)

#					#					#					#					#				
1	Ⓐ Ⓑ Ⓒ				21	Ⓐ Ⓑ Ⓒ Ⓓ				41	Ⓐ Ⓑ Ⓒ Ⓓ				61	Ⓐ Ⓑ Ⓒ Ⓓ				81	Ⓐ Ⓑ Ⓒ Ⓓ			
2	Ⓐ Ⓑ Ⓒ				22	Ⓐ Ⓑ Ⓒ Ⓓ				42	Ⓐ Ⓑ Ⓒ Ⓓ				62	Ⓐ Ⓑ Ⓒ Ⓓ				82	Ⓐ Ⓑ Ⓒ Ⓓ			
3	Ⓐ Ⓑ Ⓒ				23	Ⓐ Ⓑ Ⓒ Ⓓ				43	Ⓐ Ⓑ Ⓒ Ⓓ				63	Ⓐ Ⓑ Ⓒ Ⓓ				83	Ⓐ Ⓑ Ⓒ Ⓓ			
4	Ⓐ Ⓑ Ⓒ				24	Ⓐ Ⓑ Ⓒ Ⓓ				44	Ⓐ Ⓑ Ⓒ Ⓓ				64	Ⓐ Ⓑ Ⓒ Ⓓ				84	Ⓐ Ⓑ Ⓒ Ⓓ			
5	Ⓐ Ⓑ Ⓒ				25	Ⓐ Ⓑ Ⓒ Ⓓ				45	Ⓐ Ⓑ Ⓒ Ⓓ				65	Ⓐ Ⓑ Ⓒ Ⓓ				85	Ⓐ Ⓑ Ⓒ Ⓓ			
6	Ⓐ Ⓑ Ⓒ				26	Ⓐ Ⓑ Ⓒ				46	Ⓐ Ⓑ Ⓒ Ⓓ				66	Ⓐ Ⓑ Ⓒ Ⓓ				86	Ⓐ Ⓑ Ⓒ Ⓓ			
7	Ⓐ Ⓑ Ⓒ				27	Ⓐ Ⓑ Ⓒ				47	Ⓐ Ⓑ Ⓒ Ⓓ				67	Ⓐ Ⓑ Ⓒ Ⓓ				87	Ⓐ Ⓑ Ⓒ Ⓓ			
8	Ⓐ Ⓑ Ⓒ				28	Ⓐ Ⓑ Ⓒ				48	Ⓐ Ⓑ Ⓒ Ⓓ				68	Ⓐ Ⓑ Ⓒ Ⓓ				88	Ⓐ Ⓑ Ⓒ Ⓓ			
9	Ⓐ Ⓑ Ⓒ				29	Ⓐ Ⓑ Ⓒ				49	Ⓐ Ⓑ Ⓒ Ⓓ				69	Ⓐ Ⓑ Ⓒ Ⓓ				89	Ⓐ Ⓑ Ⓒ Ⓓ			
10	Ⓐ Ⓑ Ⓒ				30	Ⓐ Ⓑ Ⓒ				50	Ⓐ Ⓑ Ⓒ Ⓓ				70	Ⓐ Ⓑ Ⓒ Ⓓ				90	Ⓐ Ⓑ Ⓒ Ⓓ			
11	Ⓐ Ⓑ Ⓒ				31	Ⓐ Ⓑ Ⓒ				51	Ⓐ Ⓑ Ⓒ Ⓓ				71	Ⓐ Ⓑ Ⓒ Ⓓ				91	Ⓐ Ⓑ Ⓒ Ⓓ			
12	Ⓐ Ⓑ Ⓒ				32	Ⓐ Ⓑ Ⓒ				52	Ⓐ Ⓑ Ⓒ Ⓓ				72	Ⓐ Ⓑ Ⓒ Ⓓ				92	Ⓐ Ⓑ Ⓒ Ⓓ			
13	Ⓐ Ⓑ Ⓒ				33	Ⓐ Ⓑ Ⓒ				53	Ⓐ Ⓑ Ⓒ Ⓓ				73	Ⓐ Ⓑ Ⓒ Ⓓ				93	Ⓐ Ⓑ Ⓒ Ⓓ			
14	Ⓐ Ⓑ Ⓒ				34	Ⓐ Ⓑ Ⓒ				54	Ⓐ Ⓑ Ⓒ Ⓓ				74	Ⓐ Ⓑ Ⓒ Ⓓ				94	Ⓐ Ⓑ Ⓒ Ⓓ			
15	Ⓐ Ⓑ Ⓒ				35	Ⓐ Ⓑ Ⓒ				55	Ⓐ Ⓑ Ⓒ Ⓓ				75	Ⓐ Ⓑ Ⓒ Ⓓ				95	Ⓐ Ⓑ Ⓒ Ⓓ			
16	Ⓐ Ⓑ Ⓒ				36	Ⓐ Ⓑ Ⓒ				56	Ⓐ Ⓑ Ⓒ Ⓓ				76	Ⓐ Ⓑ Ⓒ Ⓓ				96	Ⓐ Ⓑ Ⓒ Ⓓ			
17	Ⓐ Ⓑ Ⓒ				37	Ⓐ Ⓑ Ⓒ				57	Ⓐ Ⓑ Ⓒ Ⓓ				77	Ⓐ Ⓑ Ⓒ Ⓓ				97	Ⓐ Ⓑ Ⓒ Ⓓ			
18	Ⓐ Ⓑ Ⓒ				38	Ⓐ Ⓑ Ⓒ				58	Ⓐ Ⓑ Ⓒ Ⓓ				78	Ⓐ Ⓑ Ⓒ Ⓓ				98	Ⓐ Ⓑ Ⓒ Ⓓ			
19	Ⓐ Ⓑ Ⓒ				39	Ⓐ Ⓑ Ⓒ				59	Ⓐ Ⓑ Ⓒ Ⓓ				79	Ⓐ Ⓑ Ⓒ Ⓓ				99	Ⓐ Ⓑ Ⓒ Ⓓ			
20	Ⓐ Ⓑ Ⓒ				40	Ⓐ Ⓑ Ⓒ				60	Ⓐ Ⓑ Ⓒ Ⓓ				80	Ⓐ Ⓑ Ⓒ Ⓓ				100	Ⓐ Ⓑ Ⓒ Ⓓ			

맞은 문제 개수: ___ /100

TEST 08의 점수를 환산한 후 목표 달성기에 TEST 08의 점수를 표시합니다.
점수 환산표는 문제집 167페이지, 목표 달성기는 교재의 첫 장에 있습니다.

✂ 자르는 선

Answer Sheet

TEST 07

LISTENING (Part I~IV)

#					#					#					#					#				
1	Ⓐ Ⓑ Ⓒ				21	Ⓐ Ⓑ Ⓒ Ⓓ				41	Ⓐ Ⓑ Ⓒ Ⓓ				61	Ⓐ Ⓑ Ⓒ Ⓓ				81	Ⓐ Ⓑ Ⓒ Ⓓ			
2	Ⓐ Ⓑ Ⓒ				22	Ⓐ Ⓑ Ⓒ Ⓓ				42	Ⓐ Ⓑ Ⓒ Ⓓ				62	Ⓐ Ⓑ Ⓒ Ⓓ				82	Ⓐ Ⓑ Ⓒ Ⓓ			
3	Ⓐ Ⓑ Ⓒ				23	Ⓐ Ⓑ Ⓒ Ⓓ				43	Ⓐ Ⓑ Ⓒ Ⓓ				63	Ⓐ Ⓑ Ⓒ Ⓓ				83	Ⓐ Ⓑ Ⓒ Ⓓ			
4	Ⓐ Ⓑ Ⓒ				24	Ⓐ Ⓑ Ⓒ Ⓓ				44	Ⓐ Ⓑ Ⓒ Ⓓ				64	Ⓐ Ⓑ Ⓒ Ⓓ				84	Ⓐ Ⓑ Ⓒ Ⓓ			
5	Ⓐ Ⓑ Ⓒ				25	Ⓐ Ⓑ Ⓒ Ⓓ				45	Ⓐ Ⓑ Ⓒ Ⓓ				65	Ⓐ Ⓑ Ⓒ Ⓓ				85	Ⓐ Ⓑ Ⓒ Ⓓ			
6	Ⓐ Ⓑ Ⓒ				26	Ⓐ Ⓑ Ⓒ				46	Ⓐ Ⓑ Ⓒ Ⓓ				66	Ⓐ Ⓑ Ⓒ Ⓓ				86	Ⓐ Ⓑ Ⓒ Ⓓ			
7	Ⓐ Ⓑ Ⓒ				27	Ⓐ Ⓑ Ⓒ				47	Ⓐ Ⓑ Ⓒ Ⓓ				67	Ⓐ Ⓑ Ⓒ Ⓓ				87	Ⓐ Ⓑ Ⓒ Ⓓ			
8	Ⓐ Ⓑ Ⓒ				28	Ⓐ Ⓑ Ⓒ				48	Ⓐ Ⓑ Ⓒ Ⓓ				68	Ⓐ Ⓑ Ⓒ Ⓓ				88	Ⓐ Ⓑ Ⓒ Ⓓ			
9	Ⓐ Ⓑ Ⓒ				29	Ⓐ Ⓑ Ⓒ				49	Ⓐ Ⓑ Ⓒ Ⓓ				69	Ⓐ Ⓑ Ⓒ Ⓓ				89	Ⓐ Ⓑ Ⓒ Ⓓ			
10	Ⓐ Ⓑ Ⓒ				30	Ⓐ Ⓑ Ⓒ				50	Ⓐ Ⓑ Ⓒ Ⓓ				70	Ⓐ Ⓑ Ⓒ Ⓓ				90	Ⓐ Ⓑ Ⓒ Ⓓ			
11	Ⓐ Ⓑ Ⓒ				31	Ⓐ Ⓑ Ⓒ				51	Ⓐ Ⓑ Ⓒ Ⓓ				71	Ⓐ Ⓑ Ⓒ Ⓓ				91	Ⓐ Ⓑ Ⓒ Ⓓ			
12	Ⓐ Ⓑ Ⓒ				32	Ⓐ Ⓑ Ⓒ				52	Ⓐ Ⓑ Ⓒ Ⓓ				72	Ⓐ Ⓑ Ⓒ Ⓓ				92	Ⓐ Ⓑ Ⓒ Ⓓ			
13	Ⓐ Ⓑ Ⓒ				33	Ⓐ Ⓑ Ⓒ				53	Ⓐ Ⓑ Ⓒ Ⓓ				73	Ⓐ Ⓑ Ⓒ Ⓓ				93	Ⓐ Ⓑ Ⓒ Ⓓ			
14	Ⓐ Ⓑ Ⓒ				34	Ⓐ Ⓑ Ⓒ				54	Ⓐ Ⓑ Ⓒ Ⓓ				74	Ⓐ Ⓑ Ⓒ Ⓓ				94	Ⓐ Ⓑ Ⓒ Ⓓ			
15	Ⓐ Ⓑ Ⓒ				35	Ⓐ Ⓑ Ⓒ				55	Ⓐ Ⓑ Ⓒ Ⓓ				75	Ⓐ Ⓑ Ⓒ Ⓓ				95	Ⓐ Ⓑ Ⓒ Ⓓ			
16	Ⓐ Ⓑ Ⓒ				36	Ⓐ Ⓑ Ⓒ				56	Ⓐ Ⓑ Ⓒ Ⓓ				76	Ⓐ Ⓑ Ⓒ Ⓓ				96	Ⓐ Ⓑ Ⓒ Ⓓ			
17	Ⓐ Ⓑ Ⓒ				37	Ⓐ Ⓑ Ⓒ				57	Ⓐ Ⓑ Ⓒ Ⓓ				77	Ⓐ Ⓑ Ⓒ Ⓓ				97	Ⓐ Ⓑ Ⓒ Ⓓ			
18	Ⓐ Ⓑ Ⓒ				38	Ⓐ Ⓑ Ⓒ				58	Ⓐ Ⓑ Ⓒ Ⓓ				78	Ⓐ Ⓑ Ⓒ Ⓓ				98	Ⓐ Ⓑ Ⓒ Ⓓ			
19	Ⓐ Ⓑ Ⓒ				39	Ⓐ Ⓑ Ⓒ				59	Ⓐ Ⓑ Ⓒ Ⓓ				79	Ⓐ Ⓑ Ⓒ Ⓓ				99	Ⓐ Ⓑ Ⓒ Ⓓ			
20	Ⓐ Ⓑ Ⓒ				40	Ⓐ Ⓑ Ⓒ				60	Ⓐ Ⓑ Ⓒ Ⓓ				80	Ⓐ Ⓑ Ⓒ Ⓓ				100	Ⓐ Ⓑ Ⓒ Ⓓ			

맞은 문제 개수: ___ /100

TEST 07의 점수를 환산한 후 목표 달성기에 TEST 07의 점수를 표시합니다.
점수 환산표는 문제집 167페이지, 목표 달성기는 교재의 첫 장에 있습니다.

무료 토익·토스·오픽·지텔프 자료 제공
Hackers.co.kr

Answer Sheet

TEST 10

LISTENING (Part I~IV)

맞은 문제 개수: ___ /100

TEST 10의 점수를 환산한 후 목표 달성기에 TEST 10의 점수를 표시합니다.
점수 환산표는 문제집 16페이지, 목표 달성기는 교재의 첫 장에 있습니다.

Answer Sheet

TEST 09

LISTENING (Part I~IV)

맞은 문제 개수: ___ /100

TEST 09의 점수를 환산한 후 목표 달성기에 TEST 09의 점수를 표시합니다.
점수 환산표는 문제집 16페이지, 목표 달성기는 교재의 첫 장에 있습니다.

자르는 선 ✂

무료 토익·토스·오픽·지텔프 자료 제공
Hackers.co.kr

MEMO

MEMO

최신 기출유형으로 실전 완벽 마무리

해커스 토익 LC

실전 1000제
LISTENING 1 문제집

개정 5판 4쇄 발행 2024년 8월 5일

개정 5판 1쇄 발행 2023년 1월 2일

지은이	해커스 어학연구소
펴낸곳	㈜해커스 어학연구소
펴낸이	해커스 어학연구소 출판팀

주소	서울특별시 서초구 강남대로61길 23 ㈜해커스 어학연구소
고객센터	02-537-5000
교재 관련 문의	publishing@hackers.com
동영상강의	HackersIngang.com

ISBN	978-89-6542-507-6 (13740)
Serial Number	05-04-01

외국어인강 1위, 해커스인강
HackersIngang.com

해커스인강

· 해커스 토익 스타강사의 **본 교재 인강**
· 단기 리스닝 점수 향상을 위한 **무료 받아쓰기&쉐도잉 프로그램**
· 최신 출제경향이 반영된 **무료 온라인 실전모의고사**
· 들으면서 외우는 **무료 단어암기장 및 단어암기 MP3**
· 빠르고 편리하게 채점하는 **무료 정답녹음 MP3**

영어 전문 포털, 해커스토익
Hackers.co.kr

해커스토익

· 본 교재 **무료 지문 및 문제 해석**
· **무료** 매월 적중예상특강 및 실시간 토익시험 정답확인/해설강의
· 매일 실전 RC/LC 문제 및 토익 기출보카 TEST, 토익기출 100단어 등 다양한 무료 학습 콘텐츠

헤럴드 선정 2018 대학생 선호브랜드 대상 '대학생이 선정한 외국어인강' 부문 1위

5천 개가 넘는
해커스토익 무료 자료!

대한민국에서 공짜로 토익 공부하고 싶으면 해커스영어 Hackers.co.kr ▾ 검색

RC 정수진 **RC 이상길**

토익 강의

베스트셀러 1위 토익 강의 150강 무료 서비스,
누적 시청 1,900만 돌파!

토익 실전 문제

토익 RC/LC 풀기, 모의토익 등
실전토익 대비 문제 제공!

LC 한승태 **RC 김동영**

최신 특강

2,400만뷰 스타강사의
압도적 적중예상특강 매달 업데이트!

고득점 달성 비법

토익 고득점 달성팁, 파트별 비법,
점수대별 공부법 무료 확인

전원 무료
*미션 달성 시

가장 빠른 정답까지!

615만이 선택한 해커스 토익 정답!
시험 직후 가장 빠른 정답 확인

더 많은
토익 무료자료 보기 ▶